Margaret Savannah Fox

5,000 Gems for the Household

A Book that Teaches Everything a Lady Would Like to Know

Margaret Savannah Fox

5,000 Gems for the Household
A Book that Teaches Everything a Lady Would Like to Know

ISBN/EAN: 9783337122775

Printed in Europe, USA, Canada, Australia, Japan

Cover: Foto ©Lupo / pixelio.de

More available books at **www.hansebooks.com**

5,000 Gems for the Household.

A Book That Teaches Everything a Lady Would Like to Know.

A COMPACT MANUAL OF RELIABLE INFORMATION.

It tells you how to make paper, wool, feather, hair and tinsel flowers; how to paint on satin, silk and velvet; full list of characters for masque ball; a chapter on bead and embroidery work; a list of over three hundred new names for children.

OVER 3,000 RECEIPTS FOR COOKING,

—AND—

1,000 Useful Receipts for Anyone and Everyone.

PREFACE.

The design of the author, in the preparation of this work, has been to furnish a book in which information for the ladies upon almost any subject can be found. Usually, this subject of ladies work or fancy work has been treated in such away as to form the contents of a dozen or more separate volumes: THE PAPER FLOWERS, HAIR FLOWERS, FEATHER FLOWERS, etc., are combined in this volume.

Attention is especially called to the manner in which the MISCELLANEOUS FANCY WORK DEPARTMENT is conducted, as all the latest novelties in the decorating line are introduced, along with the most explicit directions for forming them. Also to the PAINTING; all the different branches of painting being explained, the colors to be used, the brushes, how to mix paints and how to apply them. The reader will appreciate the patterns herein described in the CROCHET DEPARTMENT, but still more appreciate those in the KNITTING DEPARTMENT whereby instructions for skirts, dresses caps, leggins, mittens, jackets, shawls, lace and insertions of the latest designs are given, that a child who knows how to take the first simple stich in knitting and crocheting cannot fail to bring about the desired result by close observance of the directions given.

Then to the ladies who do not exactly take to fancy work, we have endeavored to put forth a few valuable receipts in the COOKING and BAKING line, and we can truthfully say that the receipts are all genuine and good, having tried most of them ourselves before placing them before the public. Then again, so nothing will go to waste, we have added some COLORING RECEIPTS which have been tried with the utmost success.

Great pains have also been taken to make this work superior to all others in its typographical arrangement and finish, and in the general tastefulness of its mechanical execution.

The author takes great pleasure in acknowledging her indebtedness for many valuable suggestions received from teachers of experience and others interested in woman's work.

How nearly the author has accomplished her purpose to give to the public, in one VOLUME, a clear, scientific and COMPLETE treatise on this subject, combining and systematizing many REAL IMPROVEMENTS of practical value and importance to women and young girls, the intelligent and skilled worker must decide.

M. S. FOX.

Albany, Oregon, May 20, 1887.

TABLE OF CONTENTS.

Paper Flowers..	6-9
Wool Flowers	10-12
Hair Flowers	13 14
Feather Flowers	14-15
Tinsel Flowers	15-16
Christmas Tree Ornaments	15-16
Feather Work	17-18
Bead Work	19-23
Knitting Department	24-62
Crochet Department	33-86
Stamping	87-88
Painting	89-61
Miscellaneous Department	92-101
Home Department	102-145
Cooking and Baker's Department	146-204
Coloring Department	205-213
Miscellaneous Cooking and Baking Recipes	214-232
Anything And Everything	233-279

PAPER FLOWERS.

There can be nothing more beautiful to the eye that loves nature, than are (within their own limits) these paper flowers. How many mothers and daughters would gladly like to fix up their parlors and sitting rooms, like some of their friends do, if they only knew how to make anything.

These paper flowers are so easily and quickly made, and material so cheap, that no house should be without them. The directions given within this book are so explicit and simple that a child can make the flowers by close observance of the directions. By practice all kinds of flowers can be made with but little patience and trouble. Any room, no matter if the furniture be not of the finest quality, can be made to look tastefull and cozy by nimble fingers. Lamp-shades, toilet sets, wreaths, boquets, fans and numberless other things, which ingenious minds will think of, can be made and decorated with paper flowers. which are one of the simplest kind of fancy work, and undoubtedly one of the most fascinating, the peculiar facination about it being unlimited variety.

We have endeavored to represent in these pages a considerate number of the most popular and ornamental flowers now used by ladies who have excelled in this direction. We will commence by giving the little field daisy which is perhaps the simplest and quickest made. It requires no rubber tubing or extra stems.

PAPER FLOWERS

Materials: Dead white paper (it might now be said that the paper is not the common tissue paper, but heavy and tough tissue paper) medium yellow paper, a piece of wire three inches long, and a pair of scissors. Have a field daisy at hand, take it apart carefully, draw an exact copy off of the lower part of the daisy, out of the white paper cut two pieces like the pattern, hold them in the finger and with the scissors curl each prong, taking care not to curl too much as the prong will turn clear under; take a pin and punch two holes, one on each side of the center of these two pieces; next cut a pattern from the upper part of the daisy, and cut of the yellow paper 20 or 30 pieces the same size; punch two holes in these pieces the same as in the white paper, turn down one-half an inch of the wire, put both ends of the wire through the holes made in the yellow paper, take the scissors and clip all around the edge as near the centre as possible, muss it with the fingers to make it round on the top so the wire will not show in the centre; now put the ends of the wire through the holes in the white paper, draw them together tightly and twist the wires, and the field daisy is finished. For just the common little daisy make just as you did the upper part of the field daisy, taking pink, red, etc.

WATER LILY.

For this, two shades of green, one yellow and one of white paper are required. If a water lily is at hand take it a part and take patterns off of its various parts; from the pattern taken from the bottom part of the lily, cut two of the darker shade of green and one of the lighter shade, also one of the white; curl each prong of each paper separately by laying the paper on the open hand and taking a large hat pin (with a round button on the end of it) and rubbing the head of the hat pin over each prong; the hand being soft and the pressure of the pin will cause each prong to curl up just like the natural flower. After all are curled in a like manner, set one in the other, putting the dark green on the bottom, the light green next and the white on top; make a yellow center like the one needed for the field daisy; set this in the lower part of the lily and fasten same as field daisy. For water lily buds, take a small piece of cotton and fasten it on to a piece of wire, cut four common leaves of green paper and tie around the cotton and gum here and there and you have the bud.

Any one with nimble fingers who has succeeded in the easy task of making the daisy or water lily, will have no difficulty in making the tulip.

Tulip.

Take a pattern from a tulip, make seven of them any shade to suit individual taste. To give it the appearance of reality, curl the leaves with the fingers slightly, turning the curled side toward the center. The petals are easily constructed over tiny wads of cotton covered with paper and fastened on very fine wires, and these wires fastened on to the main stem. To fasten the leaves on to the stem, take a peice of thread and wrap the leaves to the stem, one at a time, fastening the petals on first. To wrap the stem, either zephyr or green paper will do.

Rose.

By close observance one will find that there are five sizes of leaves in the rose. Take a pattern from each size; numbering them 1, 2, 3, 4, 5, calling the smallest size 1, etc. From size

1 make 14 leaves, size 2 make 10 leaves, size 3 make 12, size 4 also 12 and size 5 fourteen leaves. Curl them by pressing the scissor slightly on the under side, always curling two together; then from size 1 you will only have 7 after they are curled, etc. Twist the lower ends slightly with the fingers; take 3 of size 1, and turning two of them together, that is, turn them face upward together, fasten them to the wire stem by wrapping them with thread. Wrap all on in this manner turning on edge in between the preceeding ones, using the smaller sizes first; the stem may be wrapped if desired.

Poppy.

After taking a pattern from the poppy, cut one of the tissue paper any shade. The petals are made first, as described in the tulip, fasten them to the stem; take the leaf cut out of the tissue paper and crease it with the finger, the more unequal the creases the more natural is the effect; run the stem the petals are fastened on to, through the leaf and wrap the stem. The buds for the poppy are made similar to the water lily buds.

Fuchsia.

Take the fuchsia apart and take the patterns off of the parts; great care should be taken in cutting the calyx exactly like the flower; with a piece of cotton or wool wrap the wire tightly around the stem for a distance of three-fourths of an inch. Gum the small leaf form of the fuchsia on to the top of the wire, then gum the calyx on; with the scissors curl the four prongs of the calyx; make the petals as described, or they can be purchased of any dealer in such articles.

PAPER FLOWERS.

Pink.

There will be but little difficulty in making the pink, for although there are many leaves they are all of one shape, and it is only necessary to cut them of different sizes. The number of leaves depend, of course with the size of the pink. The first thing to be done after the cutting of the leaves is to make a firm ball of wool or cotton and fasten in on to the wire for a center, and gum the smallest leaf on to it, then, one by one gum the larger ones on to this central foundation, keeping of course, the largest ones for the outside and not gumming so closely as the work proceeds. The bud is made by taking a piece of green paper and notching the ends and twisting and gumming it around a piece of cotton that is fastened to the stem.

Plaques.

Beautiful and tasteful plaques can be made by making a rose, pink, a few daisies and a tulip and fastening on to the plaque, which is covered with crushed or rustic paper. To make crushed paper take a sheet or half a sheet of the tissue paper and crumple it all in the hand, then straighten it out and crumple it again; cover a plaque with this which assumes the appearance of silk. To make rustic paper, instead of crushing, plait the paper in fine knife plaits, press them between the fingers while in plaits, open out and be careful not to tear while pressing. This presents a beautiful and marked contrast to the crushed paper.

Petunias.

These pretty little flowers are very simple. Here any shade or color may be used, shaded petunias being especially beautiful. The little cup is easily made, and this is the foundation of the flower. Carefully w.. p the wire with cotton or wool for a distance of one-half inch, fasten on the calyx by gumming. A little coaxing is necessary in the settling of the leaves, and the careful touch can only be given in accordance with individual taste and judgment. After having arranged the leaves as may be considered most desirable, place the little cup around the wadded stem and gum securely to it. The most appropriate shade for this little cup is green. To make the buds the only difference from the full bloom flower being, that the center wadding round instead of long, and in working it the leaves are pinched a little upward and inward.

BUTTERCUP.

This flower is very nice for beginners to work on, as the leaf form is simplicity itself, the only trouble being in making the petals, and as the structure of the petal has already been described it is unnecessary to mention it again. After gumming the petals on to the stem, gum the leaf form on.

DAHLIA.

Make 30 leaves varying in sizes, say six sizes; wrap a bunch of yellow zephyr on the wire, then either tie or gum the leaves on in graduated sizes, commencing with the smallest size. The size of the dahlia must, of course, depend upon the number of leaves used in its construction.

WOOL FLOWERS.

Materials: Brass wire, zepher, two lead pencils, white shell beads, small glass beads, knitting needles and a heavy fine comb. To make a green leaf, use a piece of wire one-half yard long, a piece of zephyr one and one-half yards long. Place the two lead pencils together between the thumb and forefinger of the left hand, bring the middle of the wire around the pencils, and cross it under the thumb; divide the zephyr in 3 equal parts, place the ends over the crossed wire under the thumb; cross the wire again, this time over the zephyr, and not around the pencils; wrap the zephyr around the pencils, and cross the wire over it again; proceed in this manner until the zephyr is all used up; then pull the pencils out and twist the wire securely to prevent the work from coming undone; with the scissors cut the zephyr, comb until it looks like a flake of cotton, trim to give the appearance of reality Wrap the stem with split zephyr, tie up close to the leaf. A very pretty way of fixing leaves under a rose is putting them in single and in tige (i. e. 3 leaves on a stem).

Tiger Lily.

It would be lovely to make a tiger lily of pure white, the innermost heart being of yellow. Here there is a great opportunity for the display of individual taste, for although everyone would say a tiger lily was yellow or white, a kneen observer knows that those colors include shades and gradations of every variety, and in able hands the lily will become a marvel of delicate work, for zephyr can be obtained in every conceivable shade.

Make six leaves the same as the green leaf was made; for petals, wrap wire with split zephyr and pinch a tiny of yellow zephyr on the end or, wrap wire closely around a knitting needle, slip it off, and string either large or small beads on. With the remaining lengths of wire twist together, placing the petals in the center. The leaves should be bent downward with the fingers and the flower can be left open or closed, as may be considered most desirable.

ROSE.

The leaves are made the same as the green leaf, only not so large; the small leaves for the innermost part of the rose should be made with but one pencil. The little center of the rose is easily made and the flower naturally rises from it. This can be made of fluffed out wool or zephyr fastened on to the main stem. The central leaves are very small, and are 5 in number, the next size 5, next 6, and largest size 7. These are fastened together the same as the leaves of the paper rose; for buds, make a small ponpon, the same as for any kind of fancy work; comb it thoroughly; place four or five strands of green zephyr around the ponpon, and comb it also; insert a piece of wire into the center of the ponpon for a stem; wrap the stem. Dampen the fingers slightly, bring the green zephyr around the ponpon sparingly, twist together at the top, to give it the apperance of reality.

To make pansies and other flowers, the leaves are all made the same way, using one or two pencils according to the width of the leaf; for the length one must use judgment.

A very pretty way to make a few choice flowers is to weave them, as the variety is limited.

A WOVEN ROSE.

Take a long piece of wire, wrap it around a knitting needle very closely, leaving enough at each end for stems; slip this off the needle, fasten both the plain ends together, this forms a leaf; tie a piece of split zephyr on where the ends are fastened together, lay it across the center of the frame of the leaf, bring it down to the next division of the spiral frame next the stem, then up at the top again, down the bottom, and so continue until the frame is entirely filled. The number of leaves (usually 12) to make a rose varies in accordance to the size wanted; after the leaves are made they are put together the same as paper rose. These flowers are very dainty and appropriate for forming the center piece of a wreath made of the combed zephyr flowers.

HAIR FLOWERS.

Certainly nothing could be more lasting and beautiful than HAIR FLOWERS. Perhaps not as elegant as the paper or wool flowers, but nevertheless they have a certain charm about them that cannot be explained unless it is that we hold dear the material from which they are made. If we have a lock of hair of some friend, either living or dead, it is likely to be lost or destroyed by being placed here and there, but if woven into a flower and the flower placed in a wreath, it will will last for ages, and may be handed down from one generation to the other.

Materials: Hair, knitting needle, brass or steel. Take a small quantity of hair (which must be of the same length) and weave it just the same as the combed zephyr flowers using a knitting needle, instead of pencils; slip it off of the needle, but do not cut as the zephyr was out; bring the two ends together and twist securely, wrap with brown thread No. 16. This forms one of the leaves for the rose. For the outside row use more hair than for the inside row. For the centre weave yellow hair, and after it is woven coil in a round coil, leaving enough of the ends to be wtapped in with the stems. To make the center of another flower, take a bunch of hair about one-half the thickness of the little finger and about two inches in length, fasten to a piece of wire that has previously been doubled four times, tying it on securely, spread the hair out over the wire, this will gi it a spherical appearance. The vari ty of hair flowers is very limited, but any one with taste can arrange in different forms so as to amply repay the time expended on them. In case the leaf to be made should be a wide one, use two knitting needles.

FEATHER FLOWERS.

Ah! Now we have something that it is not everybody that knows how to make.

Materials: Goose feathers, wire, green tissue paper and wax (that is made by using 3 parts resin and 1 part beeswax). Trim the down all off of the quill, turn about $\frac{1}{8}$ of an inch of the wire stem, place a small piece of wax on this, put the feathers on by sticking the ends into the wax. When there are a sufficient number waxed on, wrap the stem with green tissue paper. The feathers can be cut in various shapes, and patterns can be taken from natural flowers. The flowers may be constructed on the same principle as the paper flowers. Of course there can be but one shade of feathers, but every conceivable shade can be made by mixing. Take paints turpentine and apply it to the feathers with a brush. This should be done before putting the flower together. To make a crystal flower, put a quantity of resin in a tin pan, place it on the stove; when it is hot dip the feathers quickly through. To make any color, put mixed paint in with the resin, or buy the colored sealing wax.

TINSEL FLOWERS.

Flowers can be made of tinsel foil just the same as of paper, using the same patterns and the same mode of construction. Tinsel foil can be obtained in all shades, and if not, can be painted by using the paints just as they come out of the tubes.

CHRISTMAS TREE ORNAMENTS.

First a few paper flowers will be needed for the tips of the branches, then a few sheets of tinsel foil of various shades, and cut in long narrow strips. Strew it about the tree to give it a brilliant appearance. Of course among the decorations a strand of popcorn is always acceptable. Hangings made of stiff pape of different colors making a chain, which takes a graceful form in falling is particularly effective, and when the skilled worker adds a few paper flowers it is impossible to exaggerate the pleasing effect produced. The whole room is lighted up by it. Another very pretty ornament is the little fan. This is made by taking a piece of writing paper and covering it with tissue paper on both sides; plait it in five knife plaits, sew one end and let the other go loose. Paste paper fringe all the way around the fan. The fringe is made by cutting a sheet of paper lengthwise in two-four plaits, pulled through the hands until it becomes finally creased, cut the paper crosswise very fine. Tinsel cornicopias fringed around the top and filled with candy and nuts give a world of pleasure to the little folks. Tiny slipper cases are very beautiful; also tiny baskets knit of bright colored paper and lined with something bright and having a few flowers tacked on the side. Another one that will amply repay time expended on it, is the tiny window. This is made by taking a piece of paste board 5 or 6 inches long and gathering white colored swiss on at one end; paste some pretty card on the center of the card board, make tapestry of the swiss and draw back and fasten with a piece of red paper; this will give the appearance of a dainty little window.

Still another ornament is a small quantity covered with tinsel foil or tissue paper and some green leaves placed behind this so as to represent fruit. As these bunches of fruit are very light they may be fastened on to the end of a spray which will look like a tree bearing fruit.

Plaques of tinsel may also be made to look very attractive. Paper dolls, peanut Chinamen, little Santa Claus, paper parasols and feather balls are all very popular ornaments. Feather balls are made by taking a ball of cotton, and dying some feathers, all colors, stick them onto the cotton with prepared carriage glue. This makes something that cannot be surpassed in beauty and attractiveness. There is endless opportunity for the exercise of taste and literally no limit to the variations which the fancy and ingenious mind may suggest and carry out as the most charming method of beautifying the Christmas tree.

FEATHER WORK.

What a pity that so many feathers are thrown away or burned every year, when an endless variety of beautiful, ornamental and useful things can be made from them.

Now, my dear readers, do not suppose a moment, that you are compelled to buy prepared feathers, nor do you need to slaughter the beautiful bird of the forest; merely save what heretofore you have thrown out in the alley.

First, we will take the chicken feathers and see what can be made from them. The wings can be taken just as they come from the foul, and dyed any color your taste may suggest. After taking them from the dye, have a board at hand that you may tack them on to dry; next, sprinkle the bone with powdered alum, copperas and salt petre; then stand it in the sun or behind the stove to dry. When this has been drying for a week or ten days, remove from the board and fasten them together, the points joining. Now, some loose feathers which have previously been dyed, will be needed to cover vacant places; a small bow of ribbon with long ends may be used at the base where the two wings join, and all is complete. This beautiful feather ornament is pretty and becoming if used to decorate the tops of bureaus or bedroom walls.

Another ornament has successfully been fashioned from them, which will always delight the heart of the artist, viz. a plaque. Take a piece of velvet or other material, cut it in any shape desired, stamp a large bird or foul on the cloth, dye feathers the proper colors and stick them on with prepared glue; use black beads for eyes. When finished you have something that cannot be surpassed for brightness, grace and beauty. Then again, there is still a simpler thing to be made from chicken feathers. Nothing prettier or more effective can be imagined than a picture frame covered with feathers; of course they must always be dyed and put on in such a way as to represent something.

Not long since a young lady wishing to appear as a young Irish huntress at a masque ball, was clever enough to take green calico for a shirt, trimming it around the bottom with feathers, leaving them their natural color, which gave it the appearance of fur; she also trimmed her leggins, belt and cap with the same.

Still another marvel of beauty to be made with feathers is is the landscape scenery which will show you the wonderful adaptability of them for ornamental purposes.

Turkey feathers should be saved by all means; the wings are always useful for dusting purposes around the hearth. The tail feathers may be made into a wall duster; and on one turkey there are enough downy feathers to make four yards of beautiful trimming three inches wide.

BEAD WORK.

Bead work has been somewhat neglected of late years in the rage of embroidery and painting, although beaded dress fronts are fast becoming popular.

Course net with beads sewed on in some pretty design, or sewed on in every other hole is very effective and lovely, and almost indistinguishable from the most expensive gauze or crape if nicely made. A most elaborate costume may be made this way by using a very delicate shade of pink beads. Of course one would think this tedious, but when we consider some of the specimens of men's work, which they spend months and even years to accomplish, and which are marvels of spider-web delicacy, bead work is comparatively speedy.

Beaded embroidery for children's dresses is now taking the place of silk embroidery; to do this, stamp the design to be worked, on the cloth, take linen or silk thread, sew the beads on just the same as arsene, filloselle or chenille work is done, using different colored beads for shading, etc.

Beaded work will in time become a most fascinating employment, as the result of labor expended is more marvelous than silk embroidery, and beads like silk can be obtained in almost every shade and gradation of variety. It is also much more inexpensive and durable than silk embroidery.

Gentlemens' and ladies' dressing slippers, and above all the tiny baby shoe can be beaded. This art has been learned from the Indian women who are professionals in this line of work, it being the height of their ambition to bead the moccasin for their lord. Nor must it be omitted to mention the delicate bead ball that ornaments the parlor chandalier; this is made by taking a small quantity of cotton, covering it with cheese-cloth and sewing beads all over it; if this is carefully done the success of brilliancy it will give when the room is lighted, will amply repay the time expended on it. The operator who has worked in bead work any length of time will find the most charming method of beautifying the household and adding to the attractiveness and the aesthetic influence of the home and fireside.

Recently, while visiting a friend from Illinois, my attention was called to a very attractive parlor ornament, which proved to be a bird cage, and on close examination I found it to be made from beads and even the bird itself was made of beads; in the bird's mouth was a spray of wheat also made of beads. The bird cage is made of brass wire, with beads strung on it, which is as easily done as stringing beads on thread. By looking at any bird cage the beaded wires can be fashioned into the same shape; there can be no difficulty whatever in the actual construction of the cage; all that is needed is patience, and of course some skill is required in fitting the wires tastefully at the top of the cage. The bird is somewhat more difficult and requires more skill in the making, although the body is in reality simple. A small quantity of cotton with a little coaxing may be wrapped with thread, and made to assume the appearance of a bird, with a few delicate caresses to be given in accordance with individual talant. Next, sew beads all over the bird, using black beads for eyes and beeswax for a beak; if desired the tail and wing feathers may be made of darker beads.

Beaded Lamp Screen.

Lamp screens are fast taking the place of hand shades. A very majestic one may be made by stamping on a piece of linen a small bunch of flowers and working it with beads; on another piece of linen stamp a large star or half moon and work it with beads, making the background of black beads; when both are beaded sew together and add a border of gilt beads, or if a beveled edge is desired sew on alternately large and small beads; balls of beads may be fastened on the corners and a wide chain of beads be used to fasten the screen on to the screen stand (i. e. if it be a banner screen). The result is as pretty a combination as one could wish to see. It is especially handsome and artistic in the brightly lit parlor, when the beads will shine like so many diamonds.

Beaded Purse.

The beads are sewed on fine canvas and the ground work is of dark blue beads; work a design of yellow beads in the form of wreath. Both sides may be worked alike, or, if preferred, the monogram of the cover may be worked in yellow beads on the opposite. To join the two sides place them together, and with a crochet hook and silk, work double stitches through both nearly all around, leaving a space for the opening; then work four rows of double stitches.

For the opening, work on each side separately; first row, one double into each stitch of canvas; second to fifth rows; pass over the two first and two last stitches. A steel clasp is sewed to each side of the opening. For the fringe, thread yellow beads on linen thread and sew them in loops at equal distances to the last row of double stitches.

Beaded Fischu.

These beaded fischus are a very great success. They can be either beaded only on the border, or the entire body and border can be made of beads, and clever fingers have not only fashioned beaded fischus, but reticules, bonbonmieres, mats and tidies as well, with a wonderfully happy effect. To make the fischu take a piece of bobonet a yard square; on each crossing of the net sew a bead; do the entire piece this way; for the border scallop a piece of net and with the beads button-hole stitch the edge, then sew on to the main body. A heavy couching of large beads covers the same; this makes a plain fischu. For the more elaborate ones, flowers and figures may be sewed on top of the other beads or make a background of small beads and for the design use larger beads or different shade of beads used for the back ground, which produces an admirable effect. A little neatness in beading, a little taste in the selection of colors, will make the fischu a manuel of prettiness. Another recommendation for beads would be the comparatively trifling expense, and in addition to this there is scarcely a combination which cannot be produced in beads themselves. Fringes, laces, trimmings of every kind can be made with them, and in this aesthetic age there is no material that will convey at the same time the same idea of lightness, grace and beauty. In fact, it is very difficult to say what there is that CANNOT be made with beads. And as using beads for ornamenting as well as for dress wear, we must not forget that they are used for medical purposes, and have been known to cure cases of goitre of long standing. Of course the common little bead will not do this; it requires the AMBER BEADS. These can be purchased of almost any jeweler for a nominal sum. The way to tell if you have the true amber bead is to take a pen knife and try to clip a piece off and burn it; if it will clip or burn it is good. They should be worn as tight as is comfortable over the goitre, on the neck and not on the dress.

BEADED WATCH CASE.

Cut a piece of perforated card board in the shape of a slipper the desired size; then cut off the same kind of board a smaller piece for the pocket; line it on the inside with pale blue satin, and fasten it to the larger piece; (having the blue side face the larger piece); line the large piece also with blue. On the outside work in cross stitch white beads, using blue silk thread to sew them on with. The edge is finished with a leaf ruche of blue ribbon or chenille. A brass ring button hole stitched round is fastened at the top to fasten it by.

We cannot close our brief chapter on bead work without alluding to the use of them in the nursery. Toys carefully made and covered with beads give a world of pleasure to the little folks. Doll dresses beaded, and soldier's clothes beaded will produce such an "millennium" in the nursery world that no one who has tried them will consent be without them.

A beaded ring for a very young child is always admirable; and who is it that does not love to see the string of tiny beads around the infant's neck? and while it looks pretty it prevents the neck from getting sore as the beads are always cooling to the flesh.

KNITTING DEPARTMENT.

Abbreviations: K, knit plain; n, narrow; p, purlor seam; t, twice; tog. together; tto, throw thread over; s, slip; s and b, slip and bind; st, stich.

There are still other abbreviations, such as m, make or widen; l, loop; o, over.

The following patterns have been purchased from or contributed by reliable parties.

KNITTING DEPARTMENT.

PRETTY INSERTION.

No. 1. Cast on twenty-two stitches.

1st row: K 2, o 2, p 2 tog, k 6, l 4. o 2, k 2, o 2, k 2. o 2 p 2 tog, k 2.

2nd row: K 2, o2, p 2 tog, k 2, k 1, p 1, k 2, k 1, p 1, k 6, o 2, p 2 tog, k 2.

3rd row: k 2, o 2, p 2 tog, k 14, o 2, p 2 tog, k 2.

4th row: k 2, o 2, p 2 tog, k 6, 1of 4, o 2, k 2, o 2, k 2, o 2, p 2 tog, k 2.

5th row: k 2, o 2, p 2 tog, k 2, k 1, p 1, k 2, k 1, p 1, k 6, o 2, p 2 tog, k 2.

6th row: k 2, o 2, p 2 tog, k 14, o 2, p 2 tog, k 2.

There will be 22 stitches at the end of every row.

TIDY LACE.

No. 2. Cast on twelve stiches and knit across plain.

1st row: k 3, n, o, n, o, k 3, o, k 2.

2nd row: k 2, p 1, k 3, p 1, k 1, p 1, k 4.

3d row: k 2, n, o, n, o, k 5, o, k 2.

4th row: k 2, p 1, k 5, p 1, k 1, p 1, k 3.

5th row: k 4, o, n, o, n, k 1, n, o, n, k 1.

6th row: k 2, p 1, k 3, p 1, k 1, p 1, k 4.

7th row: k 5, o, n, o, s 1, n, pull slipped stitch over, then o, n, k 1.

8th row: k 2, p 1, k 1, p 1, k 1, p 1, k 5.

There will be 13 stitches on the needle at the end of each row except the last two which will have 12.

BASKET LACE.

No. 3. Cast on 23 stitches and knit across plain.

1st row: Slip 1, k 2, o, n, o, n, k 16.

2nd row: k 1, o 3, (*) k 1, o 3, repeat from (*) until you have only 7 stitches; these you knit plain.

3rd row: s 1, k 2, o, n, o, n. Now with the right hand needle slip off from the left hand needle each knitted stitch and drop the loops. After slipping the first knitted stitch to the right hand needle drop three loops; slip the next knitted stitch and drop 3 loops; do this all across and you will have 16 long stitches on the needle and 7 stiches as a heading. Pull up the long stitches to an equal length and put the 16 long stitches back on the left needle. Then take the 5th long stitch and cast it over the 4 preceding long stitches so that it can be knit and thus transferred to the right hand needle. Cast or slip 3 more succeeding long stitches over the same 4 stitches and knit them, then knit the 4 stitches plain; you have now 8 more long stitches on the left needle; knit them in the same manner by slipping the 5th stitch over the 4th and knitting it, then the 6th, 7th and 8th, and there will be 23 stitches on the needle.

4th row: Knit plain.

LACE SIX INCHES WIDE.

No. 4. Cast on 37 stitches and knit across plain.

1st row: Purl first stitch, k 1, t t t o, p 2 tog, k 1, t t o, k 2 tog, t t o, k 2 tog, k 6, t t o, k 2 tog, t t o, k 2 tog, t t o, k 2 tog, k 6, t t o, k 2 tog, t t o, k 2 tog, t t o, k 2 tog, k 1.

2nd row: K 3, m 1, knit off all the stitches until last four t t t o, p 2 tog, k 2.

3rd row: Purl 1, k 1, t t t o, p 2 tog, k 2, t t o, k 2 tog.

4th row: T t o, k t tog, t t o, k 2 tog, k 6, t t o, k 2 tog, t t o, k 2 tog, t t o, k 2 tog. k 6, t t o, k 2 tog, t t o, k 2 tog, t t o, k 2 tog, k 1.

5th row: K 3, m 1, knit off all the stitches until last four, t t t o, p 2 tog, k 2.

6th row: P 1, k 1, t t t o, p 2 tog, k 3, t t o, k 2 tog, t t o, k 2 tog, t t o, k 2 tog, k 6, t t o, k 2 tog, t t o, k 2 tog, t t o. k 2 tog, k 6, t t o, k 2 t, t t o, k 2 tog, t t o, k 2 tog, k 1.

7th row: K 3, m 1, knit off all the stitches until last four, t t t o, p 2 tog, k 2.

8th row: P 1, k 1, t t t o, k 2 tog, k 6, t t o, k 2 tog, t t o, k 2 tog, t t o, k 2 tog, k 6, t t o, k 2 tog, t t o, k 2 tog, t t o, k 2 tog, k 6, t t o, k 2 tog, t t o, k 2 tog, t t o. k 2 tog, k 1.

9th row: K 3, m 1, knit across until last four t t t o, p 2 tog, k 2.

10th row: P 1, k 1, t t t o, p 2 tog, k 5, t t o, k 2 tog, t t o, k 2 tog, t t o, k 2 tog k 6, t t o, k 2 tog, t t o, k 2 tog, t t o, k 2 tog, k 6, t t o, k 2 tog, t t o, k 2 tog, t t o, k 2 tog, t t o, k 2 tog, k 1.

11th row: Same as 9th.

12th row: P 1, k 1, t t t o, p 2 tog, k 6, t t o, k 2 tog, t t o, k 2 tog, t t o, k 2 tog, k 6, t t o, k 2 tog, t t o, k 2 tog, t t o, k 2 tog, k 6, t t o, k 2 tog, t t o, k 2 tog, t t o, k 2 tog, k 1.

13th row: K 3, m 1, knit across until last four, t t 2 o, p 2 tog, k 2.

14th row: P 1, k 1, t t t o, p 2 tog, k 7, t t o, k 2 tog, t t o, k 2 tog, t t o, k 2 tog, k 6, t t o, k 2 tog, t t o, k 2 tog, t t o, k 2 tog, k 6, t t o, k 2 tog, t t o, k 2 tog, t t o, k 2 tog, k 1.

KNITTING DEPARTMENT.

15th row: K 3, m 1, knit across until last four, t t t o, p 2 tog, k 2.

16th row: P 1, k 1, t t t o, p 2 tog, k 8, t t o, k 2 tog, t t o, k 2 tog, t t o, k 2 tog, k 6, t t o, k 2 tog, t t o, k 2 tog, t t o, k 2 tog, k 6, t t o, k 2 tog, t t o, k 2 tog, t t o, k 2 tog, k 1.

17th row: K 3, m 1, knit across until last four, t t t o, k 2 tog, k 2.

18th row: P 1, k 1, t t t o, p 2 tog, k 9, t t o, k 2 tog, t t o, k 2 tog, t t o, k 2 tog, k 6, t t o, k 2 tog, t t o, k 2 tog, t t o, k 2 tog, k 6, t t o, k 2 tog, t t o, k 2 tog, t t o, k 2 tog, k 1.

19th row: Knit across plain until last four stitches, t t t o, p 2 tog, k 2.

20th row: P 1, k 1, t t t o, p 2 tog, knit plain across. Now reverse the pattern narrowing where you widen for twenty rows.

BEAD LACE.

No. 5. Cast on nineteen stitches.

1st row: K 3, o, n, k 2, o, n, k 1, n, o, k 2, o 2, n, o 2, n.

2nd row: K 2, p 1, k 2, p 1, n, k 1, o, s 1, n, pass slipped stitch over, o, k 3, o, n, n, o, n, k 1.

3rd row: K 3, o, n, o, n, k 1, n, o, k 1, o, k 1, n, k 6.

4th row: Cast off two stitches, k 5, o, k 3, o, s 1, n, pass slipped stitch over o, k 3, o, n, k 1.

BEAD INSERTION.

No 6. Cast on 21 stitches and knit across plain.

1st row: K 3, o, n, k 2, o, k 1, o, n, k 1, n, o, k 1, o, k 4, o.

n, k 1.

2nd row: K 3, o, n, n, o, k 3, o, s 1, n; pass slipped stitch over, o, k 3, o, n, k 2, o, n, k 1.

3rd row: K 3, o, k 3, tog, o, n, k 1, n, o, k1 , o, n, k 1, n, o, n, k 1, o, n, k 1.

4th row: K 3, o, n, k 1, o, s 1, n, pass slipped stitch over, o, k 3, o, s 1, n, pass slipped stitch over, o, k 3, o, n, k 1.

Gentlemens' Knit Slippers.

No. 7. Knit with two colors of zepher, sav scarlet and brown. These are very pretty shoes, re very comfortable, serviceable and warm. It requires 1½ oz. of scarlet and 6 oz. of brown zepher. Cast on 26 stiches and knit across with brown zepher.

1st row: L 2 with brown wool, k 2 with scarlet wool, continue in like manner until all the stitches are used but the last two; leave them on the needle.

2nd row: Turn p 2 with scarlet wool, l 2 with brown wool, repeat the same until last 2, leave them.

3rd row: Turn (*) k 2 with scarlet, l 2 with brown, repeat from (*) until last 2, leave them.

4th row: Turn (*) p 2 with scarlet, l 2 brown (*) repeat that enclosed in star until last 2, loop last 2.

5th row: (*) n 1, p 1, k 2, p 2, repeat from star until last 1, m 1.

6th row: Knit across plain.

7th row: M 1, p clear across until last stitch, m 1.

8th row: Same as 6th row.

Continue to knit like the above until your slipper is large enough at the toe. Now cast off all the stitches but one-third, and knit as before until the strip is long enough to go around the heel and fasten on the opposite side. Trim the top with knitted astrican. Finish with bow of ribbon on the front.

Oregon Lace.

No. 8. Cast on twenty stitches and knit across.

1st row: K 13, n, o, k 3, o, k 2.

2nd row: K 2, o, k 5, o, n, k 3, o, n, o, n, k 2, o, n, k 1.

3d row: K 11, n, o, k 1, n, o, k 1, o, n, k 1, o, k 2.

4th row: K 2, o, k 1, n, o, k 3, o, n, k 1, o, n, k 2, o, n o, n, k 1, o, n, k 1.

5th row: K 9, n, o, k 1, n, o, k 5, o, n, k 1, o, k 2.

6th row: K 2, o, k 1, n, o, k 3, o, n, k 2, o, n, k 1, o, n, k 2, o, n, k 1, o, n, o, n, o, n, k 1.

7th row: K 1 o, o, n, k 1, o, n, k 3, n, o, k 1, n, o, k 1, n

8th row: Cast off one, k 1, o, n, k 1, o, n, k 1, n, o, k 1, m, o, k 8, o, n, k 1.

9th row: K 5, o, n, o, n, k 3, o, n, k 1, o, s 1, m, pass slipped stitch over, over, k 1, n, k 1, n.

10th row: K 2, o, n, k 3, n, o, k 10, o, n, k 1.

11th row: K 6, o, n, o, n, k 4, o, n, k 1, n, o, k 3.

12th row: Cast off 2, k 1, o, k 3 tog, o, k 12, o, n, k 1.

Infant's Lace, 1.

No. 9. Cast on three stitches and knit across plain.

1st row: K 2, t t t o, k 2.
2d row: K 2, k 1 l, p t, l, k 1.
3d row: K 5.
4th row: Bind off 2, k 2.

Infant's Lace. 2.

No. 10. Cast on five stitches and knit across plain.
1st row: K 1, t t o, k 2 tog, t t t o, k 2.
2nd row: K 2, k 1 l, p 1 l, k 3.
3d row: K 1, t t o, k 2 tog, k 4.
4th row: Bind off 2, k 4.

Baby Lace, 1 Inch Wide.

No. 11. Cast on nine stitches and knit across plain.
1st row: S 1, k 2, t t o, k 2 tog, k 1, t t t o, n, k 1.
2nd row: K 2, k 1 l, p 1 l, k 3, t t o, n, k 1.
3d row: 1, k 2, t t o, n, k 5.
4th row: K 7, t t o n, k 1.
5th row: S 1, k 2, t t o, n, k 1, t t t o, n, t t t o, n.
6th row: K 1, k 1 l, p 1 l, k 1, k 1 l, p 1 l, k 3, t t o, n, k 1.
7th row: S 1, k 2, t t o, n, k 7.
8th row: K 1, bind off 3, k 5, t t o, n, k 1.

Fern Lace.

No. 12. Cast on twelve stitches and knit across plain.
1st row: K 2, t t t o, n, k 6, t t t o, p tog.
2nd row: T t o, p 2 tog, k 7, k 1 l, p 1 l, k 2.

KNITTING DEPARTMENT.

3d row: K 11, t t t o, p 2 tog.
4th row: T t o, p 2 tog, k 11.
5th row: K 2, t t o, n, t t t o, n, k 5, t t t o, p 2 tog.
6th row: T t o, p 2 tog, k 6, k 1 1, p 1 1, k 1, k 1 1,
7th row: K 13, t t t o, p 2 tog.
8th row: T t o, p 2 tog, k 13.
9th row: K 2, t t t o, n, t t t o, n, t t t o, n, k h, t t t o, p 2 tog.
10th row: T t o, p 2 tog, k 6, k 1 1, p 1 1, k 1, k 1 1, p 11, k 2.
11th row: K 11, take 11 back on left-hand needle and slip six stitches over that stitch, t t t o, p 2 tog.
12th row: T t o, p 2 tog, k 10.

Louis Lace.

No. 13. Cast on 12 stitches and knit across plain twice.
1st row: S 1, k 1, t t o, n, t t o, n, t t o, n, k 6.
2nd row: Second and every alternate row knit plain.
3d row: S 1, k 1, t t o, n, t t o, n, t t o, n, t t o, k 5.
5th row: S 1, k 1, t t o, n, t t o, n, t t o, n, t t o, k 6.
7th row: S 1, k 1, t t o, n, t t o, n, t t o, n, t t o, k 8.
9th row: S 1, k 1, t t o, n, t t o, n, t t o, n, t t o, k 8.
11th row: S 1, k 1, t t o, n, t t o, n, t t o, n, t t o, k 9.
13th row: S 1, k 1, t t o, n, t t o, n, t t o, n, t t o, k 10.
15th row: All plain.
17th row: S 1, n, t t o, n, t t o, n, t t o, n, t t o, n, k 8.
19th row: S 1, n, t t o, n, t t o, n, t t o, n. t t o, n, k 7.
21st row: S 1, n, t t o, n, t t o, n, t t o, n, t t o, n, k 6.

23d row: S 1, n, tt o. n, t t o, n, t t o, n, t t o, n, k 5.
25th row: S 1, n, t t o, n, t t o, n, t t o, n, t t o, n, k 4.

CLYDE LACE.

No. 14. Cast on 7 stitches and knit across plain.
1st row: S 1, k 1, t t o, p 2 tog, k 1, o, k 2.
2nd row: K 2, p 1, k 1, t t o, p 2 tog, k 2.
3d row: S 1, k 1, t t o, p 2 tog, k 2, o, k 2.
4th row: K 2, p 1, k 2, t t o, p 2 tog, k 2.
5th row: S 1, k 1, t t o, p 2 tog, knit the rest plain.
6th row: Cast off 2 stitches, k 2, t t o, p 2 tog, k 2.

PLAYTHING FOR THE BABY.

No. 15. This is a charming little plaything for a baby, and very easily made. Set up 24 stitches with single zephyr (blue) and knit across plain 22 times. Then bind off, and leave an end long enough to sew up the sides. Take a needle with strong thread and run through each stitch on one end, and draw up firmly and fasten; then stuff with cotton; before it is quite filled, put in a twisted cord of blue and gold zephyr a little more than a quarter of a yard in length; then fill up and fasten as you did the first end. Make two more pieces, one of red and one of orange, stuffed as the first, and fasten to twisted cord; sew a little round bell on the end of each and attach the cord to a rubber ring. The cords should be an eighth of a yard long when finished.

BABIE'S KNITTED SHIRT.

No. 16. Long sleeves and high neck.

KNITTING DEPARTMENT.

Materials: Two skeins of three-threaded cream white Star Light Saxony yarn. Two fine bone needles.

BACK.

1st row: Cast on 78 stitches; knit across plain once.

2nd row: All seamed or purled.

3d row: Knit plain.

4th row: K 1, * n, k 3, m 1, k 1, m 1, k 3, n, *; repeat from star to star till last stitch which is knitted plain.

5th row: All seamed or p.

6th row: Same as 4th.

7th row: All seamed.

8th row: Same as 4th.

9th row: All plain.

10th row: All seamed.

11th row: All plain.

12th row: Same as 4th.

13th row: Same as 5th.

14th row: Same as 4th.

15th row: Same as 5th.

16th row: Same as 4th.

And so on repeating until there are 4 finished pattern rows, that is, 4 times 3 rows of eyelets with the ribbing between, and ribbed rows. In going across last row of border, narrow 3 stitches on each end of needle, leaving 72. Now knit 46 times across of 2 plain, seam 2. Now to shape the shoulder, n 1 at each end of needle every time across until there are

44 stitches left on needle, bind off loosely. This forms the back.

FRONT.

After you have made a border to match that of back, k 2, p 2, 36 times across. Take off one-half the stitches on another needle, and knit 10 times across still preserving the ribbing. Then narrow on outside of needle every time across until there are 28 stitches on needle. In inner end of needle (or middle of front) bind off 3 stitches every other time across (this is to hollow the neck) continuing the narrowing for shoulder as before until all are bound off, leaving yarn long enough to sew shoulder seam. Knit up the other half of front in same manner; sew up shoulder and sides on wrong side leaving space for sleeves.

SLEEVES.

Take medium-sized steel needles, k 2, p 2, alternately, till you have done 30 rows. In the 30th row widen 12 stitches, by picking them up at equal distances, making 52. Now put in the bone needles and knit 2, p 2, alternately for 40 rows. For gussets widen one stitch at each end of needle every other time across until there are six additional on each end, or 64 in all. Bind off, sew up and insert in body.

Now around the neck crochet a row of holes to put narrow ribbon in, then on this a little shell edge continuing it down the front of shirt; sew on front two little buttons; put on edge round cuff of sleeves and turn it up.

EDGING.

No. 17. Cast on twenty stitches.

1st row: Knit across plain.
2nd row: K 14, t t t o, n, k 1, t t t o, k 3.
3d row: K 10, t t t o, n, k 1, t t t o, n, k 6.
4th row: Like 2nd, also the sixth and eight.
5th row: K 12, t t t o, n, k 1, t t o, n, k 5.
7th row: K 14, t t t o, n, k 1, t t t o, n, k 4.
9th row: K 16, t t t o, n, k 1, t t t o, n, k 3.
10th row: Knit across plain.
11th row: S 1, n, k 1, t t t o, n, k 1, t t t o, n, k 15.
12th row: K 5, t t t o, n, k 1, t t t o, n, k 13
13th row: Like 11th.
14th row: K 6, t t t o, k 1, t t t o, n, k 11.
15th row: Like 11th.
16th row: K 7, t t t o, n, k 1, t t t o, n, k 9.
17th row: Like 11th.
18th row: K 8, t t t o, n, k 1, t t t o, n, k 7.

Whenever the thread is thrown over twice, knit the first loop and drop the second   T t t o, meaning throw thread twice over.

Another Edging.

No. 18. Cast on seven stitches and knit across plain.
1st row: K 2, t t t o, p 2 tog, k 1, t t t o, k 2.
2nd row: K 2, k 1 1, p 1 1, k 1, t t t o, p 2 tog, k 2.
3rd row: K 2, t t t o, p 2 tog, k 5.
4th row: Knit and bind off 2, k 2, t t t o, p 2 tog, k 2.

KNITTING DEPARTMENT.

KNITTED TIDY.

No. 19. Cast on eighty-nine stitches and knit across alternately eleven times plain and pur —plain when the smooth side is nearest the knitter and purl when the rough side is nearest.

1st row: K 12, n, * t t o, n, t t o, n, t t o, n, o, k 1, o, k 2, s 1, k 1, throw the slipped stich over or bind, k 4, s and b. k 2, repeat from star twice, o, k 12.

2nd row: Purl, all even rows the same.

3rd row: K 11, n, * t t o, n, t t o, n, t t o, n, t t o, k 3, t t o, k 2, s and b, k 2, s and b, k 2, repeat from   r twice: t t o, n, t t o, n, t t o, n, o, k 13.

5th row: K 10, n, * over and narrow three time , o, k 5, o, k 2, s and b twice, k 2, repeat from star twice then over and narrow 3 times, o, k 14.

7th row: K 12, * over and narrow 3 times, over, k 2, s and b, k 4, s and b, k 2, o, k 1, repeat from star twice then over and narrow 4 times, k 12.

9th row: K 13, * over and narrow three times, o, k 2, s and b, k 2, s and b, o, k 3, repeat from star twice then over and narrow four times, k 11.

11th row: K 14, * over and narrow three times, o, k 1, s and b twice, k 2, o, k 5, repeat from star twice, then over and narrow four times, k 10. Repeat from first row as many times as required then knit across eleven times alternately plain and purl. Add fringe or lace at the ends.

TWINING LEAF PATTERN.

No. 20. Cast on twenty stitches and knit across once.

1st row: K 2, o, n, o, k 1, o, n, p 1, n, p 1, s 1, k 1, and pass slip stitch over, p 1, s 1, k 1, pass slip stitch, o, k 1, o, n, o, k 1.

2nd row: Pu l knitting, except the stitches purled in the last row, which are now to be knitted.

3rd row: K 2, o, n, o, k 3, o, k 3 tog, p 1, s 1, k 2 tog, and pass over the slipped stitch, o, k 3, o, n, o, k 1.

4th row: Same as second.

5th row: K 2, o, n, o, k 5, o, s 1, k 2 tog, and pass slipped stitch over, m 1, k 5, o, n, o, k 1.

6th row: All purl.

7th row: K 2, o, n, o, k 1, n, p 1, n, k 3, n, p 1, s 1, k 1, and pass slipped stitch over k 1, over, n, o, k 1.

8th row: Like second.

New Pattern.

No. 21. Cast on 18 stitches for each pattern.

1st row: P 1, s 1, k 1, and pass slipped stitch over, k 3, o, n, o, k 3, o, s 1, k 1, and pass slipped stitch over, m 1, k 3, n.

2nd row: P 17, k 1.

3rd row: P 1, s 1, k 1, pass slipped stitch over, k 2, o, k 2, o, k 1, s 1, k 2 tog, pass slipped stitch over, k 1, o, k 2, o, k 1, n.

4th row: Like second.

5th row: P 1, s 1, k 1, pass slipped stitch over, k 1, o, k 3, o, k 1, n.

6th row: Like second.

7th row: P 1, s 1, k 1, pass slipped stitch over, m 1, k 2,

KNITTING DEPARTMENT.

n, o, k 1, o, s 1, k 2 tog, pass slipped stitch over, n 1, k 1, o, s 1, k 1, pass slipped stitch over, k 2, o, n.

8th row. Like second.

KNITTED ASTRAKAN.

No 22. Cast on as many stitches as deemed necessary. For astrakan 3 inches wide put on 19 stitches and knit across plain three times.

1st row: * K 1, place needle in next stitch and while thus holding wrap the zephyr around the needle of the right hand and the fore-finger of the left hand seven times, then draw the thread around and knit through the same stitch, k 1.

2nd row: Knit all plain.

3rd row: Knit all plain.

Repeat from star.

ROSE LEAF LACE.

No. 23. Cast on twenty-eight stitches, knit across plain.

1st row: K 3, o, n, o, k 3, o. n, p 1, n, p 1, n, p 1, n, o, k 3, o, k 2, o, n, * o twice, k 2.

2nd row: S 1, k 2, p 1, * k 2, o, n, p 6, k 1, p 1, k 1, p 1, k 1, p 6, k 2, o, n, p 1.

3rd row: K 3, o, n, o, k 5, o, s 1, n, pass slipped stitch over, n, o, k 5, o, k 2, o, n, * k 4.

4th row: S 1, k 1, * over, n, p 8, k 1, p 8, k 2, o, n, p 1.

5th row: K 3, o, n, t t t o, k 1, n, p 1, n, p 1, o, s 1, n, pass slipped stitch over, n, o, k 1, n, p 1, n, k 1, t t t o. k 2. o, * n, o twice, n, t t t o, n.

6th row: S 1, k 1, p 1, k 2, p 1, k 2, * o, n, k 1, (the first of the over twice), p 3, k 1, p 7, k 1, p 3, k 3, o, n, p 1.

7th row: K 3, o, n, o, k 1, o, k 1, n, p 1, n, k 3, n, p 1, n. k 1, o, k 1, o, k 2, o, n, * k 6.

8th row: S 1, k 7, * o, n, p 5, k 1, p 5, k 5, o, n, p 1.

9th row. Same as first row to star, t t t o, n, o, twice, n. t t t o, n.

10th row: S 1, k 1, p 1, k 2, p 1, k 2, p 1, then like second after star.

11th row: Same as third row to star, k 9.

12th row: S 1, k 10, then like the second after star. Then same as 5th to star. Then narrow three together, over twice, n, over twice, n, over twice, n, over twice, n.

13th row: Same as 5th to star, then narrow three together, over twice, n, t t t o, n, o twice, n, o twice, n.

14th row: S 1, k 1, p 1, k 2, p 1, k 2, p 1, k 2, p 1, k 2. Then like 6th row after star.

15th row: Same as 7th row to star, then k 12.

16th row: Bind off 10, k 3, then like 7th after star.

Nice Knitted Edging.

No. 24. Cast on eight stitches and knit across plain.

1st row: Yarn around the needle and purl two tog, k 2, o twice, n, k 2.

2nd row: K 4, p 1, k 2, o twice, purl 2 tog.

3rd row: Yarn around the needle, p 2 tog, k 7.

4th row: K 7, o twice, p 2 tog

5th row: Yarn around the needle, p 2 tog, k 2, o twice, n, o twice, n, k 1.

6th row: K 3, p 1, k 2, p 1, k 2, o twice, p 2 tog.

7th row: Yarn around needle, p 2 tog, k 9.

8th row: B off three stitches, k 5, o t, p 2 tog.

KNITTED MATS.

No. 25. These mats are knit in three sizes; for the largest size cast on thirty-six stitches, and the smallest twenty-four.

1st row: K 3, turn and k the same 3 stitches over again.

2nd row: K 6, turn and k the same six stitches.

3rd row: K 9, turn and k the same nine stitches.

4th row: K 12, turn and k the same twelve stitches.

5th row: K 15, turn and k the same fifteen stitches.

Continue knitting the rest of the stitches in the same way only knitting three more stitches each time, and after knitting to the end of the needle, turn and seam back to the beginning: this forms a gore, and it takes 20 gores to form a mat; after knitting the last gore do not seam back to the beginning, but bind off the stitches and then sew the mat together.

A border may then be crocheted in colored worsted.

LADIES' KNITTED SCARF.

No. 26. Take a half-pound of double-scarlet zephyr, and 4 oz. of black-split zephyr and two large wooden needles. Cast on one hundred stitches.

1st row: Knit across 15 times with the black. Bind off, tie on the scarlet, knit across twice; continue knitting ten rows of black and two of scarlet until the scarf is long enough, and knit 15 times across to correspond with the beginning. Gather up the ends and place a ribbon bow on them, of black or scarlet, to harmonize with the color of the zephyr.

OLD LADIES' SHOULDER SHAWL.

No. 27. Use No. 9 wood knitting needles. Cast on three hundred stitches and knit across plain. To shape the shawl decrease by knitting two together at the end of every row. The above is knit of whole black zephyr.

2d to 9th row. Knit with whole scarlet zephyr.

10th row. Knit with black. To form the diamond-shaped pattern, when knitting the first and second stitch pick up and knit the corresponding stitches of the last row of the black with them, knit 8 stitches, then pick up and knit the corresponding stitches of the first row, and so on.

11th row. Knit with black. Repeat from the second row, reversing the pattern formed in the tenth row by picking up the stitches between those picked up in the tenth row. The edge is finished by crocheting a scolloped border of black.

CHILDS' LEGGINS.

No. 28. These leggins are knit lengthwise and then joined together. Knitting them in this way they keep their shape much better than when worked round. Cast on 24 stitches for the first row, which will be at the back seam when finished. This number must be increased to 70 stitches in 18 rows. The increase is made in this way: after knitting the second row cast on six more stitches at the end, making the increase in this way at the end of every second row. This will make the added stitches all on the lower end, the top being left straight, and will form the shape for the leg. At the end of the 20th row cast on 30 more stitches, which will make the length of the leggins 100 stitches. Knit 15 rows, then 12 more rows may be knit with some contrasting shade to form the side stripe; after knitting 12 rows in this way knit 15 more rows of the foundation color, then cast off the first eight stitches of the 16th row, leaving the remainder of the stitches on the needle for the present. The gore at the lower edge is now made by fastening the yarn to the first of the cast off stitches by which the first stitch is made; at the end of every forward row cast on two extra stitches, and in every backward row catch in one of the cast off stitches, which will all be taken up in 15 rows. In the 14th row cast on 14 stitches instead of 2 to form the part covering the instep; knit on next 40 rows the whole length of the leggin; cast off twelve stitches in the 40th row, and knit 16 stitches for the opposite gore; this will have 17 stitches on the needle. Decrease the gore by decreasing one stitch at the end of each row and casting off the last stitch. Now collect the eight stitches and knit 40 rows the whole length for the inside of the leggin; cast off thirty stitches from the next row and reduce the remaining 76 stitches to 24 in the next 19 rows and cast off. This finishes the foundation. To form holes for lacing, the first row of stitches on either side of the trimming stripe may be taken up and three or four rows knit, the holes being formed in next to last row by decreasing and increasing after every fifth stitch. Now seam the leggins together at the back, and take up the stitches at the top and knit 18 rows of two plain and two purl and cast off. Crocheted scollops at top and bottom are very pretty. These directions are for the right leggin, the left should be knit opposite in order to bring the stripe on the outside.

Ladies' Knit Wristlet.

No. 28. Knit with number 16 needles. If using Saxony yarn cast on 65 stitches using 4 needles. Knit two at the back and purl two alternately till 30 rows are knit, then purl three rows, increasing one stitch each in second and third rows. This finishes a fancy top. For the plain part of the wristlet knit at the back and purl alternately till five rows are knit, then reverse (knitting the stitch that was purled and purling the stitch that was knit) and knit five rows: This makes two divisions of the pattern. The increase for the thumb is now begun; this is done by making a stitch between the 4th and 5th stitches from the end of a pin. This extra stitch is made after a purled stitch so as to bring the stitches knitted at the back beside each other Knit out the four remaining stitches on the needle and four from the next needle, then increase or make another stitch for the other side of the gore. This increase is repeated in knitting every fresh division of five rows of the pattern, the second time the new stitch is made after a stitch taken at the back, that is between the 5th and 6th stitches from the end, this will bring the made stitch directly under the one in the last row, and will leave five more stitches on the needle to be knit or ten stitches between the two increased stitches. Continue alternately these two methods of increasing, making the new stitches under each other which will increase the number of stitches between the sides of the gore by two in each division. After increasing twelve times the top of the gore is reached, when the widening part consists of 32 stitches; knit two more divisions without widening before commencing the thumb. The thumb is knit with 3 stitches in the gore and 13 additional stitches taken from the other needles and caught together in a ring, the 45 stitches of the thumb are taken off at the beginning and end of the rows of next two divisions, then three more divisions or 17 rows more are to be knit with the 32 stitches, then three purl rows, then one whole row and three more purl rows, the thumb is then cast off. To complete the hand the 13 gore stitches are again picked up and knit with the other stitches of the hand; six of these 13 gore stitches, three on each side, are, however, decreased while knitting the next division; five more divisions are knit and then finished off like the thumb. These are finished with a crochet edge and a bow of ribbon.

KNIT EDGING.

No. 29. Cast on 14 stitches and knit across plain

1st row: t t o, 1, p 2 tog, t t t o, p 3 tog, k 3, t t t o, n, k 3, t t t o, n.

2nd row: Knit plain to the last four stiches, t t t o, p 2 tog, t t t o, p 2 tog.

3rd row: t t t o, p 2 tog, t t t o, p 2 tog, k 4, t t t o, n, k 3, t t t o, k 1.

4th row: 6th, 8th and 10th rows like 2nd.

5th row: t t t o, p 2 tog, t t t o, p 2 tog, k 5, t t t o, n, k 3, t t t o, k 1.

KNITTING DEPARTMENT.

7th row: t t t o, p 2 tog, t t t o, p 2 tog, k 6, t t t o, n, k 3, t t t o, k 1.

9th row: t t t o, p 2 tog, t t t o, p 2 tog, knit the rest plain.

10th row: n, t t t o, n, k 3, t t t o, n, k 4, t t t o, p 2 tog, t t t o, p 2 to .

11th row: 13th and 15th rows like 9th.

14th row: n, t t t o, n, k 3, t t t o, n, k 2, t t t o, p 2 tog, t t t o, p 2 tog.

ANOTHER KNIT EDGING.

No. 30. Cast on nine stitches and knit across plain.

1st row: k 3, n, t t o, n, t o, k 1, t t o, k 1.
2nd row: k 1, p 1, k 1, p 1, k 1, p 1, k 4.
3rd row: k 2, n, t t o, n, t t o, k 3, t t o, k 1.
4th row: k 1, p 1, k 3, p 1, k 1, p 1, k 3.
5th row: k 1, n, t t o, n, t t o, k 5, t t o, k 1.
6th row: k 1, p 1, k 5, p 1, k 1, p 1, k 2.
7th row: k 3, t t o, n, t t o, n, k 1, n, t t o, n.
8th row: k 1, p 1, k 3, p 1, k 1, p 1, k 3.
9th row: k 4, t t o, n, t t o, k 3, tog, t t o, n.
10th row: k 1, p 1, k 1, p 1, k 1, p 1, k 4.
11th row: k 5, t t o. k 3 tog, t t o, n.
12th row: k 1, p 1, k 1, p 1, k 5.

KNITTED TIDY.

No. 31. Cast on any number of stitches divisible by 5 with 3 extra for edge.

1st row: k 4, * slip the third stitch over the last, k 1, s 1, k 1, s 1, thread over three times, k 3, repeat from *. At the end there are only two stitches to knit after putting the thread over.

2nd row: * k 3, p 1, loop, k 1 1, k 3, repeat from *.
3rd and 4th rows knit plain.
5th row: Like the first.

LADIES' KNITTED MITTEN.

No. 32. Cast on 64 stitches and knit six rounds plain.
7th round k 2 tog, t t o, repeat to the end of round.
8th round: t t o, k 6, k 2 tog, repeat.
9th round: k 1, t t o, k 5, k 2 tog, repeat.
10th round: k 2, t t o, k 4, k 2 tog, repeat.
11th round: k 3, t t o, k 3, k 2 tog, repeat.
12th round: k 4, t t o, k 2, k 2 tog, repeat.
13th round: k 5, t t o, k 1, k 2 tog, repeat.
14th round: k 6, t t o, k 2 tog, repeat. Repeat from 8th to 14th rounds six times, which completes the fancy top; the rest of the mitten is plain knitting. Take the first two and the last two stitches of the last round for a basis for a thumb, purling one stitch each side of the three, and in the next round and in every fourth round thereafter make two stitches for increase of width of thumb, at the same time continuing in every round the two purled stripes which outline the same, until you have 23 stitches in thumb exclusive of purled stripes. The increase should be made the next stitch to be purled stripes. When you have 23 stitches in thumb, knit

three rounds plain, now slip the 27 thumb stitches on a piece of twine and tie securely, and with the remaining stitches continue the hand, knitting all plain and narrowing as thought best to shape the hand, and continue thus until the hand has reached a sufficient length. To narrow and finish off the hand, commence at the end, stitch off one of the needles. Knit 7, and narrow by knitting two together, repeat until the stitches on all the needles are reduced so as to be devisible by nine. Next round knit plain, then knit 7, narrow and repeat to the end of the round, knit 7 rounds plain, then knit 6, narrow, repeat and knit 6 rounds plain, then knit 5, narrow, repeat and knit 5 rounds plain; then knit 4, narrow, repeat and knit 4 rounds plain; now narrow once on each needle in every round until four stitches are left on each needle, then narrow twice on each needle and cast off.

To finish the thumb, place the 24 stitches on the 3 needles and pick up three stitches from the base of the gore found between the hand and thumb, then knit around once and narrow once or twice in the next two or three rounds; knit to sufficient length and finish off by narrowing once on each needle till all the stitches are disposed of.

KNITTED LACE.

No. 33. Knit to and fro 23 stitches as follows:

1st row: Slip one, knit 1, 4 times alternately, cotton forward, decrease 2, twice cotton forward, decrease 1, knit 2 together, cotton forward, decrease 1, knit 1.

2nd row: All rows with even numbers, knitted, knit 1, purl 1 in the double made stitches.

3d row: Slip 1, knit 2, 3 times alternately cotton forward, decrease 1, then knit 10, cotton forward, knit 2.

5th row: Slip 1, knit 1, 3 times alternately cotton forward, decrease 1, knit 2 together, twice cotton forward, decrease 1, knit 5, knit 2 together, twice cotton forward, decrease 1, knit, cotton forward, knit 2.

7th row: Slip 1, knit 2, twice alternately cotton forward, decrease 1, then knit 5, twice alternately cotton forward, decrease 1, then knit 5, cotton forward, knit 2.

9th row: Slip 1, knit 1, twice alternately cotton forward, decrease 1, then knit 4, cotton forward, decrease 1, knit 3, cotton forward, decrease 1, knit 2 together, twice cotton forward, decrease 1, knit 1, cotton forward, knit 2.

11th row: Slip 1, knit 2, twice alternately cotton forward, decrease 1, then knit 5, cotton forward, decrease 2, cotton forward, knit 5, knit 2 together, cotton forward, decrease 1, knit 1.

13th row: Slip 1, knit 1, 3 times alternately cotton forward, decrease 1, then knit 2 together, twice cotton forward, decrease 1, knit 3, knit 2 together, cotton forward, decrease 1, knit 1.

15th row: Slip 1, knit 2, 3 times alternately cotton forward, decrease 1, then knit 9, knit 2 together, cotton forward, decrease 1, knit 1.

After the 16th row repeat the 1st to the 16th row as often as necessary.

Childs' Knitted Skirt.

No. 34. This skirt is knit with two knitting needles, the

upper part ma'e with fine needles, and the border v' '' course this makes the skirt hang fuller at the bottom. Commence with the border. Cast on 200 stitches.

_st row: Knit plain in red wool.

'nd row: Change to blue and purl.

3rd row :Knit plain.

4th row: Knit 1, make 1, knit three together, knit, knit 2, make 1. Repeat from the beginning of the row.

Fifth, seventh and ninth rows are purled; the sixth, eighth and tenth are knit like the fourth row:

The tenth row finishes one row of the scallops of the border; to make the other rows of scallops repeat from the first to the tenth row three times more. The plain part of the skirt is very easily done, and is worked by purling three and knitting three alternately, observing that the stitches that are purled in one row must be knitted when knitting back in the next row, and those that are knitted must be purled.

When about half the length of the skirt has been knitted, change the needles and take the smaller ones.

When the proper length has been reached, cast the stitches off and sew the sides together to within abo.. .. .. of the top, then sew the top to a linen band.

LADIES' KNITTED JACKET.

No. 35. Materials: 12 ounces single wool. It is begun at the waist

Cast on 108 stitches, and knit the first two rows backward and forward.

3rd row: Slip the first stitch, * then the wool forward, knit 2 together: repeat from * to the end of row. Coming back knit 1 row plain, then 9 rows, alternately, 1 stitch plain and 1 purled, so as to form narrow ribs, work another plain row, then repeat the 3rd row, and coming back knit 1 row plain. Over this wasteband continue to knit in the following manner: knit odly the first 3 stitches of the last row, increasing 1 stitch between the 2nd and 3rd, then in returning knit plain. Begin again and knit 5 stitches, increasing between the 4th and 5th, and in return in plain knitting; in coming back knit 7 stitches, increasing between the 6th and 7th. Now begin the increasing for the chest by making 2 stitches in the 4th stitch; repeat this, increasing in every 4th row, put 1 stitch further each time, so as to form a slanting line, the same as a dress plait. To prevent repetition we shall no longer mention this increase. In the next row knit 10 stitches working the 10th into the 3rd hole of the 3rd row of the waistband; in the next row knit 12 stitches, the 12th in the same 3rd hole of the open row, and come back. Increase once more in the 4th hole of the open row, then work 1 row all around the waist-band, and from a similar pointed piece or gore on the opposite side, coming as far as the 4th hole in the open row of the waistband. Go on with the jacket in plain knitting always increasing slanting. After having thus knitted 4 plain rows, begin the increasing for the back. For this count 23 stitches on each side, beginning for the center, and increasing on each side of these 46 stitches in every 2nd row, placing the increasings each time 2 stitches each side; in the 56 row the armhole will be reached; to form this armhole count 47 stitches on each side for the front, and 74 in the middle for the back; cast off the stitches between the back and the fronts; first work the fronts, knitting 64 rows plain, then knit on the sides of the shoulders the two stitches together before the last, in every 2nd row at the same time on the side near the neck; knit 7 times, once in every row, and afterward in every 2nd row, two stitches before the last together, until no stitches are left. As the shoulders form a point by increasing 15 stitches from the selvage, begin at the armhole with the 2nd stitch of the selvage, just under the decreasing for the shoulders. Over these 15 stitches knit plain along the armhole, but knitting together the 2 stitches before the last at the other end of each row, until the pointed piece is finished. When the 2 points are completed work 44 plain rows in the back; in the next 32 rows decrease 2 stitches at the end of each row, then sew or knit the piece together at the shoulders. After this; beginning at the waist and going up to the neck, along the front, work first one plain row, and then 1 row of open knitting (like that at the waist,) then 2 more plain rows, and cast off the stitches The sleeves are also knitted plain. They are begun at the top, cast on 32 stitches and increase 1 stitch in every row until you have 68; knit 9 rows plain; in the 10th row knit two last stitches together and repeat this, decreasing 9 times, knitting 9 plain rows between each decreasing; then work 2 plain rows, then 9 rows, alternately 2 plain stitches and 2 purled, so as to form ribs; work one plain row, one row of open knitting then 3 more rows, and cast off stitches, sew up the sleeves, and sew it into the armhole; finish the jacket by sewing on buttons and making loops.

Knitted Lace.

No. 36. Cast on eight stitches and knit across plain.

1st row: Yarn around the needle, purl two together, knit

2, over twice, narrow, knit 2.

2nd row: Knit 4, purl 1, knit 2, over twice, p 2 tog.
3rd row: Wool around the needle, p 2 tog, k 7.
4th row: K 7, over twice, p 2 tog.
5th row: Yarn around the needle, p 2 tog, k 2, over twice, n, over twice, n, k 1.
6th row: K 3, p 1, k 2, p 1, k 2, over twice, p 2 tog.
7th row: Yarn around needle, p 2 tog, k 9.
8th row: Bind off three stitches, k 5, over twice, p 2 tog.

Repeat until the required length is reached.

Infants' Sleeveless Shirt (knitted).

No. 37. Cast on 100 stitches, knit two rows clear across, plain; then purl two rows and knit two rows plain; then knit 40 stitches, and leave the remaining 60 stitches on the needles until you have knit 22 rows with the 40 stitches; this will form the front; leave these on the needle, now cast off twenty stitches, by passing one stitch over the other; this will form the shoulder; now knit 22 rows with the remaining forty stitches, knitting two and purling two, as before; this will form the back. Now knit another row, and at the end cast on 20 new stitches, and then knit the forty stitches left on the needle from the front, you will now have 100 stitches again on your needle, which should be continued five rows more and cast off. The shirt is then sewed up, leaving the arm holes open. An edging is then crocheted around the neck and sleeves.

KNITTING DEPARTMENT

Knit Lace.

No. 38. Cast on twenty stitches.

1st row: Knit 4, t t o, n, * knit plain to last 2 st., t t t o, p 2 to.

2nd row: Put thread over needle, p 2 tog, knit the rest plain.

3rd row: Knit 8, t t t o. n, repeat 1st row from *

4th row: 4.h, 7th, 10th, 13th and 16th rows like the 2d row.

5th row: 5th, 8th, 11th and 14th rows like 1st row.

6th row: Knit 8, t t t o, n, t t t o, n, repeat 1st row from *

9th row: Knit 8, t t t o, n, t t t o, n, t t t o, n, repeat the first row from *

12th row: Knit 8, t t t o, n, t t t o, n, t t t o, n, t t t o, n, repeat the first row from *

15th row: Knit 8, t t t o, n, t t t o, n, t t t o, n, t t t o, n, t t t o, n, knit 1, and slip it on to the left needle and pull all the stitches over it but one, put t t to and p 2 tog. On the first scollop there are 20 stitches as the beginning and 25 at the end.

Knitted Insertion.

No. 39. Cast on 12 stitches.

1st row: Knit 2, make 1, knit 2 tog, t, t t t o, knit 2 tog, knit 2, make 1, knit 2 tog.

2nd row: Knit 2, m 1, k 2 tog, k 2, p 1, k 3, m 1, k 2 tog

3rd row: Knit 2, m 1, k 2 tog, k 6, m 1, k 2 tog.

4th row: Same as third row. Repeat from 1st row.

Knit Edge.

No. 40. Cast on 15 stitches and knit across plain.

1st row: Slip 1, k 2, t t o, k 2 tog, t t o, k 2 tog, k 3, t t o, k 2 tog, t t o 3 times, k 2 tog, k 1.

2nd row: Slip 1, k 1, k 1st loop, p 2 1 loop, k 3,1 loop, k 2, t t o, k 2 tog, k 5, t t o, k 2 tog, k 1.

3rd row: Slip 1, k 2, t t o, k 2 tog, k 1, t t o, k 2 tog, k 2. t t o, k 2 tog, k 5.

4th row: Slip 1, k 3, k 2 tog, k 5, t t o, k 2 tog, k 1.

5th row: Slip 1, k 2, t t o, k 2 tog, k 2, t t o, k 2 tog, k 1. t t o, k 2 tog, k 5.

6th row: Slip and bind 2, k 4, t t o, k 2 tog, k 5, t t o, k 2 tog, k 1. Repeat from 1st row.

Rose Leaf Lace.

No. 41. Cast on 10 stitches

1st row: Slip 1, k 1, t t o, n, t t o, n, t t o 3 times, n, t t o, p 2 tog.

2d row: T t t o, p 2 tog, k 3, p 1, in next loop k 1 and p 1, (that is after drawing thread through in knitting,) and before slipping off stitch, bring thread foward and purl stitch in same loop, k 1, p 1, k 1, p 1, k 2.

3d row: Slip 1, k 1, t t o, n, k 1, t t o, n, k 4, t t t o, p 2 tog.

4th row: T t t o, p 2 tog, k 5, p 1, k 2, p 1, k 2.
5th row: Slip 1, k 1, t t o, n, k 2, t t o, n, k 3, t t t o, p 2 tog.
6th row: T t t o, p 2 tog, k 2, p 1, k 3, p 1, k 2.
7th row: Slip 1, k 1, t t o, n, k 3, t t o, n, k 2, t t t o, p 2 tog.
8th row: T t t o, p 2 tog, k 2, p 1, k 4, p 1, k 2.
9th row: Slip 1, k 1, t t o, n, k 4, t t o, n, k 1, t t t o, p 2 tog.
10th row: T t o, p 2 tog, k 2, p 1, k 5 p 1, k 2.
11th row: Slip 1, k 1, t t o, n, k 5, t t o, n, t t t o, p 2 tog.
12th row: Bind off 3, then take the stitch on right hand needle and put it on the left hand, t t t o, p 2 tog, k 5, p 1, k 2. Repeat from 1st row.

Knit Insersion.

No. 42. Cast on 6 stitches.
1st row: Knit 1, n, t t t o, n, k 1.
2d row: K 3, p 1, k 2. Repeat.

Knit Lace.

No. 43. Cast on 6 stitches, knit across plain,
1st row: Knit 2, t t o, n, t t o, k 2.
2nd, 4th, and 6th rows knit plain.
3d row: Knit 3, t t o, n, t t o, k 2.

5th row: Knit 4, t t o, n, t t o, k 2.
7th row: Knit 9.
8th row: Bind off 3, knit 5.
Repeat from 1st row.

Zig Zag Lace.

No. 44. Cast on 12 stitches, knit across and back plain.
1st row: Slip, 1, k 1, t t o, n, t t o, n, t t o, n, t t o, k 5
2nd and every alternate row knit plain.
3rd row Slip 1, k 1, t t o, n, t t o, n, t t o, n, t t o, k 4.
5th row: Slip 1, k 1, t t o, n, t t o, n, t t o, n, t t o, k 6.
7th row: Slip 1, k 1, t t o, n, t t o, n, t t o, n, t t o, k 7.
9th row: Slip 1, k 1, t t o, n, t t o, n, t t o, n, t t o, k 8.
11th row: Slip 1, k 1, t t o, n, t t o, n, t t o, n, t t o, k 9.
13th row: Slip 1, k 1, t t o, n, t t o, n, t t o, n, t t o, k 10.
15th row: This row all plain.
17th row: Slip 1, n, t t o, n, t t o, n, t t o, n, t t o, n, k 8.
19th row: Slip 1, n, t t o, n, t t o, n, t t o, n, t t o, n, k 7.
21st row: Slip 1, n, t t o, n, t t o, n, t t o, n, t t o, n, k 6.
23rd row: Slip 1, n, t t o, n, t t o, n t t o, n, t t o, n, k 5.
25th row: Slip 1, n, t t o, n, t t o, n, t t o, n, t t o, n, k 4.
Repeat from 1st row.

Saw Tooth Edge.

No. 45. Cast on 7 stitches and knit across plain.
1st row: Slip 1, k 1, t t o, n, t t o, n, t t o, k 1.

KNITTING DEPARTMENT.

2nd, 4th, 6th, 8th and 9th rows knit plain.

3rd row: Slip 1, k 2, t t o, n, t t o, n, t t o, k 1.

5th row: Slip 1, k 3, t t o, n, t t o, n, t t o, k 1.

7th row: Slip 1, k 4, t t o, n, t t o, n, k 1.

10th row: Cast off until there but six stitches on left hand and one on the right. Repeat from 1st row.

KNIT CURTAIN STRAP.

No. 46. Begin by crocheting a loop loosely with 18 chain and one slip stitch. Then place the stitch on the knitting needle, and knit to and fro as follows:

1st row: Twice alternately cotton forward, and decrease 1 (that is, slip 1 as for purling, k 1, and pass the slipped stitch over the knitted one.)

2nd row: Twice alternately cotton forward, decrease 1: repeat the 2nd row as often as necessary, cast off, crochet a loop of 18 chain as above.

KNITTED LACE.

No. 47. Cast on 11 stitches.

1st row: Knit plain.

2nd row: Slip 1, k 2, t t t o, n, bring the thread forward, n, k 2.

3rd row: Bring thread forward, k 2, p 1, k 2, p 1, k 3, thread forward, k 2.

4th row: Slip 1, k 2, bring thread forward, n, knit plain to end.

5th row: Cast off 3, k 7, bring thread forward, n, k 2, repeat from 2nd row.

KNIT LACE.

No. 48. Cast on 12 stitches and knit across plain.

1st row: T t o, k 2, t t o, k 2 tog, k 8.

2nd row: Slip 1, k 1, t t o, k 3 tog, t t o, k 2, k 2 tog, t t o, k 4.

3rd row: T t o, k 5, t t o, k 2 tog, k 6.

4th row: S 1, k 1, t t o, k 3 tog, t t o, k 2 tog, t t o, k 7.

5th row: S 1, k 4, k 2 tog, t t o, k 1.

6th row: S 1, k 1, t t o, k 3 tog, t t o, k 3, t t o, k 2 tog, k 2, k 2 tog.

7th row: S 1, k 1, k 2 tog, t t o, k 9.

8th row: S 1, k 1, t t o, k 3 tog, t t o, k 5, t t o, k 3 tog. Repeat.

GERMAN LACE.

No. 49. Cast on 7 stitches and knit across plain.

1st row: S 1, k 1, t t o, k 2 tog, t t o, k 1, t t o, k 2.

2nd row: T t o, k 2 tog, p 4, k 1, t t o, k 2 tog.

3rd row: S 1, k 1, t t o, k 2 tog, t t o, k 3 tog, t t o, k 2.

4th row: T t o, k 2 tog, p 6, k 1, t t o, k 2 tog.

5th row: S 1, k 1, t t o, k 2 tog, t t o, k 1, t t o, s 1, k 2 tog, pass s over, t t o, k 1, t t o, k 2.

6th row: T t o, k 2 tog, p 8, k 1, t t o, k 2 tog.

7th row: S 1, k 1, t t o, k 2 tog, t t o, k 3, t t o, k 1, t t o, k 3, t t o, k 2.

8th row: T t o, k 2 tog, p 12, k 1, t t o, k 2 tog.

9th row: S 1, k 1, t t o, s 1, k 2 tog, pass s over, t t o, k 2 tog, k 1.

10th row: T t o, k 2 tog, p 10, k 1, t t o, k 2 tog.

11th row: S 1, k 1, t t o, s 1, k 2 tog, pass s over, k 2 tog, t t o, s 1, k 2 tog, pass s over, t t o, s 1, k 2 tog, pass s over, k 2 tog.

13th row: S 1, k 1, t t o, s 1, k 3 tog, pass s over, t t o, s 1, k 2 tog, pass s over, k 1.

14th row: t t o, k 2 tog, p 2, k 1, t t o, k 2 tog. Repeat.

Knitted Twilight.

No. 50. Cast on 150 stitches for the width of the twilight. Knit 2 plain rows.

3rd row: Slip 1, make 1, k 4, * k 3 tog, k 4, make 1, k 1, make 1, k 4, repeat from *.

4th row: Knit plain quite round.

5th row: Same as the 3rd; repeat these two rows three more times, then repeat again, working each stitch in each row, with the wool twice around the needle; in the following row work in the same manner; this will give it the appearance of a fine thick stripe and a very open one, without changing the needle.

Knitted Breakfast Cape.

No. 51. Cast on three stitches, at the end of every row make a stitch until you have 150 stitches on the needle.

Then begin to decrease again to a point by knitting two together at the end of each row until there are only three stitches left on the needle. These are cast off together. The pattern of the shawl is made by every four rows being worked thus:

1st row: Knit plain.

2nd row: Purl.

3rd row: Knit 2 together throughout the row.

4th row: Knit 1, make a stitch by knitting 1 on the thread between the last stitch taken off and the next one on the left needle, k 1.

Begin again at the 1st row and go on repeating these four rows until the shawl is finished. Add a fringe.

KNITTED SHAWL PATTERN.

No. 52. Cast on any number of even stitches and knit a row plain.

1st row: Plain knitting.

2nd row: Slip 1, k 1 *, wool forward, k 3 tog, repeat from * to end of row, k 1.

3rd row: Knit 2, * in the over stitch k 1, p 1, k 1, repeat from *.

4th row: Knit plain.

5th row: Knit plain.

6th row: Knit plain, repeat from 2nd row.

KNITTED CARRIAGE ROBE.

No. 53. Materials: Largest size steel knitting needles, a

KNITTING DEPARTMENT.

ball of green carpet wrap, and some cl an angora wool; procure the wool from some wool dealer and wash it thoroughly, dip it in blue or red dye, dry it and then it is ready for use. Set on 10 stitches and after knitting a row or two to make a firm beginning, go on as if you were making a garter, but with every other stitch lay a small bunch of wool across the needles; after knitting the stitch take the end of the wool, which shows on the wrong side, and turn it toward the right side, knitting a stitch above to secure it; then put in another thread of wool and repeat the process, using altern te colors of the wool. The back of the strips should have something the appearance of body brussels carpet, while the front should be like a sort of thick, long wrapped plush.

When the strips are all finished they must be sewed together at the back; it is only for convenience that they are knitted in strips, the robe as a whole, would be very cumbersome to handle.

KNITTED RUG.

Procure remnants of tapestry brussels, ravel out and cut in lengths of 18 inches. With colored carpet wrap knit the old fashioned garter stitch with 15 stitches. After setting up the stitches turn, knit the first stitch, lay a raveling between the stitches, having it the same length on both sides; knit the second stitch, then take the end which is back of the work and bring it over on the same side with the other end; now lay another raveling and treat the same as the first one. Do this with every stitch. When knitting back on opposite side knit first stitch, then put your needle under the raveling which forms a loop on wrong side, pull it up over the needle and knit it with the stitch the same as one stitch; this holds it in place. Knit five rows across plain, sixth row treat as the first, five more rows, sixth row like the first, etc Make this row as long as you wish the rug; bind off and make a second, and so on until your rug is as wide as you wish. Four rows make a nice width. Sew the rows together over and over on the wrong side, line with some dark material and finish with fringe.

CROCHET DEPARTMENT.

Abbreviations in crochet:—Ch, chainstitch. This is the foundation of all crochet, and is simply a straight series of loops, each drawn through the preceeding one.

Single crochet, or S C: Put the needle in a stitch of the work, bring the thread through in a loop and also through the loop on the needle at the same time.

Double crochet, or D C: Put the needle in a stitch of the work, bring the thread through, then take it up and bring it through the two loops on the hook.

Treble crochet or T C: Turn a thread round the needle put it in a stitch, bring the thread through then take it up and bring it through two loops twice.

Long treble or long: Put the thread twice around the hook and work like treble crochet, bringing the thread through two loops three times.

Extra long: Put the thread three times round the needle

and work like treble crochet, bringing the thread through two loops four times.

Picot: Make a certain number of chain loops, then put the hook through the first of the loops, catch the thread and draw it through both first and last loops at once.

Crochet Sacque for Baby.

No. 1. Material: Five ounces of four-ply saxony and a long bone hook.

This very pretty sacque is done in variety of Afghan stitch and is made to open in the back after the fashion of our German friends.

Make a chain of 40 stitches.

1st row: Put hook through foundation chain, raise a loop from second chain; you have now three loops on hook; draw wool through two loops (a) put hook through loop made from second stitch, and through next foundation chain draw wool through two loops on hook, repeat from (a) to end of row; finish off as in plain Afghan stitch.

2nd row: One chain, put hook in this chainstitch and through next loop as in plain Afghan stitch; raise a loop from Afghan stitch, draw wool through two loops on hook (b) put hook in loop raised from Afghan stitch, and through next Afghan loop, draw wool through two loops on hook; repeat from (b) to end of row and finish off in the usual way.

3rd row to 8th row like 2nd.

9th and 10th rows widen 1 stitch on the end of the row.

CROCHET DEPARTMENT.

11th and 12th rows, widen two stitches on the end of the row.

Next six without widening.

19th row: Before you begin this row make with the other end of the wool a chain of 21 stitches, break off and continue the pattern on 26 stitches, leaving the last 20 stitches unworked; take the 21 chain and work the pattern on them, this forms the arm hole; there should be 46 stitches on the row.

Next six without widening.

27th and 28th rows, narrow two stitches on the end of each row.

29th and 30th rows, narrow one stitch on end of each row.

Next 16 rows, without narrowing.

Repeat the directions from the 9th row once, crochet the shoulders together, and work one pattern row on the neck and two on the bottom. For the looped edge on the front and bottom work as follows:

One single crochet in first two Afghan stitches, seven chain, two single crochets in next two Afghan stitches; repeat this all the round. For sleeves make a chain of 40 stitches, 13 rows all straight without widening or decreasing.

14th row: In finishing off the rows crochet the 20th and 21st loops together.

Next two rows without narrowing.

17th row: Narrow one stitch like 14th.

Next two rows without narrowing.

23rd row like 17th.

Next two straight.

Finish with lace to match the body, crochet the sleeves together and sew in body.

Silk Watch Chain.

No. 2. Take button-hole twist, make nine chain and joining in a ring. Put the needle through the first chain and draw the thread through both the chain and the loop on the needle, and work the remaining chain stitches the same way round and round until you have the desired length; always take one-half of the chain next to you.

Crochet Edging.

No. 3. 1st row: Make sixteen chain stitches and turn work.

2nd row: In the sixth chain from the needle make a double crochet, two chain, skip one chain and make a double crochet in next, skip one and make three double crochet in next, two chain, three more double crochet in same chain, six chain, fasten in first chain stitch of the work, turn.

3rd row: * One chain, twelve double crochet in loop formed by six chain, three double crochet in next hole formed by two chain, then two chain, and three more double crochet in same hole, and double crochet in next hole, two chain, one double in next hole, two chain, one double in next hole, then turn work.

4th row: Four chain, one double crochet in first hole of last row; two chain, one double in next hole, three double in next hole formed by two chain, then two chain and three more double in same hole, one double crochet in beginning of 12 double crochet, two chain, one double crochet between second and third double crochet of preceding scollop, two chain, one double crochet between fourth and fifth, and so on all around the scollop, then there will be six holes. Turn your work.

5th row: One single crochet and double crochet in each of the six holes, three double in next hole formed by two chain, then two chain and three more double crochet in same hole, one double crochet in next hole, two chain, one double crochet in next hole, turn.

6th row: Make four chain, one double crochet in first hole, two chain, one double crochet in next hole, three double crochet in next hole formed by two chain; then two chain, three more double crochet in same hole, one double crochet at each of the three double crochets in last row, six chain, and fasten between the first and second of the little scollops with a single crochet. Repeat from star.

Crochet Sofa Pillow.

No. 4. This is an excellent way to utilize short bits of different colored zephyrs that accumulate. Sofa spreads may be made in the same way to harmonize with the pillow, and are light and bright as well as comfortable.

Take green zephyr or yarn, make a chain of six stitches and join in a ring.

1st round: Under the ring work four groups of three trebles each, separate by two chain, after making the last chain join the first treble of the first group with a d c, break off.

CROCHET DEPARTMENT.

2nd round: Take red, 3 trebles, 2 ch, 3 trebles all under the loop of 2 ch that separate the first and second groups of the previous round(*) 2 ch, 3 trebles, 2 ch, 3 trebles under the loop of 2 ch that divides the next two groups, repeat from star twice, 2 ch, join with a d c to the first treble of the first group; break off.

3rd round• Take light green and proceed as in the second round.

4th round: Take black and work as in the previous round. This completes one square. Make as many as are preferred. In working the last round always use black wool but, the rest may be off different colors.

Crochet Scarf.

No. 5. Take four skein of Saxony yarn. Crochet (in crazy) the scarf 14 inches wide, in length as preferred. Finish the end with suitable crochet lace and bead it according to fancy, using for the beads as heavy silk thread as your needle will carry. The sides of the scarf are to be ornamented also with crochet beaded lace.

Crochet Lamp Mat.

No. 6. Take an ounce and a half of olive green, half an ounce ruby sephyr and one skein of ruby embroidery silk. The mat is round and is divided into sections. Sew the sections together and with ruby embroidery silk work each in star or cross stitch as preferred.

CROCHET DEPARTMENT.

With olive green and medium sized steel hook make a chain of 25 stitches.

1st row: Raise the work back 12 loops in Afghan stitch (13 loops on needle) raise the 12 loops of the previous row and two more of the 25 chain, work back; continue in this manner in each of the following rows, until all the loops of the 25 chain are taken up; this will form one-half of section; go on and for the other half decrease by taking up all the loops except the last one in each row until you have decreased to one stitch, break off; this finishes one section. Make 7 more in the same way and then with the ruby wool work one d c in each of the points made by the unworked stitches, one of each section, and in each of the 25 chains at the beginning. Next sew these sections together and place them over a circle of card-board which must be lined with black silesia or silk. For the fringe tie suitable lengths of wool of both colors in the edge stitches around the mat, and for the second row divide the strands and knot them again together, thus forming a diamond shaped heading.

CROCHET TRIMMING.

No. 7. Take thread, either cotton or linen, No. 24 or 30 and a fine steel hook and make a chain the length required.

1st row: Miss 4, 1 treble in the 5th, (*) 2 ch, miss 2 loops, 1 treble in the next; repeat from star to end of row.

2nd row: 2 ch, 1 treble in first loop of 2 ch, (a) 2 ch, miss 2 stitches, 1 treble in first loop of next 2 ch, repeat from (a) to end of row.

3rd row: 2 ch, 1 treble in each loop of 2 ch of the previous row (b)1 ch,1 treble in each loop of next 2 ch, repeat from (1)

4th row: 2 ch for first treble, 1 treble on first treble 3 ch, 2 treble in the loop of 1 ch (c) 7 ch, miss 9 stitches, 1 d c in next stitch, 7 ch, miss 9 stitches, 2 trebles in next stitch, 3 ch. 2 trebles in loop of 1 ch; repeat from (c).

5th row: 5 ch, (d) 7 trebles under 3 ch, 5 ch, 2 long trebles separated by 1 ch in d c of the previous row; repeat from (d).

6th row: 4 ch, (e) 1 treple on first treble of the 7 trebles, 1 treble between the first and second trebles. 1 treble on each of the next 5 trebles, 1 treble between the 5th and 6th trebles, 1 treble on last treble, (nine trebles) 4 ch, one d c in the one chain that divides the long trebles, 4 ch, repeat from (e).

7th row: 7 ch, (f) 1 d c on first of the nine trebles, 5 ch, 1 d c in fourth of 5 ch, (this forms a picot) 1 ch, 1 d c between the second and third trebles, 3 ch, 1 d c in fourth of 5 ch, (second picot); 1 d c between the third and fourth trebles (g) a picot between the next two trebles, repeat from (g) three times, six picots in all, 7 ch, repeat from (f).

This finishes the pattern.

Gents' Leisure Cap.

No. 8. Crochet a chain of four and join; make two single crochet in each one of the chain, taking up both threads at once; for the second row take two single crochet in every stitch of the first row; third row take two stitches in every third stitch, one each in the other; fourth row take two stitches in every fourth, and so on, widening enough to keep the work nearly flat till the size wanted is reached, then crochet without widening till the cap is finished.

A Crochet Rose.

No. 9. 1st round: Make a chain of four stitches and join. In this loop work twenty trebles.

2nd round: Work one ch and one treble over each treble of the last round.

3rd round: * On the treble and next chain make a leaf thus: The zephyr twice round the needle, take up the stitch, work through two, zephyr on the next needle, draw through two, zephyr on the needle, take up the stitch again, work through 2, zephyr on the needle, work through 2, zephyr on the needle, take up the next stitch and work all off the needle 2 loop at a time, then 4 ch. Repeat from *.

4th round: 1 d c on the middle of the 4 ch, * 5 ch, 1 d c on the middle of the next 4 ch; repeat from *.

Crochet Lace.

No. 10. 1st row: * Make 22 ch, close the last 8 in a circle, 12 double in a circle, 1 slip stitch in 1st of of 12 double, 7 ch, 5 long treble with 3 ch between each in the next double stitches, 7 ch 1 double in the next stitch, twice alternately 5 ch, 1 double in every second stitch, then 5 ch, 1 slip stitch in last s'ip stitch, 2 double, 1 treble, 2 long treble in next 7 ch, 3 ch, 2 long treble, 1 treble, 1 double in same ch, 4 times alternately 1 double, 1 treble, 2 long treble with two ch between, 1 treble in 1 double in 3 ch, then 1 double, 1 treble, 1

CROCHET DEPARTMENT.

long treble in 7 ch, 3 ch, 2 long treble, 1 treble, 2 double in same 7 ch; repeat from *.

2nd row: * 1 treble in center of 5 ch scollops; 9 ch, 1 treble in center of 13 ch, 9 ch; repeat from *.

3rd row: * 1 long treble, 1 ch, miss 1, 1 long treble, joining the center stitch to center of last long treble, 3 ch, miss 3; repeat from *.

WOOL TIDY OF TWO COLORS.

No. 11. Use No. 6 needle, make a chain of 150 stitches of blue zephyr, turn, throw the thread over and make a shell of six double crochet stitches into the fourth stitch of the chain, skip four and make another shell of six double crochet, and so on to the end of the row, break off the blue and join the white, turn, make a chain of two, then make six double crochet into the loop between the shells of the first row, catch down tight without putting thread over between the shells; repeat and continue in this way, making the row of blue and white to alternate. Make a deep shell border of the two colors, four rows on the side and two on the top and bottom.

CROCHET SHOE.

No. 12. Begin at the toe, make a chain of 15 stitches, work back in single crochet, working three stitches in the center stitch of chain; work 18 rows in this way, always being particular to take up the back stitch and widening each time by working three stitches in the center. For the back, work back and forth on the first twelve stitches till the piece is long enough to go around the heel, the crochet to the other side; or the opposite 12 stitches may be crocheted out and the joining be done at the back. Crochet a row of scollops around the top, run elastic in and finish with a bow of ribbon or ponpons and plush balls. The sole is finished by sewing on a lamb's wool sole, sewing it on the wrong side, and turning the shoe after it is done. These soles can be had at any shoe store.

Double Twine Bag.

No. 13. This work is easy and simple in itself, but very troublesome with the connecting rows of chain stitch. We would advise the reader to try common carpet warp for this work, as it is very cheap and durable. Make a chain of 224 stitches, cut off the thread, which must be done at the end of every row; the ends must be left long, as they are knotted together afterward to form the fringe.

1st row: 1 treble on the first ch, * 1 ch, miss 1 ch, 1 treble on the next, repeat from * until you have 46 trebles. You then join to the 11th treble stitch from the 1st, 60 ch, have 60 ch of the foundation row, 1 treble on the 61st, 1 ch, miss 1 chain, one treble in the next, repeat until you have 46 trebles which brings you to the end of the chain, but at the 36th join to the first of these 46.

2nd row: 1 treble on the 1st treble of the last row, 1 ch, 1 treble on the next; repeat until you come to the treble just over the 60th ch, join to the 60th ch or the flaps will not fall right, 1 treble on the 1st treble of the next piece, work 1 ch, 1 treble, 35 more turns, join neatly, finish the row. You must cross the chain stitches between the rows of treble, so that the end of the pieces will fall well as flaps over the bag.

Cut the thread off again. Work in this way until you have 18 rows, then knot the fringe; add a fringe on the row forming the ends of the bag.

Baby Carriage Robe.

No. 14. Cast on a foundation of 19 stitches and crochet 2 rows in wave stitch (to which follow two plain tunis) rows with very raised round shapes. For these six chains are crochet in the first rows in going forward, first five draw off loops, then three times after four of the same these are left untouched in the next single tunis row, but are formed into long loops by the crowding together of the perpendicular bars. In going backward in the now following row, all the loops made are drawn off the hook by putting the wool once this, the next perpendicular bar is then to be pierced with the hook by uniting with the thread loop drawn through to the front to loop of the raised shape on the hook. The perpendicular bars are again to be collected till the process as just described is repeated at the next stitch loop. This last row is formed by collecting the perpendicular bars on the left side, again into the first wave row. Curves each of one single worked into the the first edge stitch, and five double into the third, ornament both sides of the strip. In sewing the strips together you may use one of plain crochet and one ornamental. A silk or wool lining is very nice.

Tidy in Tricot.

No. 15. 1st row: Make a chain the length required, work off in tricot.

2nd row: One chain, * put the hook under the chain between the two next tricot loops, pull up a loop, work up the next tricot loop, now pull through two loops on the hook together, work up the back perpendicular loop of next tricot loop, keep the loop on the hook, repeat from *

3rd row: Coming back pull through each loop repeatedly. The second and third rows are repeated for the entire length.

CROCHET TRIMMING.

No. 16. Materials: A coarse crochet hook and a ball of carpet warp, any color that may be desired.

1st row: Make a chain as long again as the trimming required, and crochet from left to right as follows: * join to 1st stitch, 7 chain, join to same stitch, 3 times alternately 7 chain (crochet first of each 7 in the last of the preceding 7 like a slip stitch; all the chain scollops are crocheted like this and the description will not be repeated) miss 2, join to the next stitch, then 1 chain, miss 5, 3 times alternately join to next stitch, 7 chain, miss 2, then repeat from *

2nd row: Along the other side of the work, like the preceding row but in reversed position. To make raised knobs at the end of the vandikes take a different color of the warp, and begin from the center with the chain, close into a circle and work 4 rounds of chain stitch so that there are 10 stitches in the 4th round. The wrong side of the work is the right side of the knob, which is then sewn on to the border with fine stitches.

OPERA CAPE OF WHITE WOOL.

No. 17. Make a chain of 84 stitches, which will make 12 gores.

CROCHET DEPARTMENT.

1st row: Work 1 treble or long crochet in each of the first and second chains, 3 trebles, crochet in the third, 1 treble 1st row in each of the 4th and 5th, skip two of the chain to form t gore. If it is intended to finish with ribbon, make one single chain before taking up the first stitch for the second gore, continue after skipping the two stitches by working 1 treble in each of the next two stitches of the chain, 3 in the third, 1 in each of the 4th and 5th, repeat to the end of the row.

2nd row: Turn and work 1 treble crochet through the first and 1 through the second stitch of the first row, being particular to take the stitch through the back loop, then take 5 treble crochet through the next stitch (these five stitches are worked into the center of the three widening stitches of the the previous row), then work 1 treble in each of the two following stitches, repeat to the end of the row, continue with treble crochet stitches, making the rows as follows:

3rd row: * One each in first 3, 3 in the next, 1 each in next 3, repeat from *

4th row:* 1 each in first 3, 5 in next, 1 in next 3, repeat from *

5th row: * 1 each in first 4, 3 in next, 1 each in next 4, repeat from *

6th row: * 1 each in first 4, 5 in next, 1 each in next 4, repeat from *

7th row: 1 each in first 5, 3 in next, 1 each in next 5, repeat from *

8th row: * 1 each in first 5, 5 in next, 1 each in next 5, repeat from *

9th row: * 1 each in first 6, 3 in next, 1 each in next 6, repeat from *

10th row: * 1 each in first 6, 5 in next, 1 each in next 6, repeat from *

11th row: * 1 each in first 7, 3 in next, 1 each in next 7, repeat from *

12th row: 1 each in first 7, 5 in next, 1 each in next 7.

Repeat each of the following rows in the same manner as the preceding ones:

13th row: 1 each in first 8, 3 in next, 1 each in next 8.

14th row: 1 each in first 8, 3 in next, 1 each in next 8.

15th row: Same as 14th.

16th row: 1 each in first 8, 5 in next, 1 each in next 8.

17th row: 1 each in first 9, 3 in next, 1 each in next 9.

18th row: Same as 17th.

19th row: Same as 18th.

20th row: 1 each in first 9, 5 in next, one each in next 9.

21st row: 1 each in first 10, 3 in next, 1 each in next 10.

22nd row: Same as 21st.

23rd row: Same as 22nd.

24th row: 1 each in first 10, 5 in next, 1 each in next 10.

25th row: 1 each in first 11, 3 in next, 1 each in next 11.

26th row: Same as 25th.

27th row: Same as 26th.

28th row: 1 each in first 11, 5 in next, 1 each in next 11.

29th row: 1 each in first 12, 3 in next, 1 each in next 12.

30th row: Same as 29th.

31st row: Same as 30th.

32nd row: 1 each in first 12, 5 in next, 1 each in next 12.

33rd row: 1 each in first 13, 3 in next, 1 each in next 13.

Finish by scolloping the edge.

GENTLEMAN'S SKULL CAP.

No. 18. Make a chain of three, unite, work in double crochet, always taking up the back of the loop and increasing gradually to keep the work flat until you have worked twelve rounds. By increasing of course is meant taking two stitches in one loop; this must be done whenever you see the work beginning to draw up around the edges, it must be perfectly flat.

13th round: 3 chain stitches, miss 2 d c, 1 treble in the next, that is miss 2 stitches or loops in the preceding row, and take a treble stitch in the third loop). Repeat this 27 times; in the 9th, 18th and 27th repetitions leave one stitch only between the treble stitches instead of two stitches as in the first.

14th round: * 3 chain, one treble over the next 3 ch, 3 ch, 2 treble over the next 3 chain, repeat from *

15th round: 3 chain, 1 treble over the next chain, in this round work 2 trebles as often as necessary to keep the work quite flat. Repeat this round three more times.

19th round: * 3 d c, 1 d c on the treble, repeat from *. 11 more rounds of d c, increase in each to keep the work flat.

31st round: * 3 ch, miss 2 d c, 1 treble, 3 ch, miss 3 d c, 1 treble, repeat from *

32nd round: * 3 ch, one treble over the next 3 ch, repeat 3 more times, then 3 ch, 1 treble, 3 ch, 1 treble over the next ch, repeat from *

33rd, 34th and 35th rounds: * 3 ch, 1 treble over the next 3 ch, repeat from *

36th round: 1 d c on each treble, 4 d c over each 3 ch.

37th and next three rounds d c.

41st round: * 2 d c in next, 4 d c, repeat from * 14 more rounds plain d c.

56th round: 3 ch, 1 treble, * miss 3 d c, 1 treble, 3 ch, repeat from *

Repeat the 56th round 5 more times, working the trebles over the 3 ch.

62nd round: 3 d c over the 3 ch, 1 d c on the treble, 20 rounds more of d c.

Now line your work with silk to match the other material, and sew in a piece of leather 1¾ inches wide for the head, add a string to draw it up.

Crochet Trimming.

No. 19. This trimming is made by working part crosswise

CROCHET DEPARTMENT.

and part lengthwise; for the crosswise portion make a foundation of 26 stitches and crochet the first round plain.

2nd round: Pass over 9 stitches, 1 single crochet on the following stitch, then 4 times alternately 5 chain stitches, 1 sc on the following stitch.

3rd round: 3 ch, turn the work (this turning is done in each, so need not be again mentioned) 1 sc on the ch scollop, 4 times alternately 5 ch, 1 sc on the next ch scollop, then 5 ch, 1 d c on the third following ch in the preceding row.

4th round: 9 ch, 1 sc on the next ch scollop, 4 times alternately 5 ch, 1 sc on the following ch scollop, then 5 ch, 1 slip stitch on the first sc in the preceding round.

5th round: 3 ch, 1 sc on the next ch scollop, 5 times alternately 5 ch, 1 sc on the following ch scollop, then 5 ch, 1 d c on the middle of the first 9 ch in the preceding round.

6th round: 9 ch, 1 sc on the following ch scollop, then 5 ch, 1 d c on the middle of the first 9 ch in the preceding round.

7th round: 3 ch, 1 sc on the following ch scollop, twice alternately 5 ch, 1 sc on the next ch scollop, then 5 d c on the next sc, 1 sc on the following ch scollop, 5 d c on the next sc, 1 sc on the middle of the following dc, twice alternately 5 ch, 1 sc on the next scollop, then 5 ch 1 d c on the middle of the first 9 ch in the preceding round.

8th round: 9 ch, 1 sc on the following ch scollop, twice alternately 5 ch, 1 sc on the next ch scollop, then 5 ch twice alternately 1 sc on the middle of the following 5 d c, 5 d c on the next sc, then 1 sc on the following ch scollop, 5 ch, 1 sc

CROCHET DEPARTMENT.

on the next ch scollop, 5 ch, 1 slip stitch on the first sc in the preceding round.

9th round: 3 ch, 1 sc on the next chain scollop, 5 ch, 1 sc on the following ch scollop, 5 d c on the next sc, twice alternately 1 sc on the middle of the following 5 dc, 5 ch, then twice alternately 1 sc on the next ch scollop, 5 ch, then 1 sc on the following ch scollop, 5 d c on the next sc, 1 sc on the following ch scollop, 5 ch, 1 d c on the middle of the first 9 ch in the preceding round.

10th round: 9 ch, 1 sc on the following ch scollop, 5 ch, 1 sc on the middle of the next 5 dc, twice alternately 5 dc on the following sc, 1 sc on the next ch scollop, then twice alternately 5 ch, 1 sc on the following ch scollop, then 5 chain, 1 sc on the middle of the next 5 d c, 5 ch, 1 sc on the following ch scollop, 5 ch, 1 slip stitch on the next sc in the preceding round.

11th round: 3 ch, 1 sc on the next ch scollop, 5 ch, 1 sc on the following ch scollop, 5 d c on the next sc, 1 sc on the following ch scollop, twice alternately 5 ch, 1 sc on the following ch scollop, then twice alternately 5 ch, 1 sc on the middle of the next 5 d c, then 5 d c on the next sc, 1 sc on the following ch scollop, 3 ch, 1 d c on the middle of the next 5 d c then 5 d c on the next sc, 1 sc on the following ch scollop, 3 ch, 1 d c on the middle of the first 9 ch in the preceding round. Work the 11th to 17th round to correspond with the 2nd to the 8th rounds, but in reversed order, thus shaping the point of the edging.

18th round: 7 ch, 1 sc on the next ch scollop, four times alternately 5 ch, 1 sc on the following ch scollop, then 5 ch,

1 slip stitch in the preceding round. Repeat the 2nd to 18th rounds until you have made as many yards as may be required, then on the upper and under edges of the work crochet 1 round of sc each, and 2 rows of scollops similar to those of the crochet insertion. Complete the edge on the top with two rounds worked like the 6th and 7th rounds of the insertion.

Crochet Carriage Robe.

No. 20. This is worked in alternate squares of plush and blue made of Shetland wool. The stitch is crochet tricotee, or what is popularly called "Afghan stitch." Make a chain of 14 stitches with the plush wool, making 13 loops of tricotee, work on it 13 rows of pink, then take the blue wool and continue, working 13 rows, then take the pink again, work ng t us in alternate squares until the required length is reached.

The next stripe begins with the blue wool and is worked in alternate squares in the same way.

The stripes are joined together by a row of chain stitch, in either pink or blue; a plush square must always be next to the blue one, and vice versa. In the center of each square may be embroidered in blue or silk any pretty flower or figure.

The robe is to be finished with a fringe which is crocheted thus:

1st row: With pink wool, 1 s c (single crochet) * 7 chain, miss 2 loops, 1 s c in the next loop, repeat from * all round.

2nd row: 1 s c on the 4th loop of the first 7 chain, 1 ch, 1 s c on the 4th of the next 7 ch of the preceding row, continue all round. This row is worked with blue wool.

Next cut the two wools in lengths of 9 inches, and loop 6 strands into the center of each 7 ch of the 2nd row, putting the blue and white in alternate chains.

Sofa Afghan (Crochet).

No. 21. This afghan is worked in alternate stripes of Victoria crochet and cross-stitch. For the crocheted stripe proceed as follows:

Along 13 stitches crochet in red wool two patterns in ordinary Victoria stitch.

In the 1st row of the 3rd pattern take up the stitches as usual, and for the raised spots, crochet 6th chain after the 3rd, 7th and 11th stitches, drawing up the last of the 7 chain with the vertical part out of which the chain was taken, and in the return row crochet off all the stitches as usual.

In the 1st row of the 4th pattern row, when the raised loops are completed, take up the stitches as usual, but at the 3rd, 7th and 11th, in the 6th chain, take up twice alternately 1 stitch, pass the thread around the needle, then take up one stitch at the same place, and, lastly, draw up together everything that is in the needle. The return row is crocheted in the usual way.

Repeat the 3rd and 4th pattern rows, letting the raised spots occur in reversed position.

Along the long sides crochet as follows: on the wrong side *¡1 double in the marginal stitch, 4 chain, 1 treble in first 4 chain, miss 2, repeat from *; for the alternate stripes of canvass, work the pattern in cross-stitch, in fillsoelle of various shades.

Narrow Trimming (Crochet).

No. 22. Crochet as follows:

1st row: * 14 chains, 1 leaf as follows: Going back along the chain, 1 slip stitch, 1 single, 1 double, 2 treble, 1 double, 1 single, 1 slip stitch, repeat from *

2nd row: * 1 double in the 4th of the 6th full chain stitches, 3 chain, 7 treble in center 7 stitches of the leaf, working the center of the 7 treble in the point of the leaf, 3 chain, repeat from *

3rd row: * 1 double in 3 chain, 5 chain, 1 double in the center of 7 double, 5 chain, 1 double in next 3 chain, 1 purl of 5 ch, and 1 double, repeat from *

4th row: * 1 double in 5 chain, 5 chain, 1 double in 5 chain, 5 chain, 1 double in next purl, 5 chain, repeat from *

Rollpicot Edging (Crochet)

No. 23. For the center, work 4 chain, 1 roll picot into the first, 8 chain, draw through the last stitch of the 4 chain, 8 chain, 1 single into the stitch the roll picot was worked into. Repeat for the length required.

For the edge, 3 double separated by 3 chain under the 8 chain of last row, 3 chain. Repeat.

For the heading, 1 double under the 8 chain of the last row, 5 chain. Repeat.

Crochet Astrakan.

No. 24. 1st row: D c (double crochet), at the end 1 ch.

2nd row: 1 d c in the first d c, taking up the back of the loop, which is done throughout the work, take up the back of the 2nd loop, draw the wool through, pass the wool round the needle, take up the same loop again, making 3 loops on the needle in this one stitch, draw the wool through these 3, then through the two on the needle; take up the whole of this row in this manner.

3rd row: Plain d c worked from the back of the loop as before; repeat the 2nd and 3rd row.

Crochet Lace

No. 25. 1st row: * Close 20 stitches into a circle, 5 chain, 1 double in 4th chain stitch, 1 vandyke as follows: 9 chains, going back from the 8th to the 1st stitch, take up one out of each stitch and draw them all up together 1 double in the next chain but 1 of the circle, 1 vandyke as above, four times alternately 1 long treble in the next stitch, 2 chain, then one long treble in the next stitch, repeat from *

2nd row: 7 treble in the free chain of circle, 2 treble in the vertical part of the next long treble, 1 treble where the long treble was crocheted, repeat from *

Lace Edging.

No. 26. Select a narrow Valenciennes insertion, and crochet along one side of it as follows:

1st row: 1 treble, 2 chain, repeat.

2nd row: 3 double with 5 chain between each in the 2

chain, 7 chain, miss 3 treble, repeat.

3rd row: 2 double with 7 chain between in the 7 chain, 7 chain, repeat.

4th row: Along the other side of the insertion, 1 double, 1 chain, repeat.

Simple Crochet Edge.

No. 27. Make a chain of 6 stitches, miss 4, in the 5th chain make 1 single crochet; this forms a loop.

Turn, 3 chain and 3 double crochet in this first loop, turn, 3 chain and 3 double crochet in the 2nd loop formed by the 3 chain before worked, turn, 3 chain and 12 double crochet in the 3rd loop and join the last one of the 12 double crochet to the first loop of 6 chain, turn and work 2 chain and 1 single crochet between 9 of the 12 double crochet, leaving three double crochet.

2nd scollop: 3 chain, and 3 double crochet in the next loop, turn, 3 chain and 12 double crochet in the next loop, and join the last double crochet to last 2 chain worked in the 1st scollop, turn, 2 chain and 1 single crochet between 9 of the 12 double crochet, leaving 3 double crochet, repeat till the edge is long enough.

Child's Crochet Hood.

No. 28. Make a chain of 5, join in a circle, crochet round into chain, make outlets every second stitch for 3 rows; as it gets larger the outlets may be fewer, but keep flat.

Outlets are made by working twice into one chain stitch.

Work double crochet, make 20 rows all round, then leave 18 stitch (this forms back of crown).

Return the contrary way, always leaving the 18, and work backwards and forwards for 15 rows to 4 the front, always take up the back chain.

A border may be added. Work triple crochet into 1 hole 3 times, missing 1 always, 1 triple with 1. Repeat all round the cap.

A double border may be put on if wished. Triple crochet into the chain stitch at the back of the front border. Ties done separately. 9 chain for width is enough. Double crochet like cap until it is long enough.

A finished border will improve it. Work one triple with every second stitch. Sew or crochet on the ties.

CROCHET BALL.

No. 29. Take a large ball of twine, commence the cover of worsted by making a chain of three stitches joined to a circle, and work in single crochet stitches, increasing at regular intervals till the work is large enough to cover one-half the ball, then work a few rows without increase, draw the cover over the ball, and work the other half to correspond with the first half, decreasing instead of increasing at regular intervals.

STAMPING.

PERFORATED PATTERNS.

Oil a tough piece of tissue paper thoroughly with sweet oil

STAMPING DEPARTMENT.

or lard, spread out over a piece of linen for an hour or so, when it will be ready for use. Select some design from a book or picture card, lay the oiled paper on over it, when it will be seen that the most minute portion of the object can be discerned; with a lead pencil trace the object on the oiled paper. Fasten a piece of parchment on a small cushioned footstool, lay the oiled paper outline over the parchment paper, pin it all around the stool to keep from slipping. take a very fine needle and insert the eye into a cork, which makes a punch; now proceed by sticking little holes in the outline of the tissue paper, which will of course go through the parchment paper too; go all around the outline in this way, and thus form the pattern. Now what to do with the pattern after you have it made.

POWDER PROCESS.

Lay the perforated pattern on the goods to be stamped, burr side up, dip the ponset or pad into the powder, rub it over the pattern being careful not to press too heavily or the pattern will be damaged; lift the pattern gently up so as to not blur the figure; cover the figure on the cloth with a piece of heavy tissue paper, and with a hot iron press it over the tissue paper scarcely touching the paper at first and gradually pressing heavier, and the figure is then stamped.

INDELIBLE OR LIQUID PROCESS.

This is done by using paint instead of powder and a brush instead of a ponset. Arrange the pattern as in powder stamping; dip the brush into the paint and rub evenly over the pattern; remove the pattern and place the stamped article in a dry place. The pattern should be thoroughly cleaned after using by washing it with benzine (keep the benzine away from the fire).

How to Make Stamping Powder.

White powder: Use pulverized white glue, gum demar, gum copal and magnesia in equal parts; mix together and keep in a dry place

Black powder: Use all the gums mentioned in the white powder, using powdered charcoal instead of magnesia.

To make a ponset: Take an empty spool, cut a piece of felt to fit the end of it, glue it onto the spool and you have a ponset as durable as any to be obtained.

PAINTING.

Painting on Oilcloth.

To stamp the figure lay the pattern on the cloth the same as stamping on cloth, take a piece of charcoal from the fire pulverize it, tie in a piece of cloth, rub this over the cloth and just enough dust will go through to make a nice outline; mix a small portion of tube paint with turpentine, lay it around the charcoal outline and you have it permanent; fill in and shade with the same kind of mixture.

The most beautiful landscape may be painted on oilcloth with very fine effect. I hardly know where to stop when enumerating the beautiful things that one exquisitely sensitive to beauty may fashion from the material with the aid of a brush and some tube paint made thin with turpentine. It is just the thing for slipper-cases, comb-pockets, match-safes, hairpin-boxes, splashers and kitchen lambrequins. Painting on wood is done in the same manner.

Glass Painting.

Painting on glass is very much like the above In tracing your figure have the glass clean and lay it over the figure you wish to copy; mix with the paint a little demar varnish and proceed to sketch the outline; fill in with shade to suit the taste. If this is to be framed crush tin foil thesame as given in the directions for crushing paper; lay it on the back of the glass and you have something very novel in effect; or you may paint the whole back ground instead of using the tin foil.

White Velvet Painting.

Use the best white cotton velvet; lay the pattern on the velvet the same as the oilcloth was done, using the sack of charcoal for the distributor; mix the paints with turpentine and sugar of lead, being careful not to have it too thin nor yet too thick, for if too thin it will run on the velvet and if too thick it will stand on the velvet and make it look rough. Now proceed to fill in and shade using a fine camel's hair brush. Four or five painters or letters cut short to form a scrub will be needed to rub the paint into the velvet. These are all instructions needed to accomplish this bewitching art. It is hardly necessary to add that you should tack the velvet on paste-board before stamping it, and while working having it wrapped in paper with a small hole clipped in at the part you are working on.

As an artist I have always found my first work in a new study of little value; the mind needs time to adapt itself to new surroundings. It must assimilate the tone of the landscape before it can render their true spirit. So the new beginner in this work need not feel discouraged if his first work does not give that satisfaction which can only be rendered by patient practice.

Black Satin Painting.

Stamp the figure on the satin; fill in with water paints, let these paints dry on the satin; mix oil paints the same as for oil cloth painting, put these on top of the water paints with a camels hair brush. The greatest latitude is possible in point of color, and the worker can adapt streaks and shades to give the apearance of reality.

There are innumerable articles made from the satin paintings, for wear and ornaments, which naturely suggest themselves to persons of ingenious minds and dexterous fingers.

Light Satin Paintings.

This is done in a similar manner, using the water paints first and not using the oil paints at all, as the oil would run on the satin; afterward put on coat of demar varnish.

Embroidery Painting.

Materials: Brass pen or quill, tube paints, palette-knife, palette-board or small piece of glass. This kind of painting

PAINTING DEPARTMENT. 91

can be done on all most any kind of material but velvet is the most desirable; this style of painting will become so popular by reason of its own merit, that all that is needed is but a formal introduction. In case of using white velvet, put the paints out in a piece of blotting paper and let it stand over night; remove to the pallette-board with the palette-knife and the paints are ready for use. Sugar of lead is used as a dryer being mixed in with the paints. Apply the paints by taking them up in the hollow of the pen or quill holding the pen bottom side up; have a piece of cotton cloth handy for the purpose of wiping the paint from the top (or rather the bottom) of the pen so it will not be smeared on the velvet; draw the point of the pen, with the back to the material, over the outlines, turning the pen slightly so as to draw it, in order to make the outlines clear and bright. Refill the pen with paint and fill the center of the leaf or petals, drawing the pen towards center, as the stitch in silk embroidery. Shade to suit individual taste, blending colors together with the pen. This done then scratch the petals or leaf over with the point of the pen to give it the appearance of stitches, always making the leaves run toword the center. In painting leaves always begin from the outer edge and paint toward the center. For shading it is best to put on the light colors first, and then the darker ones, blending with the pen. In case of large flowers the paint may be applied with the palette-knife, and then put in the finer details with the pen. It is only necessary to remember two things: First, that accurracy in painting and blending are essential; second, the nearer the coloring approaches the natural tint the better. Any one who has succeeded in the easy task of satin painting will have no difficulty in doing the embroidery painting as the nack is caught with very little practice, and this style is especially, as it takes a delicate observer to distinguish it from embroidery.

MISCELLANEOUS DEPARTMENT.

We do not intend to try to instruct all of our readers in economy at this late date, as we do not feel equal to the task. But we will endeavor to set forth a few useful hints in that direction.

I was once pondering the question in my mind, what will I get to make my baby a coat? Just then the thought struck me of an old coat that was hanging in the next room that might answer the purpose if ripped up and nicely brushed. Thereupon I undertook the task, and after the ripping and brushing had been completed then came the making, at which point I was puzzled on account of not having anything with which to trim the garment. After studying for two or three days on the subject, I concluded (as the coat was of gray color) to get some dapple-gray zephyr and knit some astrakan trimming, which I did, also crocheting a cape of the same material and trimming it with astrakan; the whole cost of which was seventy-five cents (see astrakan trimming in knitting department, pattern No. 22). Thus papa's old coat was made into a warm and comfortable coat for baby.

Ladies' Fancy Wall Bag.

A handsome wall bag is something every lady would like

MISCELLANEOUS DEPARTMENT.

to own, and our description of one offers a suggestion to those who are beginning the preparation of holiday gifts, or to those who have homes to decorate. This useful bag may be made of cretone or cretone cotton flannel; the more expensive ones are made of silk, satin, velvet or plush. Take a piece of card-board, cut two pieces pocket shaped about six inches wide and seven inches deep; cut four pieces of the cloth the same size and shape; cut a piece of cloth one yard long and one-half yard wide, gather it lengthwise around one of the pocket-shaped pieces; take up the opposite side of the long piece of cloth to another one of the pocket-shaped pieces; line each one of the small pieces, leaving enough space to permit the inserting of the paste-board forms; embroider a piece of flannel and sew on to the side intended to hang next to the wall, this is for needles. For the outer facing of the bag make a neat pocket and tack on to the paste-board portion, ornamenting the same with a little bow of ribbon; make six loops of cloth or get metal rings and attach to the bag, run a cord through them and fasten and your wall bag is complete.

A Mammoth Boquet.

This is most exquisite in design. It is commenced by making a foundation from a board about eight inches long and boaring a hole through the center about one-half inch in diameter; cover the board with any kind of cloth that may be at hand, making a hole in the cloth also; next a round stick two feet long is needed and this is wedged into the hole previously made in the board; cut three pieces of paste-board 24 inches long and three inches wide; cut one inch of the corners off of each piece. Get some field grass, of which there are many varieties that will last for years and still be as fresh and pretty as when first cut. Sew small branches on the paste-board, placing one layer on the other like the shingles on the roof of a house until the entire piece of paste-board is covered, do all three in like manner; place the grass covered pieces of paste-board around the stick already mentioned tacking them together at the top (the ends with the corners cut off at the bottom); take fine gray spool cotton and wrap around them being careful to get the thread under the grass. Cover the foundation with dry moss gathered from the wood that has previously been dipped in green dye, using prepared glue to fasten the moss on to the board. Make paper roses, daises, pinks etc. having long stems and stick the stems down in between the thread that fastened the grass to the paste-board; bend the heads of the flowers downward to give the appearance of reality. Another way of filling the boquet is to take the little white everlasting flowers and use instead of paper flowers, leaving some of them their natural color and coloring others different colors.

Traveler's Bolster.

A convenient and very pretty bolster is given in our instructions. They are exceedingly comfortable to place under the neck when lying down, and one frepuently sees them among travelers, who place them back of the neck while riding in the cars. Make a case the required size and stuff with feathers. Make the outside of knitted astrakan (see knitting department) knit in stripes of different colors, brown and scarlet being a very pretty combination, and crochet together:

or, if desired use plush for the outside and finish with cord and tassel.

Precious Jewel Case.

Take a small box, round or square and mount it onto three knitting needles, or China chop sticks will answer the purpose. The upper ends are fastened to the box and are tied together in the middle with a small piece of gold cord. Cover with tiny shells, which are of course stuck on with prepared glue; or the first teeth of the little ones may be saved and fastened on in the same manner. This makes the jewel case more precious than the jewels which it may hold.

Blocks for Children.

This is something every man or woman can make, and you know the little folks must not be forgotten because they are small; this simple little toy will give them a word of enjoyment, besides being instructive, as it teaches them their letters, and if figures be placed on one side it teaches them how to count. A piece of board about two inches wide and the length in accordance to the number of blocks to be made, is needed; saw them off so they will be two inches square, and paper the edges: mark the letters on with a lead pencil, and then paint them on with oil paints mixed with turpentine. The brush needed for this work can be made by cutting off a lock of human hair and sticking it into the end of a quill.

Instructions for Crazy Patchwork.

Take a piece of muslin or firm goods the size you want the article. Upon this foundation baste the satin, silk, velvet or plush pieces in all sorts of irregular shapes, turning in the edges. Then work the blocks together with different kinds of embroidery silk stitches. The work is much improved by working sprays of flowers, outline designs of children, dogs' heads, bugs, etc.

TABLE SCARF WITH PATCHWORK BORDER.

A beautiful scarf appropriate for mantels, tables, stands, pianos, etc., is made of felt, edged at the ends with fringe formed of heavy silk tassels alternating with large silk pendants. About four or five inches above the fringe is applied a broad band of patchwork. Decorate with a variety of fancy stitches done with different colors of embroidery silk. Bordering the patchwork on each side is a row of wide velvet ribbon, blind-stitched on.

Borders for crazy patchwork are simply broad bands of plain or brocaded velvet, silk, satin or plush.

ORNAMENTAL FANS.

The ordinary large palm leaf fan can be made very decorative by painting in water colors a group of large sunflowers upon its irregular surface and tying a cord with yellow zephyr poupons on the end, around the handle. The fan is to be placed over a door, shelf, picture or bureau top.

MOSS CROSSES.

Pretty crosses can be made by covering wood crosses with moss. Stick the moss on the cross with glue. Bitter-sweet berries are pretty in them; also small white everlasting flowers; the red berries and green leaves are pretty in a white cross made of tissue paper. Baskets are pretty covered with fringed paper; and it is also pretty sewed around a vase or amp-mat. If natural moss is used it should be dipped in a green dye and it will never fade. The everlasting flowers may be dyed any color.

A Dainty Ottoman.

This little article can readily be made at home. Take a square or round box six inches in height. Cover the box with black farmers satin, placing a little wadding on the top, and paint in water paints or oil paints a wreath. Around the top of sides finish with wool fringe and full plating of satin ribbon, or if preferred, pink out strips of cloth two inches wide and fasten on with brass headed nails around the top.

A Picture Frame of Pit Work.

Any old picture frame that has been thrown aside will answer for this work. Cover with acorns, beach nuts, fruit pits, etc. These are stuck on to the frame with prepared glue, and touched here and there with copal varnish. An innumerable variety of things may be made of this kind of work, such as, hanging baskets, fancy boxes, brush cases, wispbroom holders, etc. They are also very pretty for covering a parlor woodbox. We consider it not necessary to give directions for these as they are so simple.

Fancy Pin-cushion.

This fancy pincushion is made on a circular cushion seven inches in diameter. The bottom being of pasteboard, the sides of strong mumie cloth or satine, and the stuffing of wool. Cover the bottom with satine, sew a strip of satine six inches wide around the edge, take up the other side of the satine strip so as to hold the wool, and stitch a small round piece of satine over the gathers. Take two strips of garnet silk two inches wide, either pinked or hemmed on one side; one strip must be longer than the other, pleat up the long strip into sixteen double pleats, and sew them on the cushion. Now cut out a star shaped figure in blue velvet, embroider the dessign with zephyr, filoselle, tinsel or silk, fasten it to the top of the cushion so that the point of the star fits in between the pleats of silk.

A Beautiful Dress.

A dress of mineral-blue and golden brownchecked-wool this forming the skirt and bodice; the front drapery and lower half of the sleeves of blue watered silk trimmed with three bands of blue galloon dotted with white beads; the silk front is a wide square apron, pleated in at the top; the bodice has two bands of galloon, one on the edge and one above; the galloon outlines a deep pointed plastron, with linen chemisette and collar; two bands of galloon trim the sleeves, one where silk and wool join and one above.

Chemisette.

Chemisettes are now very fashionable. Some of them have incertion in the center, through which collored ribbon is run with folds on either side and high collar of mull. Others have alternate rows of embroidery and plain mull, while still others are made of rows of embroidery with a high collar, covered by a band of embroidery. Chemisettes cut square in the neck have opening bordered by full ruching; those for mourning have the ruching run with black silk; those of Fedora lace have loops of ribbon among the lace.

MISCELLANEOUS DEPARTMENT.

Saving Odds and Ends.

Bits of ribbon, silk linings, odds and ends left from the crazy quilt, even the silk of a brown umbrella, every conceivable color and shade. These all may be cut into strips half an inch wide and sewed together at random, so as to color in one long piece and wound forming a large ball. This sewing can be done, either by hand or machine; in the latter case, cut the strips after sewing. Now cast from the silk forty stitches upon medium size tidy needles and knit in loose, plain stitch, back and forth. The blending of colors will be found very pleasing, the work rapid and fascinating, and the result most satisfactory. The pieces can be knitted of any desired size, and be applied to numberless uses and ways for ornamenting. To use long strips of this knitted material by alternating them with the same width of satin for window curtains, is effective. It also makes a very handsome piano scarf, the ends finished with a heavy, mixed silk fringe.

Housekeeper's Friend.

A large wall bag to a housekeeper, is what a desk full of pigeon holes is to a business man. It is a large piece of strong gray drilling with a dozen (more or less) pockets sewed on, three rows of four pockets, or four rows of three according as you have a long or broad wall space on which to hang it. These pockets are from six inches deep and five broad, to twelve by ten, according to the stowing room you require; they are stitched on, and on each is written in large plain letters with ink the contents; for instance, buttons, tapes, ribbons, braids, curtain rings, etc; in short, all the articles that may be to useful to throw away, yet because they are not new or seldom used, may not find a place in the work-basket. Ribbons a little soiled, just the thing to line or bind with, tapes still strong, or buttons from a garment old fashioned but sure to come in again; odd buttons too, that only encumber the regular button box. All the odds and ends we may think it a sort of duty to keep, if we have a thrifty soul, yet which are a nuisance if we constantly come across them, may find appropriate homes in these bags.

Toboggan Hood.

The Toboggan hood is more suitable for larger girls; and while it does not protect the throat so effectually, although strings may be easily added, it will keep the ears warm. The toboggans are made in wool, plush, velvet, or any soft warm material, and trimmed with bows of ribbon or ponpons in front. In some instances the brim is lined with fur. One-half yard of goods twenty-four inches wide will be required for the size for six years.

Pen-Wiper.

Make a roll of soft cotton material, then cut a strip of cloth, or blue silk, three inches wide and seven inches long, put it round the cloth, and make straps of zephyr cord, finished with balls.

Hair-Pin Holder.

Materials: Small round tin spice box; small piece of cardboard, and zephyrs light red, dark red, and green. Cut a piece of the perforated cardboard the size around the box, and work a small rose vine on the cardboard. Then place it around the box and fasten with a stitch here and there. For top and bottom, make a dozen tiny pompons and tie them to a zephyr cord about one quarter of an inch apart. Fasten these to the top and bottom with thread and needle.

Table Cover.

This cover is composed of navy-blue flannel, with a border pinked on both edges. The tendrils are worked in overcast stitches with brown silk, edged with olive green silk.

Watch Case.

The slipper is of blue silk, ornamented with an applique design in colored silk, trimmed at the edge with chenille cord. It is sewed to a sole, covered on both sides with silk. The edge is finished with chenille cord. A brass ring button-hole stitched round, fastened at the top to hang it up by.

A Rag Bag.

A useful present for a young lady to give to her mother is a rag-bag. A new way to make one is to take a strip of material the size of an ordinary chair-back; linen or woolen stuff will do; embroider it at one end and fringe it, turn over the other end, and work it to match, so that the two rows of fringe and work appear one above the other. Sew a piece of muslin at the back to make the bag, and some rings at the top through which run cord; hang it on the wall of the sewing-room, where it will be convenient to put scraps in.

THE HOME.

A Pretty Room.

A young friend of mine, who was no mean artist in a small way, had one of the most charming rooms I ever entered. She furnished it, as far as possible, with her own hands The beadstead, dressing case and chairs had been purchased in a very plain state, and she made them beautiful with her hand painting on the panels. The chairs were simple in style and only cane seated at that, but every one of them had been covered by her deft fingers into an upholstered chair, with an embroidered design to harmonize with painted panels of the furniture. Pictures, panels and plaques of the fair owner's onw make, just enough and no more, found their proper places in that room. Rugs, fashioned by her herself in imitation of Turkish by a familiar process known as" drawing," adorned the room and saved the carpet at the same time. A bunch of lillies of the valley in wax, and so dainty as to invite you to smell them, stood in a tiny vase on the bracket of the girl's own carving. Mosses and ferns with the aid of her brush to execute back-grounds, grew into charming pictures more beautiful than landscape painting, and a dozen other means of adornment did the girl devise to make her room beautiful, careful always that the work should be of her own work, executed with as little expense to her father as possible. And it was a fairyland of beauty.

Home Saving.

We know not who is the author of the following noble

plea, but trust that it may have a wide reading and influence. "In regard to bedroom furnishing don't get a plain, cheap furniture for your own use and put a handsome suite in the guest chamber for the benefit of the occasional visitor. Get one bedroom suit of as handsome a style as you can afford, knowing it will never wear out, and if nice in the beginning will always remain so, though it may grow old-fashioned, and you have no idea with what tenacity these relics of your early housekeeping will cling to your heart in after years. In the first place decide if possible, on the exact sum you wish to use for your house furnishing; then go into your mother's kitchen and pantry and make a complete list of the things which you must have first of all, though there be no carpet in the parlor or lamp in the hall. Deduct the cost of these from the first amount, and to the expenditure of the remainder devote your very best judgment, taste and forethought. Never, never buy expensive furniture and carpets at the sacrifice of books, music, pictures and other things which so much more truly help to make the sunshine of our days. Better, far better have painted and varnished floors, with ingrain or even matting for rugs with these, than without them to indulge in these creature comforts of elegance.

Strive to make home a heaven of rest to the tired hearts and minds as much as the wearied bodies of your friends, administering refreshment by your intellectual and bright surroundings, just as truly to the former as to the latter, when they sit around your board, and you will find that your abode will be an alluring spot to many a worn pilgrim on life's way, and you will feel something of the joys of creation, having created that sweet, rare thing, true emblem of heaven ly rest—a true home."

Doll's Furniture.

Any article for her doll never fails to please a little girl. Common spools are quickly metamorphosed into toy ottomans by covering with a bit of gray chintz or silk, putting a little wadding in at the top for a cushion and tying a piece of ribbon around the center. A cigar box set on end makes a doll's wardrobe if furnished with rows of small white tacks on which to hang the tiny dresses. A little varnish or polish improves it. A wooden box can be converted into a doll house by setting it up on end and running one or two shelf like partitions across to divide it into rooms, the lower serving for kitchen and the upper for parlor and bedroom. The wall should be nicely papered or painted and the floor carpeted; then furnish with chairs cut out of card-board and a bedstead made out of paste-board and furnished with spread and pillows. A toy stove and a set of dishes, such as may be purchased at any toy store, will be suitable furniture for the kitchen.

Nursery Basket.

An extremely pretty nursery basket can be made by taking two of the common half bushel peach baskets, so easily to procure, stand one upside down then place the other upon it. thus bringing the bottoms of the two baskets together, making a form much like an hour-glass; now take some silesia, any color, and line the inside of the top basket neatly, cover this again with darned net making deep pockets, etc., and tacking them onto the basket with dainty bows of ribbon. It is well to make the round piece to line the bottom of the basket, separately; now begin at the outside, tack the silesia in plaits about the top rim with smallest, flat-headed furniture tacks, then drawing it down tightly, tie with a ribbon tightly around where the two baskets come together or screwed together, and then drawing the silesia to the bottom of the stand, turn the whole thing over and tack it onto the lower rim; across the bottom simply tack a piece of slate colored corset jeans, before putting on the lace. Take some carpet warp or twine and crochet some lace and beginning again at the upper part, sew on the lace putting the edge or border of he lace at the top rim of the basket and then gather the plain part in where the silesia is tied; for covering the lower basket put another flounce gathering it quite full at the center, and letting it fall loosely. At the center where the baskets are joined tie a large satin bow the same color as the silesia.

A Warm Baby Blanket.

Take heavy, soft flannel which comes for this purpose; the ornamenting consists of a three quarter wreath of ferns and dasies in the center, about fifteen inches in diameter. The dasies are worked in kensington stitch in silk of different shades of pink, and the fern leaves and the vine of delicate olive green. The edge is cut in squares, every other one taken out. A pretty cream lace is then frilled under-neath them.

At the Foot of the Bed.

Wall pockets to hang at the foot of the bed are very popular at present. They are to hold the diary, pocket-book, handkerchief, and watch, and the novel one is reading, and are most convenient to one who dislikes to get out of bed.

A good way to make one is to take two pieces of silver card-board, of a size to suit the taste, one piece being four inches wider and six inches shorter than the other. The wider piece forms the pocket; join them together with scarlet or blue wool, and before doing so work on the outside some motto such as, "Early to bed, early to rise" or "Rest ye tired one." More elaborate ones can be made of satin, hand-painted, and covering the card-board.

Ladies' Purse Bag.

The lower part of the purse-bag is formed of black silk, in spider-web lace, lined with common silk, as also the upper part of the bag. Cord of crimson silk to draw the purse together near the top, and tassels are placed at each division and one at the bottom.

Dining Room Pictures.

I want to tell the sisters living in the States where we are obliged to use so much canned fruit how to use the pictures that are on the cans. Tomatoes and all kinds of fruit work in nicely. If the paper sticks tight to the cans, steam it over the tea-kettle a few minutes, and it will come off easily. When you have about 25 pictures, get a large piece of black or brown card-board from any printing office, cut out the pictures neatly, and arrange them along the bottom of the sheet, contrasting with taste and using judgment in grouping; make the next short at each end, and so on until you have formed a pyramid; now get some small transfer picture, leaves and flowers, and fill in the spaces, so as to give the picture a connected appearance. Use mucilage to fasten the pictures on.

Waste Paper Basket.

A square basket, medium sized, is much prettier for this purpose, and neater than a round one. The decoration consists of half a yard of brown velvet, quarter of a yard of gold-colored felt; quarter of an ounce of each of the following shades of crewels, light and dark olive green, blue, brown and yellow, one yard and a quarter of worsted ball fringe made of different shades of brown and green, six yards of double faced satin ribbon, one side dark brown and the other gold colored. The ribbon must be three inches wide. Cut a strip of the felt an eighth and a half yard wide, and long enough to fit smothly around the basket; work on this strip with the crewels alternate bunches of cat-tails and yellow daisies or coreopsis, spacing them so that two bunches shall come on each side of the basket. They must be shaded in working them, the cat-tails brown, the daisies yellow with brown center; the leaves should be varied with different shades of green; a strip of velvet an eighth of a yard wide and the same length as the cloth, is then sewed on above the embroidery; the seam must of course be on the wrong side. Work on the right side a fancy stitch all along where the edges are joined; this piece is then fitted smoothly around the basket, allowing the seam to be at one of the corners; the velvet must be about two inches from the top of the basket; the ball-fringe is then sewn around the lower edge of the cloth, which finishes the bottom of the basket. The ribbon is then made in a full ruche of double box plait, having the gold colored on the inside of the ruche. Full bows of the ribbon are tied on each of the handles. The ruching of ribbon is sewed around the top of the basket just above the velvet, but having the edges meet. The basket when finished is a rich and tasteful one.

Dressing Old Frames.

Old mirror frames are painted to match the paint in the room and then draped with any pretty material used for tapestry.

The Porcupine Pin-cushion.

One of the prettiest novelties suited for fairs or for gifts for a ladies' work-basket, is a porcupine pin-cushion. Of course the mere mention of the name will give a good idea of the appearance and shape of the article which we are to describe. To begin take a card-board and cut two oblong pieces, which are intended for the base, and may be about six inches long; cover these and sew them together as for a flat pin-cushion; then cover with green crinkled sephyr, to represent moss. The shaded zephyr will be the best for the purpose. For the pin-cushion itself take another piece of card-board cutting it the shape of a porcupine, with round body and short, tapering nose, and of brown silk of the same shape, only an inch larger all around, two pieces; these are to be worked with eye-lets of yellow silk all over except the head; put in black beads for eyes, and represent the mouth by a small circle of button-hole stitch at the extreme end, with two red dots for nostrils; sew the silk edges over and over along the edge of the card-board, stuffing it out with wool until the body is firm and of a proper shape. For quills stick the pins into all the eyelet holes, and from the under side make small, flat feet with a darker shade of silk. Secure the whole upon the base with a few strong stitches and your porcupine is complete.

Crepe Vails Bad for the Health.

Dr. Rober B. Morison of Baltimore, in a public lecture, expressed the opinion that the long thick crepe veil is very injurious to the complection and that Baltimore exceeds other cities in the wearing of them. The rough crepe, he is reported to have said rubs the skin off, and the poisnous matter is taken into the circulation in that way as well as carried into the lungs in breathing. Such a vail worn for two consecutive years seldom fails to produce evil results. Simular goods about the neck, and black silk and black cotton goods, also produce bad effect. Paris has a feather dyer's disease, produce from the dye in which the feathers are dipped.

Cleaning Carpets.

Carpets should be thoroughly beaten on the wrong side first, and then on the right side, after which spots may be removed by the use of gall or ammonia and water.

Clay Pipe Plaques.

A beautiful and tasty plaque may be made by covering a plaque with velvet or plush, and getting three clay pipes, paint one gold, one silver, and one red; cross one over the other placing the red one in the center, tie where they cross with blue ribbon, fasten to the plaque.

Glove Sachet.

This dainty sachet is made of ruby-colored plush and old

gold quilted satin. The plush is 16 inches deep by 12 wide, and the satin is one inch wider each way. Embroider the top with silk applique embroidery. If applique embroidery is used they may be tinted with liquid bronze applied with the brush. The reinings and French knots at the centers are worked with brown silk. Turn up the edge of the lining and slip-stitch the plush down upon it with the lining projecting half an inch at the edge. Put in an interlining of stiff canvas for a foundation. Fold the sachet through the middle, and if desired turn up one corner for reverse, finish with a bow of ribbon.

Women Who Read.

The pursuance of a regular system of reading is more easily preached to than practiced by busy women. There is a great many of those who declare that they have not an hour in the day they may call their own. But with even ten minutes a day some-thing may be achieved. A book kept on hand for odd moments may be finished in time, and the habit of reading, once rooted, is a strong point gained. As children grow older a great deal may be accomplished by the practice of reading aloud. When this is begun by little children, the system is not apt to be dropped as they grow older. By judicious care the mother may make herself the intelectual center of the family.

Sofa Pillow.

Materials: Three-quarters of a yard of black velvet, three yards of heavy cord, four tassels, three quarters of a yard of old-gold satin. Paint a wreath in Kensington on the velvet; paint the monogram of the owner in water-colors on the old-gold satin; sew these together. Make a pillow of some common material, fill it with curled hair, then slip the fancy cover on over it, finish the edge with cord leaving loops at each end, adding the tassels.

USE OF PERFUMERIES.

There are few ladies who can resist the pleasure of using perfumes and if they are not in too great quantities they are not objectionable. It is a better plan to use only one kind of perfumery, such as violet, heliotrope, rose-geranium, etc. Instead of satuating the handkerchief use perfumes in sachet powders. Put them in cotton in small bags of muslin, silk or satin, and strew them in every part of the bureau and wardrobe, so that a delicate, fresh, almost nameless perfume prevades every article of dress from the hat to the boots. Sachets filled with powdered orris root will give a sweet, wholesome oder that never becomes so strong as to be disagreeable. It is hardly needful to say that the use of strong extracts of perfumery is not considered in good taste.

PERFUME SACHET.

Cut two pieces pale cashmere any size desired,' lay a little cotton between, with some perfume powder, button-hole stitch the edges together with white floss; chain stitch some small figure on with fine sewing silk.

CHEST FOR SOILD LINEN.

Take an ordinary cracker box, line it with paper muslin, and on the outside cover it with cretonne laid in box-plaits; around the top finish with a lambrequin of turkey red with cretonne flowers transferred on the center of each vandyke;

cover the lid with cretonne inside and out and put a full plaiting of the same around the edge; for tassels on the lambrequin use zephyr to correspond with the color of the cretonne. By stuffing the lid of this box it can stand in a room and be used for a seat.

Parlor Door Mat.

Materials: Piece of brussels carpet three-quarters of a yard square: cut three strips of cloth for ruffles, one of green one blue, and one yellow. Cut one edge in small vandykes or pink it, and box-plait or ruffles, sew the green ruffle on first all around the piece of carpet, then yellow and then the blue, laying one ruffle a trifle over the other. In the center put a piece of velvet upon which some design has been embroidered or transfer cretonne figures on the piece of carpet.

Lambrequins.

An elegant lambrequin for a bedroom may be made of white oilcloth, by cutting it in deep vanduykes or saw tooth style, and painting a vine of bunch of flowers upon it. The lambrequin should be lined with pink or blue paper muslin. The vines and flowers inside the vandykes should be painted to imitate the tapestry stitch with shaded green and brown. A profusion of small tull tassels of the mixed colors used in painting, made of wool or silk, are sewn on and between each vanduyke; large polished silver beads or the white shell beads should be sewn all around the lambrequin.

White Oil-cloth Slipper Case.

Cut a large piece of card-board the size desired; cover it with white oil-cloth on one side and paper muslin on the other;

then cut of card-board two smaller pieces for pockets; cover them with oil-cloth and paper muslin, and fasten them to the large piece. Paint on each of the pockets a large bunch of grapes and grape-leaves; paint a vine of grape-leaves all around the back ground of the case. Finish around the edge with a full ruching of satin ribbon; also around the pockets where they are sewed on to the main part of the case. To hang it, sew two large brass rings at the back of the top.

Needle Book.

Cut a piece of card-board about eight inches long and three inches wide; on this card-board work a border in cross-stitch; also a figure in the center (before doing this the card-board should be doubled in the middle so as to form the back of the book) of one of the backs, and the word 'needles' on the other. Cut of blue satin or cashmere a piece the same size of the back, over-hand them together, this forms the linimg of the book; for the leaves cut three pieces of white flannel the same size of the other pieces, pink them all around and sew them into the book. Sew narrow ribbons on to tie the covers together.

Lattice Stitch.

A stitch used in ticking work and other ornamental embroideries for borders, and formed of straight interlaced lines. To work, trace along the edge of the border two straight lines half an inch apart, and in between these lines work the lattice stitch. Carry five straight but slanting lines of silk across these in contrary directions with five other lines, interlacing these with the finest laid by passing each thread over one line and under one line as they cross. Miss the one-eighth of an inch and commence to throw the five lines again across the space and interlace these as before mentioned.

BROOM CASE.

Cut a board back the shape of a star and cover with plush. The front is of card-board sufficiently large to form a pocket. Cover this on the outside with plush, on which some design oas been painted. Line inside with plain satin. Fasten the top and bottom of the front in the frame with the back. The broom is slipped in at either side.

COLLAR BOX.

A satin box to hold collars is quite easily made, and is a very suitable present for a gentleman and one that will be appreciated. Take a common collar box and cover the outside in ruby-colored satin, the inside with pale-blue silesia or quilted satin. On the lid paint a design in water colors, having the principal flowers of blue and white. Around the sides put antique lace and finish the edges of the box with a silk cord corresponding with the flowers. For the feet and knobs use gilt beads, strung on coarse linen thread, and a tiny bead to hold the thread to place.

OIL CLOTH SPLASH: R.

Take a piece of white oil-cloth twenty-four inches long and eighteen inches wide. Paint some design on the center some design of children to be preferred with motto such as, "Splash, splash," or "Be careful of the carpet," Arise, the sun is high," "Make haste your breakfast is waiting." If any such design or motto be painted it is not necessary to fill them in, but simply to paint the immitation of chain or outline stitch. Around the edge put crochet lace or a full ruche of satin ribbon; finish with a large bow of pink satin ribbon in the center of the top edge.

Umbrella Case.

Material: Brown or black oil-cloth; bind with braid and work the edges with a feather stitching of coarse silk; work the monogram of the owner near the top; finish with straps and buttons.

Sofa Roll.

This roll is made of quilted satin; the ends are joined together and quilted ribbon placed around and finished in the center with a heavy cord and tassel. Work two strips of velvet long enough to go around the roll, filazelle or arrasene. Chain stitch the strips on to the roll, laying a plait in the pillow under the bands at the top. The pillow-case is much nicer if filled with curled hair.

A Gipsy Table.

Any old table can be used for this purpose, by being varnished over with ebony varnish; then paint the monogram of the owner in the center and a wreath of flowers around that; varnish the entire surface with colorless varnish. Or cover the top with the same material as the lambrequins and embroider a design to correspond with the one on the lambrequins. The border is cut in vandykes and a design embroidered in each point. Make the stitch very long and spiky and the effect is much more desirable. Old gold satin with a running vine of maderia, is particularly effective and the same on cream color would be quite novel. When the embroidery is finished line the border with satin or silesia, by running the edges of the points together and turning, which is all the finish the edge requires. Put a large full tassel on each of the vandykes.

Card Rack.

A novel card rack is one fashioned of a pine cone. Select a large, perfect one, sew on either side at the top a cord to hang it by, with a tassel covering where the cord is attached to the cone. On the lower end of the card-rack sew another tassel. Then gild or varnish the cone, and when dry it is ready for use.

Night-Dress Case.

Made of turkish toweling embroidered in red or blue marking-cotton as the fancy may dictate. Cut the pique for the case thirty inches long and eighteen inches wide, and round one end for the floss, embroider some small design on the flap and on the part that forms the front when folded over, and execute the work in outline stitch in colors to suit the taste and character of design. Fold the pique in the manner one would seal an envelope, sew up the sides, and hem the top and the flap. Finish around the edge with colored linen lace.

Stove Mats.

These are made of cloth; take two pieces of cloth 5x6 inches lay a layer of cotton between them and overhand them together. On one side the monogram of the owner can be worked and on the other side some humorous design be outlined; fasten a loop on one corner to hang it up by; finish around the edges with crochet lace.

A Rack for Keys and Hooks.

Take a small rolling pin, cover it with velvet all over except the handles, paint in Keusington some vine, fasten six or seven brass hooks on one side; to hang it up take a yard of yellow ribbon and tie to each handle making a small bow on each end.

Lambrequin for Cupboard.

The lambrequin may be made of any kind of cloth. An applique design cut of blue perforated card-board and sewn on with blue and gold colored silk thread is very novelistic. There may also be a feather stitching of red and a chain stitching of blue floss. Lay the pattern of the lambrequin on the perforated card-board, to get the edge the same size as the cloth. Work a star in each vandyke of the lambrequin in alternate colors of red and yellow; finish with fall tassels.

Ornamental Bracket.

This bracket is made nicely may pass for an objet dart, and find a place in the moist elegant boudoirs. It is 14 inches wide and ten inches wide including the frame. The small should be made with hinges on so it can be folded down at pleasure; it is ment to hold a small statuette, a vase of flowers or any small knick-knack. The frame is fitted up with Java canvas in slanting stitches of old-gold colored silk forming squares' when the canvas is this worked all over, the bracket of carved wood is fastened in the center. The outer edge of the canvas is covered with ruby plush, over which wooden beads are sewn on with small white beads so as to form a raised frame. The canvas should be previously lined with stout card-board, covered on the outside with paper muslin.

Bedroom Rug.

Take a common salt sack, cover it with Java canvas, work in slanting stitches of crimson zephyr forming squares, which may be crossed over with royal blue zephyr to give more brilliance to the grounding. The rug is finished with zephyr fringe, to which little tufts are added, made by twisting zephyr over a pencil and fastening each twine with a twist of very fine mounting wire.

Spittoon Mat.

Cut a piece of brussels carpet the size of a saucer. Then cut strips for two ruffles, one of red and the other of blue. Have one edge of each psnked, and box plait all round, laying one ruffle a trifle over the other. This mat is very nice for the slop bowls in the bedroom and may keep drops from the carpet.

Fancy Woodbox.

This wood-box is made of a box three feet long and one and one-half feet high, same width, and having a cover made with hinges. Line the inside with zinc, and bring it over the edges of the box, round the top, cover the outside with heavy navy blue cloth and to finish the edges tack on a narrow moulding. The sides and ends are ornamented with a lambrequin of large vandykes, embroidered in various colors of wool. When the embroidery is finished, press on the wrong side, then line with foundation, and finish the edges with a heavy cord, and a long tassel in the center of each point. The top is to be embroidered to correspond with the sides and ends. It is better to have casters on the box so it can be easily moved from one part of the room to another.

Comb Pocket.

Cut of card-board, one piece ten by fifteen inches (back) a half circle, ten inches diameter (bottom) and another piece four by twenty inches (front). Cover the back, and front with red leather. On the front of the back either paint or embroider some simple design. Treat the front of the pocket in a similar manner. Overhand the three pieces together, and trim the front, top, and bottom with tiny roses made with pink and white leather, which can be procured in almost any shade; finish the sides with tassels.

Bedroom Commode.

Have a round box made 9 inches high, and large enough to admit the vessel. The cover should be on hinges Cover he top with cloth padded with curled hair. Line the box on the inside with muslin. Cover the outside with cloth. On two sides and the top paint or imbroider a spray of flowers. Around the top, up one side, and at the bottom, is a loose puffing of light colored satin with variegated tassels.

Transom Tidy.

Take a piece of green felt the size of the transom, pink it all around the edges; on the side that is to face the street, embroider a vine around the edge; in the center work the name in large letters, the outline of each letter to be made of gold tinsel and the filling to be of silver tinsel; line with pale blue satin upon which some design is painted in water colors. Blind stitch the two pieces together, leaving the green felt about one-half inch wider all around than the blue satin; finish with a dainty bow of ribbon on each corner of the blue satin.

HANDKERCHIEF SACHET.

This sachet requires a box six inches square and two inches high. Line the inside with pink satin quilled on the sides; the outside is covered with pink velvet and embroidered; the leaves are outlined in stem stitch with reseda and yellow crewel, then filled in satin stitch with wool of a darker shade; the veins are in stem stitch. A small flower is outlined in ruby crewel, and filled in satin stitch and point Russe with a darker shade. The outer petals are light blue, the center of darker blue. The top is covered and embroidered to correspond with the sides. Finish around the bottom and around the edges of the lid with a full plaiting of pink satin ribbon.

EMBROIDERY AND PAINTING SCRAP BOOK.

Any old book will answer for this purpose; take out all the eaves, cover the back with blue satin, paint in water colors hinges in immitation cross stitch, and in the middle of the upper side a monogram. For leaves paint on all kinds of material, and in all the different methods of painting, also embroider in Kensington, Brier-stitch, Herring-bone, French knot, etc., on various kinds of cloth. This makes a very neat sample case for showing your own handiwork.

DOOR BRICK.

Take a common brick, cover it with cloth; plait a puff at the bottom of the brick, and finish with a cord; then place a layer of curled hair round the brick and draw the puff up loosely over it, and fasten around the top of the brick, then finish the edge with fringe or lace, and over that sew cord. Fasten the cover for the top on three sides, then put in the hair to suit fancy. Tack the remaining side of material down, and sew on cord. The center of the top is ornamented with a tidy of Java canvass, edged with lace or a piece of the same material the brick is covered with, embroidered in colors.

Lamp Shade.

Take a sheet of colored tissue paper, mark out some design on it, and then with a sharp pair of scissors cut away all the outlines so that when the lamp is lighted the effect produced is that of a pictured scene. Finish around the top and bottom with a row of paper flowers.

Shaving Case.

This dainty little article is made by taking two pieces of card-board cut nearly square, covered on the outside with crushed paper and lined with any contrasting color, filled with fancy colored papers, which can be pulled out for use as they are wanted, then filled again; a handle of plaited paper fastened at the top with mucilage; form rows of fringe at the bottom, flowers on the outside.

Decorated Fans.

Handsome fans are made by covering Japanese fans all over with paper fringe with bows of ribbon or bunches of flowers placed in the center. The back is covered with plain, stiff paper of the same shade or white, covered with tissue paper of the color of the fan, put together with mucilage.

Sitting-room Basket.

Nothing is more attractive in a room than a basket of flowers; the basket itself should be of dark-colored paper, and made without any bottom, simply with a wire ring, the paper being placed in folds; the flowers are then placed in the basket. The handle is made of wire covered with paper; around the handle twine some climbing flowers such as morning glories, flowering-beans, etc. If covered with a glass shade one can scarely distinguish them from wax.

Boys's Jersy Caps.

Take a piece of cloth the size of the boys' head and about seven inches wide; blindstitch a hem on the right side; gather the top; sew the two ends together making the seam in the back; draw the top together and place a button on it; make or buy a long tassel and fasten it on with the bottom. A brown jersey with gold cord and tassel around the edge forms a pretty combination.

Waste Basket.

Procure a common scrap basket, line it with silesia. The basket is covered with puffings of pink satin and tabs of navy blue velvet, edged with narrow antique lace. The tabs are two and one-half inches wide and three long, pointed at one end. Some design should be worked on each tab in satin, chain and feather stitch and in point russe. A heavy fancy cord is arranged in loops around the basket and finished with a large satin bow.

HOME DEPARTMENT.

Toilet Sets.

Make a case the desired size, fill it with wool; cover the top with crushed paper, make a very full puff around the sides; make a mat three inches larger than the cushion, cover it with crushed paper; sew four rows of paper fringe around the edge, make a paper cord for a heading, fill the space between the cushion and the fringe with paper flowers, also put a bunch of flowers on the top of the cushion.

Bed Valance.

Material: Dark green cloth, gilt cord and fringe, small white beads, yellow and brown silk floss. A scroll pattern of the gilt cord, and leaves of brown and yellow floss, the flowers of beads, and fringe on the edge makes a lambrequin that it is impossible to exaggerate the pleasing effect produced; it is safe to say it is a marvel of prettiness.

Letter Sachet.

Take a piece of silver perforated card-board, fourteen inches long by seven inches wide, double it in half, and on the part to form the top, work some small design in silk floss or split zephyr, or work the word "Letters" or "Notes." Quilt a piece of pink satin the size of the case, and fasten it to the inside of the case. Around the edges, put a narrow trimming of ostrich feather band, and finish with tiny loops of satin ribbon. Across the top lay satin ribbon, and finish the ends with bows. A perfume sachet placed underneath the quilted lining is a great addition.

Parlor Wood Basket.

Material: Basket without ends, twenty large tassels, thirty-two small ones, bottle green cloth, garnet velvet, spangles and a bottle of gilt and brushes. Gild the basket around the edges, the handles and the entire inside. Fasten a strip of the bottle green cloth across the sides, and over that make a vandyke of the garnet velvet, and spangle it thickly. The tassels can be made of worsted with a few strands of silk on the outside, and would look well if a few colors were mixed. These baskets can be had at any large basket house, and are called fire-wood baskets. Most of the houses in this conntry burn wood and this fancy little article will be found very useful as well as ornamental.

Bureau Scarf.

This scarf is made of felt or canton flannel; across the ends are colored velvets and braids laid in points and straight bands. To brighten the whole, feather and cat stitch the braid and velvet with various colors of floss. Finish the ends with deep antique lace, and work some of the heavy spots in the lace with floss, and on each of the points hang different colored tassels. Or another very pretty way is to put a broad strip of velvet across each end of the scarf and upon this sew a band of satin with a conventional design in kid applique and tinsel couching or floss and gold thread embroidery. A heavy couching covers the seams.

Chair Cushion.

Make a case the desired size, stuff wiih feathers or curled hair; cover with a fancy cover made after the old log cabin style. A thick twisted cord. silk tassels, and a puffing completes the edge of the cushion. This style of work is very old, but never the less it is very effective, and can be worked by an unpracticed hand.

French Knot Embroidery.

The French knot is formed by bringing the needle up through the material, winding the silk or thread around the needle two or three times, and putting it back in the same place it came up, being careful not to tangle the thread as it passes through.

Folding Screens.

Folding screens are very useful as well as ornamental, and can be easily made. First, have a plain frame made at a carpenter shop after your own direction. Those having three panels are, perhaps, more useful than those having two. They can be made of various materials from muslin to the elaborate embroidered ones so common in fashionable drawing-rooms. A very effective one may be made by making each panel differently; for instance cover one with Turkish toweling, another with coarse muslin nailed tightly down each side, and a strip of garnet plush or velvet turned over the wooden edges, and tacked round to form the binding; for the panel use the unbleached muslin, upon which embroider a design of one or two long stalked ox-eyed daises, with a few leaves and blades of grass, and several rich hued butterflies. On another, cover with striped bed-ticking, divide it into squares and oblongs by lines of brier stitch or herringbone in china blue crewel, leaving the central division larger than the rest. In each of the irregular divisions thus obtained, work with crewel in two shades of blue, pointed with stitches of filoselle, geometrical patterns not to minute in detail. If desired this pattern may be worked with applique cut from dark colored linen. It adds very much to finish the top of the screen with gilded balls; these can be purchased at almost any toy shop. The screen above mentioned is but a simple one, yet it adds to one's chamber, and one has little idea, unless they have used them, how very convenient they are. For home every day use this simple one is pretty.

A Convenient Letter Carrier.

These are very convenient to carry letters to and from the post office and are made of leather or any other material may be used. Take a large sized envelope, cut out a piece of red leather large enough to make a case for it, and leave a flap like the envelope; embroider something pretty on the back of the case. I prefer the name of the owner best, and work a border around the edges. Line with silk or merino; put a full ruching of leather around the edges. Use a handsome cord and tassels to correspond with colors used in the case to make the handles. Another pretty way to make the handles is to cover a small piece of rope with leather, shot with silver.

Children's Bibs.

Children's bibs are are made of Turkish toweling. These are cut out to fit the neck, and the edge is ornamented with a fril of linen lace.

Fancy Penwiper.

A pretty, small penwiper is made of two two-inch-and-a half squares of celluloid for covers, with two or three leaves of chamois. On one cover is painted a branch of wild rose blossoms and leaves, with the legend, "Extracts from the pen of———" The name of the recipient to be inserted if used as a gift. The covers and leaves are tied together with a bow of narrow gros-grained ribbon.

Chain-Stitch Embroidery.

The chain is formed by a loop made first upon the upper side of the material, and the needle passed through securing the loop. The needle is then passed back near where it was drawn up, a stitch taken toward you, and each time this is done the loop is left around the needle, forming a link in the chain.

Bathing Slippers.

These slippers are made of substantial bed-ticking, with either a felt, cloth, cork or rope sole. Bind the edges with a bias piece of the ticking and make a full bow of red oil calico for the top. The straps to go over the foot and around the ankle are made of cloth button-hole stitched on the edge.

Childs' Carriage Cushion.

Materials: Pink and light blue cloth and a heavy cord and tassals. Make a cushion with ticking a foot square; fill it tightly with wool or feathers, then make a case of the pink cloth and in the seam around the edge of the case pull in one edge of the piece to from the puffs, then turn it up and turn in the upper edge and box-plait it and sew it firmly on the top of the case, leaving a space in the center about nine inches square. Cut of the blue cloth a piece for the center and braid it with gilt-edged and canary colored braids, having the edge of the center (which is star shaped) pinked.

Fasten the star to the cushion in each point with a large bead and finish each corner with a tassel. Draw the cord around the cushion firmly and tie in a knot, leaving a loop in the center to lift it by.

Hair-receiver.

The foundation is a small lard pail. The pail is covered with perforated card-board, with the word hair-receiver worked on it. Draw the card-board tightly over the pail first turning in the edges; the top is made of satin, and drawn up with cord and tassel; the handle is covered on both sides with the card-board, and bound or button-hole stitched together at the edges; finish on each side of handle with bow of ribbon.

Embroidery Rings.

This stitch is much used in cotton embroidery; it is first run round and then cut out with a pair of scissors, a small margin being left to turn back where it should be neatly button-hole stitched.

Boy's Marquerite Caps.

To make a cap for a boy four years old you will require twenty inches of gray cloth one-half yard in width, and one yard of gray cord and a darker tassel; make same as the jersey cap until you come to the top. This is taken up and laid in a tripple box-plait and brought over and fasten to one side; next take the cord and trim the top bringing it over the plait and fasten at the side and then add the tassel.

Satin Stitch Embroidery.

The satin stitch is used in working the leaves and flowers

in all kinds of em' .o'dery; the stamp d pattern should first be run 'ound, then after sewing in a few threads in long, loose stitches lengthwise of the leaf, the stitches are sewed in closely side by side in a slanting and contrary direction, fol- o r .; carefully the defining line of the pattern.

Book Mark.

Make the marker of cardboard and cover one side with silk. Paint flowers and birds in gold and other colors on the s k. T a satin ribbon through a hole at one end. Work the ini- tials on the cardboard side.

Waste Paper Basket.

Take any ordinary scrap basket and run stripes of wine col- ored cotton flannel through the splits. Around the top, make a valance of garnet plush cut in vandykes, and pink these, then stud it with beads. Add to each point a tassel of canary color in wool. Line the basket throughout with silesia, and cut strips of the same two inches wide; notch both edges. plait in full box plait and secure firmly around the top of the basket inside.

Herring Bone Stitch Embroidery.

Herring bone stitch is made by sewing backwards and all ternating loose loops of button hole stitch.

Baby Basket.

The material required for covering one of these baskets is three yards of light blue silk, two yards of dotted Swiss, and twelve yards of tatting or narrow lace for edging the fluted border. The basket should be first lined with the colored material and afterwards with the white muslin.

Bath Room Picture Frame.

For the foundation use a stiff piece of cardboard. The whole is first neatly covered with brown glazed paper, and afterward ornamented with little chips and pieces of wood of various sizes and shapes which can be collected at any carpenter's shop; or they are more to be preferred if from the cabinet shop. Glue them on securely. The thin chip should form the border; the heaver pieces the center. When the chip work is finished, the back may be covered with a piece of cloth. When finished, brush over with a good copal varnish. In order to enliven it, a few of the chips may be touched with gold and silver leaf.

Kensington Stitch Embroidery.

The stitch is taken the same as the outline stitch; they should be evenly laid and dovetailed one into another; the outline of the design should be carefully followed, but the interior of the leaf or petal filled in according to the shape. The stalks of the flowers should be worked in stem stitch.

Dinning Room Crumb Cloth.

This is made taking a large unbleached sheet and embroidering it in applique cut from red linen. Or treat it in a similar fashion, and work puppies and ragged robins in geometrical squares. Black cotton may be used for the veining, and coarse linen fringe sewed around the edge. Outline work is the most simple method of arriving at an effect in this branch of decoration. To vary the result, a darned-in-background is often added. Of this work a few varieties may be described: A design of large passion flowers, outlined in chocolate brown crewel on linen crash, has a background of old gold threads of crewel darned in wavy lines. The artichoke plant is outlined on linen in shades of orange, the back-ground covered with arrow-head stitches of dull yellow crewel, suggesting the seeds of the plant.

BED SPREAD AND SHAMS.

A bed spread and shams, easily made and highly effective, is cretonne canton flannel, finished around the edges with crocheted lace. Or a stout linen sheet, divided into squares and oblongs by lines of brier stitch or herring bone in china blue crewel, leaving the central division larger than the rest. In each one of these divisions work some design not to minute in detail.

Darned netting is still used, a sixteenth century bed cover having been recently copied. It has twelve squares, each one with a figure representing a month of the year, outlined in colors. Madras muslin, in all its varieties of faint hues, quaint designs, soft and lovely texture should be advanced as the chief among bed covering. If needle work be added to the ground of Madras muslin, it must be in the shape of outlines, or darned lines of filoselle introduced upon the woven pattern of a plain cream tinted stuff.

A TABLE SCARF.

A scarf table cover of pink satin diagonal has for the decoration of the border a band of scroll work. This is worked in darned stitch with brown, yellow and pale red filoselles. Below is a smaller border of deep red plush, with a heavy fringe of pink. A square cover er may be made of double width canton flannel of a deep wine color; the border has a stripe of heavy cretonne about six inches wide set fully six inches from the edge of the cloth. The ground was light blue covered with sprays of flowers. The cretonne was simply blind stitched on; a fancy stitch would have detracted rather than added effectiveness. A fringe was made by slashing the edge of the flannel in quarter inch widths two inche deep. A mantle lambrequin may be make by using similar bands of cretonne on a foundation of Java canvas applied by fancy stitches in filosettes of several colors.

Railway Stitch Embroidery.

Railway stitch is made by winding the thread over the needle a number of times, or as many times as the space to be filled will require. No running out is necessary for this stitch, but a tracing only.

Pocket Pin Cushion.

Cut two pieces of card-board any desired shape, then take two pieces of velvet and paint a spray of flowers in each corner; then round the edge lay a fine gold thread, and catstitch over it with some bright color, and scatter tiny flowers in the center. Draw the velvet tightly over the card-board and overhand the edges together, and stick the pins in nicely.

Child's Ball.

This may be made by making a ball of rags the required

size and covering it with bright pieces of cretonne, or by crocheting a cover of some fancy stitch, using first red wool, then yellow, then using blue till the work is large enough to cover one-half of the ball, then make one red row, draw the work over the ball, and work the other half to correspond with the first half, decreasing at regular intervals. A pattern of bright flowers worked with worsted round the center, adds greatly to the ball's attraction to a child.

Chair Cushion.

This may be made of odd bits of silk, cut in diamond shape. Silk cord finishes the edge, and a tassel on each point. A button is drawn down through the center and fastened firmly. Curled hair is the most desirable filling for the cushion. The diamond pattern is five inches long and two and a half inches wide.

Doylies.

Housekeepers will find something very pleasing in the line of drapery by making doyleys of linen crash, fringing the edge and working some conventional design in the center, but these are all done in brown tints, scarcely varied by other colors, and in the finest of silk. Still others have Japanese and Chinese pottery designs done in the lightests blues, reds and olive greens.

Dress for Flower Pot.

Material: Green, red and yellow floss. Black, blue and orange flannels. Cut a piece of card-board the shape of the flower pot; sew it together, and make a full puff of the black flannel on the outside. Then cut four diamond shaped pieces of the orange flannel, and notch the edges, or better still, have them pinked. In the center of each diamond applique small pieces of the blue flannel feather stitching with the flosses. When all the pieces are finished, fasten them on the outside of the cover at the top, allowing the points just to reach the bottom outside. This design may also be used for covers for toilet bottles.

Eyelet Holes Embroidery.

The pattern, be it a leaf or hole, is first run round, then the material, after being slashed with a pair of pointed scissors, or pierced with a stiletto, is turned back and sewed neatly and firmly over and over.

Monograms.

For marking handkerchiefs, make a half moon, horse shoe, or circle, and place the letters in the center.

Children's Leggings,

Are very pretty, made of striped Jersey cloth and buttons sewed on the outside.

Hem Stitch Embroidery.

A few threads are first drawn out of the material to be hem-stitched, and with the needle, three, four or more threads are taken up, and the stitch caught in the hem.

Baby Comfortable.

A very neat comfort may be made for baby, of dark colored blue muslin, with a wide bold design traced all round for braiding with coarse white, or if preferred, white wool, use and chain-stitch it. Holland used as a border on light blue satin cover, and the Holland worked with blue floss or worsted, makes a very pretty cover.

Tray Cover.

A servicable cover may be made of fine linen, and a border of knotted fringe embroidered in the center. The embroidery should be of colored washing cottons, blue or red worked in cross-stitch.

Outline Stitch Embroidery.

Outline stitch is simply the back stitch, and is generally used in outlining designs upon linen, and is very popular for embroidering the ends of towels for splashers, doyleys, etc. It is usually done in cotton, but may be done in etching silk, which comes for the purpose.

Pelerine.

Cast on thirty-five stitches; knit eight turns straight, then thiry-six turns, increasing one stitch on one end of each row. Decrease one stitch for 21 rows on the staight side to form the back part of the neck, still increasing on the other side. Then knit twelve turns quite straight, the center of these twelve turns is the center of the Pelerine, and the other side must be knitted in reverse.

Cap Basket.

This is useful for ladies to take along when driving out. A round is formed of silver paper it is lined, and at each side there is a crimson silk or satin bag, drawn with a silk cord.

If preferred, cardboard covered with java canvass and worked in cross-stitch can be submitted for the silver paper. This can also be used for carrying fancy work and materials.

Double Chain Stitch Embroidery.

Double chain stitch is done much the same as the single chain stitch, except that the needle is put in further to the left, and twisted a little as it passes through.

Tissue Paper Dresses

Are a very great success; They can be either all paper or just trimmed in paper. Of course these dresses are only or the ball room. The pretty dresses that can be made of tissue papers are familiar to every one who looks into a fashion store, and a little neatness in the trimming, a little taste in the selection of colors will make a tissue paper dress a manuel of prettiness.

Piano Cover.

For the material of the cover use olive green velveteen, and for the border have a design of blossoms or deep yellow sunflowers. Or another design is to have the cover of old gold felt, worked with gorgeously colored humming-birds and tall grasses.

Boot Pin Cushion.

Dmall china boots are sold in the toy shops all ready to receive the cushions that are to make them useful. In this one the boot portion is of old gold satin, and the cushion is in harmony. Gold cords are pretily arranged about the top and the tiny tassels that finish them seem a wee touch of croquetry. The cushion should be firmly stuffed, and if the little boot is to be given to a bachelor the sender should not forget to have it full of pins.

Umbrella and Cane Holder.

This receptacle for canes and umbrellas is made of willow and may be purchased ready for the trimmings at any willow-ware establishment. Ribbon is run in and out through the open work left between the solid fancy work and is as wide as the space calls for; the ends are tied in large, soft bows diagonally across the front of the holder. The ribbon may be of any color and variety preferred, sometimes three different shades of ribbon are effestively used; again only two shades are selected, and oftentimes only one color is seen, so ones' taste can be exercised in producing a very original combination.

Embossed Top for a Lamp Ornament.

Fasten a small piece of wire in the end of the top to fasten the top onto the lamp; then cover the top with silver foil and gild the peg and the ornament is completed.

Paper Receiver.

This receiver is made by covering two three cornered pieces of card-board with pale blue satin. Upon the front is a half wreath cluster of applique roses which is put on in perfect smoothness. Heavy crimson silk cords are fastened from corner to corner; while the pocket is suppended by crimson satin robbons which, starting from different points, all meet at the center and form many loops. For a room furnished in pale-blue or crimson this pocket is very becoming. In arranging the pocket the colors used for the decoration should be in perfect harmony.

Table Cover.

For a square or oblong table this is a handsome and elaborate looking cover. The material is cloth of dimensions to hang gracefully deep at all sides of the table. A wide band of velvet is arranged a little above the edges and fastened down at its edges with fancy stitches done with contrasting silks. It is also richly embroidered near the top and bottom with simple stitches, which only require care in producing a very elaborate and pretty effect.

Lace Lamp Shade.

In the development of this dainty and beautiful piece of work Spanish lace is used, the color being chiefly rose-red. The lace is mounted on rose colored tarlatan properly shaped, and is in three rows, the upper row being finished for a heading and having narrow ribbon run through it. The result is very dainty. Any color preferred may be chosen, and often a row of beading for the ribbon is added to the upper ruffle.

Fancy Work Stand.

A positively masculine air may be given to this little table because it is evident that somebody's brother has been robbed of his felt hat and then cajoled into giving up three of his walking sticks. The outer side of the hat is covered with strips of many colored ribbon arranged in rainbow fashion. The inside and brim are lined with pale blue satin. A tripod formed by three canes is caught in the center by an enormous bow of blue satin ribbon deftly tied. This basket will be found especially convenient for cards or for one's vinaigrette, fan or the many little trifles of the boudoir.

Photograph Case.

This case is made by cutting three pieces of Bristol cardboard the desired shape and covering them with deep crimson plush. The edges are bound when required with narrow ribbon the same shade, the sewing of the pieces together over this making a less bulky seam than plush. Sprays of flowers are embroidered upon each frame. Small bows of ribbon decorate the corners of the center picture. Velvet, satin or brocade may be used, if preferred to plush.

Tobogganing Cap.

This handsome cap is made of pure silk, with Roman stripes up to five inches; from this point are shown narrow one and two stripes followed by two inch navy and cardinal bars. The top is finished in full Roman stripes and is provided with a heavy tassel.

Tam O'Shanter Cap.

Make a chain of three stitches, join, and in each of these stitches make two single crochets and in each of these make two single crochets in the same way, working round and round, but not fastening at the ends of the rows. After the second row one single crochet only is made in each stitch, except when it is needful to widen so as not to make the work "cappy," two crochets being made for this purpose whenever needed. All that is to be considered in the further progress of the crown is to have the work neither cap nor ruffle the least bit, and judgment will have to be exercised in introducing the two single crochets in one stitch, as no rule can be followed in this matter. Crochet very tightly and evenly and do not widen regularly at certain places, for this will spoil the circular shape needful. Forty rows are necessary to complete the crown. The part for the side and brim is made separately from the crown. Start with a chain of as many stitches as there are in the last row of the crown and join the ends of the chain; then make a single crochet in each chain. In the second row make as many stitches as in the second row from the last in the crown, skipping a stitch when necessary to obtain the right number; each succeeding row should also contain only the same number of stitches as the corresponding row in the crown, until twenty rows are made. When correctly made this portion will be perfectly smooth when laid upon the outer part of the crown. The twenty-first row is made without widening or narrowing and seven other rows are needed for the brim and to complete the cap. In making these last seven rows widen a little on each row, only enough, however, to make a band that will fit the head of the person that is to wear the cap. When the last row is made finish off securely and neatly, then place this portion on the crown with the right sides together; with a piece of the worsted crochet them together by lifting the corresponding stitches in the two parts and making half stitches. The cap is then completed and ready for the pompon, which should be sewed on with strong thread at the center of the crown.

HOME DEPARTMENT

Match Receiver.

This receiver has two divisions; the upper division being used for burnt matches, and the lower one for unused matches. The foundation is card-board covered on the outside with velvet or plush, and on the inside with Surah put in slightly full. A tin box is placed in each compartment, but should not be visible. Fancy stitches done with silk or floss decorate the edges of each compartment, a variety being used. The word "Matches" is embroidered with tinsel on the lower compartment. A strap of ribbon joins the two parts at the end, and over each end of each strap is placed a bow of ribbon having long loops and ends. Ribbons extending from the bows on the upper compartment are used to suspend the receiver, being tied in a bow at the point of suspension. The receptacle is exceedingly dainty, and the colors, materials and stitches will depend altogether on individual taste.

Work Basket.

Somebody's archery box has been riffed for three arrows which form the stand for this unique looking basket. The arrows are arranged with their heads down and are tied together with ribbons a little above the heads. Between the arrows, just at the end of the feathers, are fastened three fine brass rods, which are run in and out through the meshes of a net bag, which is make of cord. Ribbons are run through the meshes just below, and tied in bows with long loops and ends at each arrow. The arrows may be gilded or painted any perferred color, and the ribbons may be in one or more colors and of any variety.

Catch-all Bag.

In any apartment this bag will be useful and decorative, and it may be hung in a corner, on the back of a chair or the side of a table. The lower part is card-board rolled cornucopia fashion and covered with silk, with lapped edges of different lengths, producing a pretty effect. All the edges are bordered with gold braid, and in the top is fastened a deep bag of silk that is gathered at the lower edge before being attached and is drawn in closely near the top by narrow fancy edged ribbons run in casings. The top is finished to form a frill above the casings, and the ribbons are tied in long looped bows. One of the loops thrown over the chair or nail will support the bag in the most artistic manner. Sometimes velvet, plush or fancy silk is used to cover the stiff portion.

Decorated Fans.

A simple palm-leaf fan of good size can be carefully painted with gold liquid paint and beautified by a cluster of three ostrich tips fastened to droop gracefully near the handle and a strip of ribbon passing from under the tips along the sides, terminating under the edge. The tips may be some that have done service on a hat or bonnet, and the ribbon may match or contrast with the tips and be of any preferred variety. Such fans are fastened against the wall or artistically placed on the table or mantle. A bunch of paper or artificial flowers may be used instead of the feathers, if preferred.

Sachet.

Three varieties of pretty ribbon are joined to form this

beautiful sachet and fancy stitching in colored silk is made along the seams. The shape is three cornered and applied points of ribbon decorate one side, while the bottom is decorated with the ribbons gathered to the lower corners and tied together near the left corner. Scraps of fancy ribbons, silks and velvets may be thus utilized and frequently the three will be seen in one sachet. Of course the customary filling of cotton well sprinkled with sachet powder is requisite, but it should not be too compact.

Toilet Cushion.

A piece of brocaded silk showing a large detached pattern is used for this cushion, the silk being cut off so that only part of the pattern will come in one corner. The cushion is bordered with a thick silk cord which is looped in rosette fashion in the upper corner.

Ornamented Scarf.

To throw over a towel rack, a table or the back of a large chair; this scarf is useful as well as decorative. The fabric is China silk, and the end which hangs over is decorated with a row of applied velvet dice edged with tinsel cord. A crocheted ring is fastened to the bottom of each disc and through it is fastened a bunch of silk floss to form a large tassel. A tassel made of floss is also fastened where the disc touches and also at a similar point to the outer discs; the other end, which falls much deeper, is bordered with two bands of velvet edged at each side with tinsel cord arranged in single scroll; the lowest band is directly at the edge, and pendants formed of crocheted rings and floss tassels are tacked to form a fringe all across the edge; the other band is a short distance above and a row of crocheted rings depends from it.

Fancy Apron.

The material of this apron is scrim. A deep hem is made at the bottom, at the sides and across the top, a wide ribbon being inserted in the hem at the top to draw the apron in and to tie about the waiste; the hems are held with button-hole stitches of yellow floss; threads are drawn above the bottom hem to form three rows of squares, which are filled in with long stitches of the floss radiating from the center to the edges; these stitches produce the effect of daisies and are soft and beautiful. Narrow ribbon the color of the embroidery silk is run in to show in the openings at the corners of the squares. The stitches may be shaded hues, heliotrope, pink scarlet, pale-blue or green. A row of button-hole stitching is also made across the apron at the top of the squares. Extreme care is needful in drawing the threads to produce the regular effect which is so desirable to the good finish of the work.

Paper Pocket.

An ordinary wire toaster or broiler is used for the foundation of this pocket. The toaster is painted with gold liquid paint, and wide ribbon in two shades arranged to alternate as run in and out through the wires, each strip of ribbon being in one continuous piece all around thus banking the sides; the ends are neatly joined at the back. A ribbon bow is fastened to the top at the sides, and ribbon is also tied in a bow near the top of the longest handle by which the pocket is suspended. The ribbon may be in two shades of one color or in two contrasting colors or each row may be of a different shade or color. When contrasting colors are chosen care should be taken to produce a pleasing harmony.

COOKING AND BAKER'S DEPARTMENT.

Yeast Cake.

Good yeast, one pint; rye or wheat flour to form a thick batter; salt, one teaspoonful; stir in and set to raise; when risen, stir in Indian meal until it will roll out good; when again risen roll out very thin; cut them into cakes and dry in the shade or by the stove; if dried in the sun they will ferment.

Potato Bread.

Boil six common sized potatoes; when thoroughly cooked mash them fine adding a teaspoonful of salt, and one yeast which has been well dissolved in a cupful of lukewarm water; two quarts of warm water and with sufficient flour make a soft dough moulding it thoroughly; let it stand over night in a warm place to rise; in the morning when light mold into small loaves and bake.

Compressed Yeast Bread.

Place one Compressed Yeast Cake in a cup of warm water; when dissolved rub quite smooth; make a sponge in a large pan of flour with two quarts of warm milk or water, a teaspoonful of salt and the yeast; stir all together thoroughly making a stiff batter; cover with a thick cloth and set it in a warm place over night to rise; in the morning make it into a stiff dough by adding more flour and knead it for half an hour; put it aside to rise again, when light mold into six loaves, place in pans, cover and let stand a short time for further rising, and bake in a moderately hot oven

Graham Bread No. 1.

Two quarts graham flour, a small cup of molasses or sugar, one cup baker's yeast, a little salt, warm milk or water enough to make a well beaten thick batter; place this in tins and when light bake in moderately hot oven.

Graham Biscuits.

Take two quarts of graham flour, one quart cornmeal, one-half cup of butter; one cup molasses, sour milk to wet it up with saleratus as for biscuits. Bake in the usual way,

Breakfast Rolls No. 1.

Two quarts of flour, one tablespoonful of sugar, one tablespoonful of butter, one-half cup yeast, one pint scalded milk or water and set to rise until light, then knead until hard and set to rise, and when wanted make in rolls, place a piece of butter between the folds and bake in a slow oven.

Brown Bread.

Take a large cooking bowl, into it put one cup Indian meal, one cup rye meal, also one cup graham meal, and a pinch of salt. Mix all thoroughly while dry. Put a teaspoonful of saleratus into a tin pint measure, take teacup sour milk, pour it onto the soda and stir till foamy; turn into the dry meal; add one cup sweet milk and beat all together. Lastly add one-third cup molasses, beat again and turn into a buttered brown bread tin. The baking pan should have a tight cover. Steam three hours. bake half an hour.

Graham Bread No. 2.

Set a sponge at night with white flour. In the morning take enough to make two loaves, add a cup of molasses, and knead it well, adding only graham flour.

Graham Bread No. 3.

Take enough luke warm water and flour to make a thin batter, add one-half teacupful of bakers's yeast, beat well together; when light, mix in graham flour, one cup of warm milk or water, half a cup of sugar, making a stiff dough; mold with a little wheat flower, put it into a pan, and, when light, bake.

Breakfast Rolls No. 2.

At night take two lbs. of flour, rub in an ounce and a half of lard; make a hole in the flour and add half pint of cold milk, half gill good yeast, 1½ oz. sugar, the yolk of one egg and a little salt, let it stand till morning; then mix, let stand for an hour or so; then roll out and bake in hot oven.

Buns.

To a pint of warm milk add half cup good yeast, four eggs and cup and a half sugar beaten together, one cup butter well rubbed into some flour dry; mix all together, using enough flour to make a stiff batter, let it rise over night. When quite light, add flour and mold into small buns, place in bake pan; after rising more bake twenty minutes.

Another Kind of Roll.

Take bread dough after being raised, spread lumps of butter over the top, and sprinkle flour over the butter. Knead till the butter is worked in thoroughly, then roll out and cut with a cutter. Have melted butter at hand and rub over the rolls which are cut, and fold one-half over the other half. Let them stand in a warm place till very light, and bake in the usual way.

Another Roll.

Take two tablespoonfuls of butter, two of sugar, and a pinch of salt well worked together; make a sponge with warm milk or water, add one cup yeast and a little flour. When light add more flour and mold for twenty minutes; let rise again. Roll it out, cut into cakes, butter the tops, fold them half over, set to rise again and bake in a hot oven.

Rusks.

To a pint of luke warm milk add half cup yeast and a little salt, make a sponge and let it rise; then add one teacupful of sugar, two beaten eggs, a cup of butter, worked well into dough adding more flour; let it rise. Roll into a sheet, butter it and cut into biscuits, fold them over, place in tins separate a little, let them rise again for a short time, then bake.

Albany Rolls.

One cup yeast, 3 cups sweet milk, 5 oz butter, the yolk of 5 eggs, 3 oz of sugar, 1 oz. salt, all the flour it will take up. Set in a warm place to rise, then bake.

French Rolls.

Three-fourths pint of milk, ¼ pint of yeast, little salt, 1 oz. white sugar, 1 oz. lard, 2 lbs. flour; set in the morning with about one-half the flour; at noon add the remaining portion of the flour and work up stiff; at 4 o'clock in the afternoon, knead well and make into rolls. Should be brushed a little, then baked.

Vienna Rolls.

Two pounds of flour, 1 pint of milk, 1 cake compressed yeast, little salt, 1 teaspoonful of sugar. Make the milk luke warm and dissolve the yeast in it. Set sponge at 8 in the morning, at 11 add the salt and sugar and make up stiff dough. Let rise till about 3. Then knead well on the table. Roll out the dough in thin sheets and divide it off in small divisions, then take each piece and form into a crescent. Place in pans, let rise for half an hour, then bake ten minutes.

Wheat Flour Griddle Cakes.

One pint of warm milk, one beaten egg, ¼ cup yeast, pinch of salt, and flour to make a batter, let rise over night, bake on a hot greased griddle.

Wheat Hot Cakes.

One quart flour, 1 cup yeast, little salt, 1 tablespoonful of syrup, ½ teaspoonful of saleratus. Mix flour and yeast together over night, in the morning add other ingredients, also enough luke warm water to make a thin batter. Bake on hot griddle.

Corn Bread.

Scald 1 quart of corn meal; when cooled add a little salt, half pint wheat flour, ½ cup yeast; mix up with warm milk or water as stiff as can be kneaded, set to rise in a warm place; when light, bake, or steam two hours.

Buckwheat Griddle Cakes.

Use with one quart of buckwheat flour, a pint of corn meal, a teaspoonful of salt, and water to make a thin batter, after adding 1 cup of yeast.

Rusks.

Make a dough of 1¼ lbs. of flour, two ounces sugar, two ounces butter, ¼ cup of baker's yeast, and a little salt and milk; proceed as for other rolls.

New Englbnd Rolls

Two quarts flour, one-half pint warm milk, one pint warm water one cup yeast, stirred into a stiff batter and set to rise; when light add one tablespoonful of butter, one of sugar and two well beaten eggs; knead well adding flour if necessary; roll out thin, cut into small cakes, place in pans, and when light bake in a hot oven.

Baking Powder Biscuits.

Sift together two or three times dry, one quart of flour and two teaspoonfuls of baking powder; rub in a tablespoonful of butter or lard and a little salt; have your oven hot; with cold sweet milk or water stir all up to a stiff batter or soft dough as can be handled; roll out and cut the biscuits and bake immediately.

Graham Rolls.

Three cups graham flour, one cup wheat flour, two teaspoonfuls of baking powder well mixed together dry; lump of butter the size of a walnut, a little salt, two tablepoonfuls of syrup, one beaten egg and cold sweet milk enough to make a soft dough; roll out, cut and bake as once.

French Sweet Rusk.

One pound light dough, two ounces sugar, two ounces of butter, two yolks of eggs, half cup of milk and flour to make a soft dough.

Oatmeal Gems.

Soak one cup of oatmeal over night with one cup of water; in the morning sift together dry, one cup of flour and two teaspoonfuls of baking powder and a little salt; mix in the meal, wet with sweet milk to stiff batter, drop into your gem pans and bake at once.

Graham Gems.

One-half pint of graham flour sifted dry with three teaspoonfuls of baking powder, rub in a tablespoonful of butter, add one pint more graham, a little salt, one egg and half cup sugar; stir all with cool sweet milk to a batter, drop in gem pans and bake in a hot oven.

Waffles.

Two cups milk, two eggs, three cups flour, one teaspoonful cream-tartar, one half teaspoonful soda, a little salt, small lump of butter; sift the cream-tartar into the flower with the salt; dissolve the soda in hot water; beat the eggs well; add the flour last **and** if the batter is too stiff pour in more milk.

Hot Cross Buns.

Three cups of sweet milk, one cup yeast, and flour to thick batter; set this as a sponge over night; in the morning add one cup sugar, one-half cup butter melted, half a nutmeg, a little salt and flour enough to roll out like biscuits, knead well and set to rise five hours; roll half an inch thick, cut into round cakes and lay in rows in a buttered baking pan; when they have stood half an hour make a cross upon each with a knife and put into the oven at once; bake to a light brown and brush over with the white of an egg beaten up stiff with white sugar.

Muffins.

Beat well the yolks and whites of four eggs separately; to the yolks add three pints of sweet milk, two teaspoonfuls of baking powder, and a little salt; stir in enough flour to make a batter; then add the whites of the eggs, one-half cup of butter; drop into gem pans and bake at once. For graham muffins use graham flour instead of white flour. If desired stir in a cup of sugar.

Doughnuts No 1.

Two eggs, one cup sugar, one-third cup of butter, a little salt, one cup sweet milk, teaspoonful of soda, flour enough to roll out, nutmeg; bake in boiling lard.

Another Gingerbread.

Two cups of molasses, one-half cup of butter, one cup of

sweet milk, one-half teaspoonful of salt, one teaspoonful of soda dissolved in a little milk and a heaping teaspoonful of ginger; stir to the consistency of dough, knead, roll thin and bake.

Tea Cakes.

One pound of light bread dough, six ounces of sugar, six ounces of butter, two eggs, one-fourth pound of flour to work in one-fourth pound of currants; take about five hours time; mix all the ingredients with the dough in the middle of the day and let it rise till 4; then beat the dough with a spoon; it will be a little to soft to handle and spread it thin on buttered pans: rise about an hour, bake and split open and butter them.

Doughnuts No. 2.

One-half pound butter, one teaspoonful of soda, three-fourths pound sugar, salt, two eggs, flavor to suit, one-half pint milk, flour to make a dough; roll out one-fourth inch thick, cut into fanciful forms and boil in hot lard; when browned on both sides drain them, lay them on a dish and sprinkle with fine sugar.

Breakfast Cake.

One teaspoonful sweet milk, one teacupful buttermilk, one teaspoonful salt, one teaspoonful soda, one teaspoonful melted butter and enough meal to enable you to roll it into a a sheet half an inch thick; spread upon a buttered tin or in a shallow pan and bake forty minutes; as soon as it begins to brown baste it with melted butter; repeat this five or six times until it is brown and crisp; cut it up and use for breakfast.

Gingerbread

One cup of sugar and molasses, one-half cup of butter, two eggs, one teaspoonful of soda dissolved in one-half cup of water, one-half teaspoonful of salt and one teaspoonful of ginger. Stir into the flour and knead as little as possible; roll in thin sheets and bake in hot oven.

Breakfast Rosettes.

Three eggs, the yolks beaten very light, add one quart of milk, a piece of butter the size of an egg, cut in little pieces into the milk and eggs, three coffeecups of flour, a little salt, three teaspoonfuls of baking powder, and lastly the whites of the eggs beaten very light and stirred quickly into the mixture. Bake in hot oven.

Flannel Cake.

One quart of milk, three-fourths cup yeast, one tablespoonful butter, melted, two eggs, well beaten, flour to make good batter, little salt. Set the rest of the ingredients as a sponge over night, and in the morning add the melted butter and eggs.

Morning Cake.

One quart "clabber" milk, about four cups sifted flour, two teaspoonfuls soda dissolved in boiling water, three tablespoonfuls molasses, salt to taste. Mix the molasses with the milk. Put the flour into a deep bowl, mix the salt through it; make a hole in the middle and pour in the milk, gradually stirring the flour down into it with a spoon. The butter should not be to thick. When all the milk is in, beat until the mixture is free from lumps and very smooth Add the soda-water, stir up fast, and bake at once.

One quart of flour, three teaspoonfuls of baking powder, a little salt, mix to a batter with milk or water and bake on a well greased griddle.

Breakfast Graham Cakes.

Two cups brown flour, one cup white flour, three cups sour milk, one teaspoonful soda, dissolve in hot water; one teaspoonful salt, lump of lard size of walnut, three eggs beaten very light.

Griddle Cakes of Graham Flour.

Equal parts of graham and wheat, or buckwheat flour, to one quart, add three teaspoonfuls baking powder, little salt, wet to a batter with milk or water.

French Sweet Rolls.

One pound of light dough, two ounces sugar, two ounces of butter, yolks of two eggs, one-half cup of milk, flour to make a soft dough.

Tea Cones.

One pound powered sugar, one-half pound grated cocoa-nut, whites of five eggs. Whip the eggs as for icing, adding the sugar as you go on, until it will stand alone; then beat in the cocoanut. Mould the mixure with your hands into small rolls, and set them far enough apart not to touch one another, upon buttered paper in a baking pan. Bake in moderate oven.

Strawberry Short Cake.

One quart of flour sifted dry, with two teaspoonfuls of baking powder, little salt, one tablespoonful white sugar, mix thoroughly, add three tablespoonfuls of butter, and milk enough to form a soft dough. Roll out in two crusts, lay one on top of the other, buttered slightly between; when baked and partially cooled, separate the crusts, place the bottom crust on a plate, cover it with a layer of ripe strawberries, sprinkle well with white sugar, lay on the other crust and cover with berries and sugar, eat while warm.

Orange Cake.

Two teacups of sugar, half cup butter, three spoonfuls baking powder, three eggs, grated rind and juice of an orange, cream for filling whites of three eggs beaten very light, one cup of sugar, and the grated rind and part of the juice of an orange with 3 cups flour.

California Cakes.

One egg, one and one-quarter cups of butter, one-half cup cold water, one-half cup molasses, one teaspoonful soda, one and one-half cup flour, half teaspoon cinnamon, half teaspoon allspice. Bake in gem pans. Heat the pan before dropping them,

Coffee Cake.

Set sponge without one ounce of yeast, half a pint of lukewarm milk, and flour sufficient; when raised add two ounces of sugar, two ounces of butter, the grated yellow rind of one lemon, a little salt, two eggs, flavor to suit, roll out and cut round or square; wash with melted butter, then dust with powdered sugar and cinnamon mixed together; set them in a warm place to rise, and when light, bake them to a nice brown color.

CREAM CAKES.

One-half pint boiling water, half cup butter and lard mixed. Place in a kettle and gradually stir in one-half pint sifted flour Boil and stir until smooth. When cool, add three eggs, one at a time. Bake in gem pans. Filling: One-half pint milk, one egg, one-half cup sugar, one teaspoonful of flour; well cooked. When cool, split the cakes and place the filling within.

COOKIES.

One cup butter, three cups sugar, one cup cream, four eggs, seven cups flour, or just enough to make nice rollable paste; two tablespoonfuls coriander seed (beaten,) one teaspoonful soda dissolved in boiling water. If sweet milk is used, add two teaspoonfuls cream-tartar.

EVERLASTING CAKE.

Butter or lard, one-half pound; molasses, one pint; soda, one-half ounce; milk or water, one gill; ground ginger, one teaspoonful; flavor, flour sufficient. Mix the ginger in the flour, rub the butter in also; dissolve the soda in the milk or water; put in the molasses, and use the flour in which the ginger and butter is rubbed up, and enough more to make the dough of a proper consistence to roll out; cut the cakes and wet the top with a little molasses and water to remove the flour from the cake; sprinkle the top with pulverized sugar. and bake in an oven sufficiently hot for bread.

Butter Cake.

Two cups granulated sugar, one-half cup butter; add four well beaten eggs, one cup sweet milk, three cups flour with two teaspoonfuls of yeast powder stirred into it. Beat all together very light; bake slowly in a buttered tin. Frosting: Beat the yolk and white of one egg together; add powdered sugar to the right consistency.

Strawberry Short Cake.

Make a crust with one-fourth more shortening than for biscuits, roll out one-third of the crust, lay it in a tin and spread butter over the top; do the same with the other thirds of the crust except not buttering the top of the last one; lay one on top of the other and bake in a quick oven; when baked the parts will separate easily; mix berries with plenty sugar and some cream, place between the layers and send to the table warm. Orange, raspberries, blackberries and others are made the same way.

Tape Cake.

One and one-fourth cup sugar, one-half cup butter, beaten together, three well beaten eggs, two-thirds cup of sweet milk, two cups flour, one teaspoonful cream-tartar, one-half teaspoonful soda; reserve two cups of this mixture for top and bottom cakes; to the remainder add one teaspoonful each of cinnamon, and cloves, one-half a nutmeg, two tablespoonful molasses, one cup fruit and one-half cup flour; bake in three cakes, place them together the dark one in the center with jelly or frosting between; the top may be frosted if desired.

Hill Cake.

Three cups sugar, one cup butter, one-half cup sweet milk, white of ten eggs, one-half teaspoonful soda and one teaspoonful cream-tartar, sifted with the flour, four and one-half cups flour, flavor to suit. Icing, white of three eggs, one pound powdered sugar, flavor; bake in small tins and fill with grated cocoanut, sweeten with powdered sugar.

Flour Drops.

One pint molasses, one-half pound sugar, one-half pound lard, one and one-half pint water, one ounce soda, two and one-fourth pounds flour, flavor with lemon; place in pans as for drop cakes.

Layer Cake No. 1.

Dark part.—Two cups brown sugar, one cup milk, one-half cup butter, yolks of five eggs, three and a half cups of flour, two teaspoonfuls of baking powder, one teaspoonful each of ground allspice, cinnamon and cloves, one coffeecupful of chopped raisins; bake making three sheets.

White part.—One-half cup butter and one cup sugar well beaten together, half cup of milk, whites of three eggs beaten to a froth, two cups of flour well mixed one teaspoonful of yeast powder; bake in two sheets.

Graham Bread, Common.

The loaf is made with a quart of bread sponge, half a teacup of molasses, and all the graham flour that can be stirred in; do not knead it. Pour into a deep pan, wet the top and smooth it, let it rise and bake till done.

Strawberry Short Cake.

Make your crust up just as you would for pies. Mash ripe berries with sugar and cream, and place between two crusts, eat warm. The sugar and berries make the juice needed.

Lemon Cake.

One pound of sugar, twelve eggs, whites and yolks beaten separately; half pound flour, juice and rind of one lemon, icing flavored with same. Ice the top.

Common Cake.

One egg, one cup sugar, one-half cup butter, one cup sweet milk, one teaspoonful of soda, two teaspoonfuls cream tartar. Flavor to suit, and use sufficient flour to make proper consistence.

Layer Cake No. 2.

Two cups sugar, half cup water, yolks of five eggs and whites of three, two teaspoonfuls yeast powder well mixed dry with two cups of flour, mix and bake in sheets; make an i-ing with the whites of two eggs and colored sugar sand, flavor to suit and spread between the sheets.

Layer Cake No. 3.

Light part—One and one-half cup white sugar, one-half cup butter, one-half cup sweet milk, one-half teaspoonful soda, one teaspoonful cream-tartar, whites of four eggs, two and one-half cups flour; beat and mix thoroughly.

Dark part—Half cup molasses, one-half cup butter, one cup brown sugar, one-half cup sour milk, one teaspoonful soda, one teaspoonful cream-tartar, two or three cups flour, yolks of four eggs, ground cinnamon, cloves, allspice and nutmeg of each one teaspoonful; beat and mix as above.

Layer Cake No. 4.

Two teacups light brown sugar, two teacups flour, two teaspoonful yeast powder, into this break six good sized eggs and beat well together; turn into long narrow tins and bake in a hot oven to light brown; when baked turn out on a table and spread quickly with jelly; roll out and wrap each roll in a clean cloth.

Excellent Cake.

Three cups sugar, one and one-half cups butter, one cup milk, four and one-half cups flour, five eggs, small teaspoonful soda, two teaspoonfuls cream tartar. Caramel for filling; One and one-half cups brown sugar, one-half cup milk, one cup molasses, one teaspoonful butter, one tablespoonful flour, two tablespoonfuls cold water, Boil this mixture five minutes, add half cake grated chocolate, boil until it is the consistency of rich custard. Add a pinch of soda, stir well, and remove from fire. When cold, flavor to suit and spread between the layers of cake, which should be baked as for jelly cake. The above quantity will make two large cakes.

Layer Jelly Cake.

Five eggs, one cup sugar, lemon flavor, one teaspoonful saleratus, two cups sour milk and sufficient flour for cake; beat the eggs, sugar and flavor together; dissolve the saleratus in the milk and mix; then stir in the flour to make only a thin batter and bake in a quick oven; three or four of these thin cakes with jelly between, forms one cake; spread jelly on while the cake is warm.

Orange Layer Cake.

Half cup butter and two cups sugar stirred to a cream, one cup sweet milk, three eggs well beaten, three cups flour, two teaspoonfuls yeast powder; bake in sheets. Frosting, white of two eggs, make a frosting as for other cakes; save enough to frost the top of the cake and add to the rest the juice and grated rind of a large orange and spread between the layers.

Wedding Cake.

One pound powdered sugar, one pound butter, one pound flour, twelve eggs, one pound currants, one pound chopped raisins, one-half pound citron cut in slips, one tablespoonful cinnamon, two teaspoonfuls nutmeg, one teaspoonful cloves, one small glass brandy. Cream the butter and sugar, add the beaten yolks of the eggs, and stir well together before putting in half of the flour. The spice should come next, then the whipped whites stirred in alternately with the rest of the flour, lastly the brandy. Bake at least two hours in deep tins lined with well buttered paper. The icing should be put on thickly. The above quantity is for two large cakes.

JELLY ROLLS.

Brown sugar, one and one-half cups, three eggs, one cup sweet milk, two cups flour, cream tartar and soda of each one teaspoonful, one teaspoonful lemon essence: beat the eggs and sugar together, mix the cream tartar and soda with milk stirring in the flour also; now mix in the flour; bake at once spreading thin on a long pan and as soon as done spread jelly upon the top and roll up; slicing off as used.

CHOCOLATE CAKE No. 1.

One cup butter, two cups sugar, one cup milk, one-half cup cornstarch, two cups flour, two teaspoonfuls yeast powder mixed dry with flour; whites of six eggs beaten stiff, add all together, flavor to suit, bake in layers. Frosting: Beat the yolks of the eggs, sweeten and add chocolate to taste, one cup milk; cook a few minutes, stirring continually, not allowing it to boil. Flavor with vanilla.

HUCKLEBERRY CAKE.

Two cups sugar, three-fourths cups butter, three cups flour, five eggs, one cup sweet milk, one teaspoonful soda dissolved in hot water, one teaspoonful nutmeg, and the same of cinnamon, one quart of ripe huckleberries thickly dredged with flour. Work the butter and the sugar to a cream, add the beaten yolks, then the milk, the flour, and spice, the soda, and the whites of the eggs beat stiff. At the last stir in the huckleberries being careful not to bruise them. Bake in a moderate oven.

CHOCOLATE LAYER CAKE.

One cup butter, one and one-half cups sugar, one cup milk, yolks of nine eggs well beaten, two and one-half cups of flour, two teaspoonfuls yeast powder, flavor with vanilla, bake in sheets. Filling: One cup milk, one egg, half a cup sugar, two tablespoons grated chocolate scalded together, flavor with vanilla.

MODEST CAKE.

One teacup of brown sugar, one egg, piece of butter size of a walnut, one teacup of sour milk, one teaspoonful of soda, two and one-half teacups of flour, one teaspoon of cinnamon, one teaspoon cloves, one teacup chopped raisins stirred in. Bake in loaf and frost when cool with the following: Beat white of one egg very stiff, and two tablespoons granulated sugar, one teaspoonful flavor. Beat until smooth, spread over the cake, place in the oven and harden slightly.

CHOCOLATE CAKE No. 2.

One cup sugar, half cup butter, half cup milk, three eggs, two cups flour, two teaspoonfuls yeast powder. Mix thoroughly and bake. Filling: Half cup milk, one square of chocolate, yolk of three eggs, flavor with vanilla, sweeten to taste.

COMMON ALMOND MACAROONS.

One-half pound pulverized sugar, five ounces flour, whites of four eggs, two drops bitter oil of almond, mix flour and

ALMOND CAKE.

One cup of butter and two of sugar worked to a cream, one cup of sweet milk, two cups of flour or more mixed dry with two teaspoonfuls yeast powder, beat the white of six eggs to a stiff froth, stir all together, add in two teaspoonfuls of extract of almond and bake in sheets. Icing, beat the white of two eggs to a very stiff froth, adding one-half pound of pulverized sugar; use the yolks of the eggs for a pudding.

BREAD CAKE.

Take from your bread dough, after its second rising, two cups dough, two cups white sugar, one cup butter, creamed with sugar, three eggs, one teaspoonful soda, dissolved in hot water, two tablespoonfuls sweet milk—cream is better, one half pound currants, well washed and dried, one teaspoonful cinnamon, one teaspoonful cloves. Beat the yolks very light, add the creamed butter and sugar, the spice, milk, soda, and dough. Stir until all are well mixed; put in the beaten whites, lastly the fruit. Beat hard five minutes, let it resi thirty minutes in well buttered pans, and bake half an hour or until done.

ORANGE JELLY CAKE.

One and a half cups of sugar, half a cup of butter, beat to a cream; half-cup milk, two and a half cups flour, two teaspoonfuls yeast powder, three eggs, well beaten, bake in sheets. Filling.—One cup of sugar, one egg; grate the rind and use with the juice of one orange, one tablespoonful of water, one teaspoonful of flour. place the dish in a kettle of boiling water and let it thicken; when cool, spread between the cakes.

SMALL SUGAR CAKES.

One teacup of sugar, three-quarters teacup of butter, one-quarer teacup sweet milk, two eggs, well beaten, two teaspoonfuls cream tartar, one teaspoonfuls soda, dissolved in hot water, flour sufficient to enable you to roll out the dough, little salt, cloves and cinnamon to taste. Bake quickly.

NUT CAKE.

One and one-fourth cup sugar, half cup butter, one cup sweet milk, two cups flour mixed dry with two teaspoonful of yeast power, whites of three eggs beaten thoroughly, bake in sheets. Filling: Whites of three eggs beaten stiff, one-half cup white sugar, one cup chopped nut meats, flavor to suit taste.

PEEL AND CITRON CAKE.

Six eggs beaten light, two cups of sugar, three-quarters cup of butter, two and one-half cups flour or enough to make pound cake dough, one-quarter pound citron cut in thin shreds, juice of an orange and one-half pound grated peel, cream, butter and sugar; add the yolks, the whites and flour by turns, the orange, and lastly, the citron, dredged with flour. Beat all up hard, and bake in two loaves.

WHITE CAKE.

The whites of seven eggs, two cups of sugar, one-half cup of butter, three-fourths cup sweet milk, three cups flour, and two teaspoonfuls baking powder. Flavor to suit taste.

Soda Cake.

One-half pound flour, two drahms soda, six ounces butter, two drahms tartaric acid, two ounces white sugar, four ounces currants, two eggs, half teacup warm milk.

Cocoanut Macaroons.

One-fourth pound sweet almonds bleached and dried, white of four eggs, one pound pulverized sugar, one pound cocoanut, grated, two pounds flour, yolks of four eggs; roll the almonds, sugar and whites of eggs together, mix in the grated cocoanut then the yellow of the eggs, then the flour, drop the size of walnuts in greased and floured pans.

Fruit Cake.

One and one-half pounds of butter, one and one-half pounds sugar one dozen eggs, well beaten, four pounds raisins, five pounds English cocoanut nicely washed, two pounds citrons cut fine, two pound sifted flour, nutmeg, mace, cinnamon, cloves, ginger, allspice, and oil of lemon.

Smll Sugar Drops.

Two pounds butter, two pounds sugar, four pounds flour, four eggs, four teaspoonfuls baking powder; make a stiff dough, roll in strips an inch thick, cut them the size of a pepper box cover, roll them in sugar and bake in a cool oven.

Cinnamon Wafers.

One-quarter pound sugar, three ounces flour, two ounces cinnamon; put the flour, sugar and cinnamon in a dish, mix in the whites of seven eggs, these are made the same as almond wafers.

Nut and Fruit Cake.

Two cups sugar, four cups flour, one cup butter, seven eggs, whites and yolks separated, one cup cold water, one cup of hickory nut kernels, one-half pound raisins chopped and dredged with flour, one teaspoonful soda dissolved in hot water; two teaspoonfuls cream tartar sifted in the flour, one teaspoonful mixed nutmeg and cinnamon. Rub the butter and sugar together to a smooth cream, put in the yolks, then the water, spice and soda, next the whites and flour. The fruit and nuts stirred together and dredged, should go in last. Mix thoroughly and bake in two large cakes.

Layer Fruit Cake.

Two cups of sugar and a half cup butter beat to a cream, half cup sweet milk, mix three cups of flour with three teaspoonfuls of yeast powder, beat the whites of seven eggs to a froth, stir all together and flavor to suit taste; bake in sheets. Filling: Whites of seven eggs beaten with sugar as for frosting, save out enough for top of cake, add one teacup raisins chopped fine, flavor to suit, spread between sheets.

Gold Cake.

Yolks of eleven eggs, five cups flour, three cups white sugar, one cup butter, one and one-half cups cream or sweet milk, one-half teaspoon soda, one teaspoon cream tartar. Bake in deep pan. Beat the eggs with the sugar, having the butter melted by the fire, then stir it in; put the soda and cream tartar into the milk stirring up and mixing all together, then sift and stir in the flour.

Yolk Cake.

Yolks of twelve eggs beaten, and two cups sugar, one of milk and one of butter; mix four cups of flour with two teaspoonfuls of baking powder. Flavor to suit taste.

Snow Cake.

Two cups powdered sugar, one heaping cup flour, ten eggs, the whites only, whipped stiff; beat in the sugar, juice of one lemon and half the grated peel, and a little salt, and finally the flour Stir in very lightly and quickly and bake at once in two loaves, or in square pans.

Marble Cakes.

Stir to a cream one pound of white sugar and half pound of butter, beat the whites of ten eggs stiff and add to the sugar and butter, three cups of flour and one teaspoonful of yeast powder, mix all together, then take one teacupful of the batter and stir into it one teaspoonful of fruit coloring. Fill a pan three inches deep, first with the white batter and then with the colored; alternate in this way until the batter is all in.

Dark Cake.

One and one-half cups molasses, one teaspoonful soda, two cups sour milk, two eggs, butter or lard the size of a walnut;

mix all by beating a few minutes with a spoon; bake immediately in hot oven.

Yellow Cake.

The yolks of ten eggs, two cups sugar, one-half cup butter, three-fourths cup sweet milk, one and one-half cups flour, and two teaspoonfuls baking powder. Flavor to suit taste.

Light Cake.

Whites of eleven eggs, five cups flour, one cup each of butter and white sugar, one and one-fourth cups sweet milk or cream, one teaspoonful cream tartar, one-half teaspoonful soda, beat and mix as for ordinary cake, bake in deep cake cake pan.

Quick Sponge Cake.

One cup flour with one teaspoonful baking powder, one cup sugar. three eggs and a little sweet milk, flavor with extract of lemon; stir briskly and bake at once.

English Currant Cake.

Rub a cup of butter and a cup of sugar to a cream, beat and add five eggs, mix together dry two cups flour and two teaspoonfuls of baking powder, and add to the same one cupful of well washed, dried and dredged currants and flavor to suit the taste.

Seedless Raisin Cake.

Take one and one-fourth pounds of light dough, one teacupful of sugar, one of butter, three eggs, one teaspoonful of soda, one pound of seedless raisins and cinnamon or cloves to taste; let it rise and bake one hour.

POUND CAKE.

One pound of flour, one pound butter, one pound sugar, eight eggs, flavor with lemon; mix all by beating a few minutes, then bake.

SPONGE CAKE WITH MILK.

One and one-half cups brown sugar, three eggs, one cup sweet milk, four cups flour, one teaspoonful each of cream tartar and soda and one teaspoonful lemon flavor; beat briskly and bake at once.

COMMON ALMOND MACAROONS.

Three-quarters of a pound pulverized sugar, six ounces flour, whites of six eggs and a little extract of lemon; mix flour and sugar together, then the whites of eggs, drop them on paper and bake.

SPONGE LADY FINGER.

Take fifteen eggs, one and one-quarter pounds powdered sugar, one pound and a half of flour, two ounces ammonia; beat the sugar and eggs light, then put the ammonia in and beat again until it gets stiff, work in the flour lightly, drop them out on paper, sieve sugar over them and bake in hot oven.

GRIND CAKE.

Two and one-half pounds flour, one and one-half white pulverized sugar, three-fourths pound butter, five eggs well beaten, two teaspoonfu!s baking powder, one pint water or milk is best if you have it.

Seed Cake.

One-half pound sugar, one-quarter pound butter, creamed with sugar, five eggs beaten very light, enough flour for soft dough, one ounce caraway seeds, mixed with dry flour, mix well, roll into thin paste, cut into small cakes, brush each over with the white of an egg, sift pulverized sugar upon it, and bake in a quick oven about ten minutes. Do not take them from pans until nearly cold, as they are apt to break while hot.

Lillie Fingers.

Two and one-fourth pounds sugar, one pound of butter, one-half pint milk; 6 eggs, flour enough to make an easy dough to ro'l out; cut them, place them on boards closely, wash them with beaten eggs and milk, seive pulverized sugar over them lightly, bake in cool oven immediately after they are sugared, flavor the dough with mace.

Jelly Mixture.

Fifteen eggs, one and one quarter pounds sugar, one quarter pound butter, one-half oz. baking powder one and one-quarter pounds flour, drop on jelly pans, spread jelly between each layer. Bake in hot oven.

Fried Nuts.

One pound of butter, one and one-quarter pound pu'verized sugar, eleven eggs, mace and and nutmeg to taste, flour to roll out stiff. This is for a large quantiiy of nuts. Rol out in thin sheets, cut into shape small cutter, and fry in plenty of boiling lard. These should be a fine yellow. If the lard becomes too hot so that the nuts brown before they puff out to their full dimensions, take the kettle from the fire a few minutes.

Spice Cup Cake.

One cup brown sugar, one of butter, one of molasses, one of milk, one teaspoonful each of nutmeg, cinnamon, cloves, mace, allspice and ginger, four eggs, four cups flour and two teaspoonfuls of yeast powder.

Fern Cake.

Work two cups of sugar and half a cup of butter to a cream, half a cup of milk, one and a half cups of flour in which is mixed dry, half a cup of cornstarch and two teaspoonfuls of yeast powder, then add the whites of five eggs beaten to a stiff froth; flavor with vanilla.

Gilt Cake.

The yolks of seven eggs well beaten, one cup sugar, half cup butter, half a cup of milk, one and a half cups of flour in which is well mixed, dry, half a cup of cornstarch and two teaspoonfuls of baking powder, then add the whites of seven eggs beaten to a stiff froth; flavor to suit taste.

Lemon Snaps.

One pound of pulverized sugar, four eggs whipped very light and long, juice of three lemons and peel of one, one heaping cup flour, one-half teaspoonful nutmeg. Butter your hands lightly, take up small lumps of the mixture make into balls about as large as a walnut and lay upon a sheet of buttered paper more than two inches apart. Bake in hot oven.

NUGGFT CAKE.

Two cups of sugar, one small cup of butter, beat to a cream, three eggs well beaten, one-half cup milk, three cups flour, one-half cup water, two teaspoonfuls of baking powder, and one of flavor; mix all together quickly and bake at once.

YOCK CAKE.

Take one pound of flour, one quarter ounce bicarbonate of soda, six ounces butter, six ounces sugar, six ounces currants, four eggs, one-half pint milk, bake for one hour and a half.

FUFFY CAKE.

One and a half cups of sugar, one-half cup thick cream, a little salt, four well beaten eggs, two cups of flour, one and one-half teaspoonfuls of baking powder, bake in quick oven.

PEEK-A-BOO CAKE.

One quart molasses, one-fourth pound lard, one ounce soda, little almond, ginger, and one gill water, flour enough to make a tight dough to roll.

SCOLLOP CAKE.

One quarter pound butter, one-half pound white sugar, two eggs, one gill milk, one teaspoonful soda, put in the milk one and one quarter pounds flour, one-half ounce cream tartar, put in the flour, flavor cinnamon and lemon oil, rub your butter and sugar together, then add your eggs and mix well, add your milk and soda, and then mix in your flour, roll them out thin and cut them out with scolloped cutter, then bake in hot oven.

Currant Jam Cake.

Rub one-half pound butter, one-half pound sugar, four eggs, together, one-half pint milk, one teaspoonful baking powder, flavor lemon extract, three fourths pound flour, lay out round, with currant jam, after icing the top and ornament with fancy jelly,

Laurent Cake.

Eight eggs beaten separately, one-half pound each of butter and sugar, a tumbler of milk, the juice and rind of a lemon, a small teaspoonful of cream tartar, one-half teaspoonful of bicarbonate of soda, and flour enough to stiffen. Bake well.

Snow Mountain Cake.

One pound of flour, one pound of sugar, one-half pound of butter, whites of six eggs, one teaspoonful cream tartar, one-half teaspoonful soda. Sugar and butter with soda are rubbed light as for pound cake, whites of eggs must be beaten up stiff and slowly mixed in, cream tartar mixed with the flour is then sifted in. Filling: One pound and a half sugar, whites of four eggs, one and a half grated cocoanuts. This will make twenty sheets divided into so many greased jelly pans, spread out evenly, and bake at once in hot oven.

This will make four cakes of five layers each; between each of the layers the following filling must be so divided that it will allow and even share for each; the whites of eggs must be beaten stiff; the cocoanut with the milk of one, and lemon, and sugar, must be mixed together. Sift sugar over them.

Ginger Snaps.

One pound and a half of flour, one-half pound brown sugar, one-half pound lard, one-half pint molasses, one-half cup water, one quarter ounce of soda, one teaspoonful ginger, little salt. Rub sugar, lard, salt, molasses and ginger together, then mix the flour and soda in the water, with it; roll out with rolling pin, and cut with plain round cutter. Set on ungreased pans one inch apart, and bake in moderte oven.

Illinois Cake.

Four cups of flour mixed dry with two heaping teaspoonfuls of yeast powder, two cups of white sugar, one cup of butter, one-half cup of sweet cream, the whites of eight eggs beaten to a stiff froth, added to the cream, flavor with extract of orange, work the butter and sugar well together, then stir in the cream, then alternate the flour and eggs until all the ingredients are in, and last of all the extract. Put into deep buttered pans and bake in a moderate oven.

Dainty Cake.

Three cups sifted flour, one and a half cups of sugar, whites of six eggs, one teacup of sweet milk, two tablespoonfuls of butter, two heaping teaspoonfuls yeast powder, and flavor to suit taste. Beat the butter and sugar to a cream, add to it the milk and eggs well beaten, then add the extract. Mix with this very slowly three cups of flour, in which the baking powder has been well mixed. Bake in a hot oven.

Folderyi Cake.

One cup butter, little salt, two quarts of flour. Rub thoroughtly together with the hands and wet up with cold water, beat well, and beat in flour to make quite brittle and hard, then pinch off pieces and roll each cake by itself, if you wish them to resemble bakers' cracker cakes.

Cocoanut Steeples.

Take equal weights of grated white part of cocoanut and powdered white sugar, add the white of eggs beaten sttff, six to a pound of cocoanut and sugar, should be eggs enough to wet the whole to stiff mixture, drop parcels the shape of small steeples separately upon buttered paper laid upon tins, and bake in a moderately heated oven.

Columbia Cake.

Take three teacupfuls brown sugar, one of butter, one of milk, four eggs, one teapoonful each extract of mace and cinnamon, one teaspoonful of ground allspice, one cup of seedless raisins, three cups of flour and two teaspoonfuls of baking powder.

Rex Cake.

One-half pound butter, one-half pound sugar, two-thirds

COOKING AND BAKER'S DEPARTMENT.   179

teacup milk; three teaspoonfuls baking powder mixed in the milk; mix the butter and sugar together, add your eggs and milk and one-fourth pound flour, roll out and cut with a round cutter, bake on greased pans in hot oven, when done ice with chocolate icing.

Cinnamon Cake.

One cup of sweet milk, two of sugar, one of butter, three well beaten eggs, three teaspoonfuls of baking powder, worked into flour enough to make a stiff dough, roll out thin and sift ground cinnamon on the sheet and roll up into a roll, cut off slices from the roll and place on tins; before baking, sprinkle, rather thickly, dry white sugar, on the tops of the slices

Orville Cake.

Two cups of sugar, one-half cup of butter, one cup sweet cream, white of seven eggs beaten stiff, one teaspoonful good extract of lemon, two cups of flour, mixed well with one heaping teaspoonful of baking powder, mix all together and bake.

Walnut Cake.

Two cups of sugar, one cup of butter, stir to a cream; whites of six eggs beaten stiff, one-fourth cup of milk, three cups of flour, two teaspoonfuls baking powder, one coffee-cup of nut meets, bake in a loaf.

Hill's High Cake.

Stir to a cream one teacupful of butter with two coffeecupfuls of sugar, add one teacupful of sweet milk, the white and yolk of six eggs beaten seperately, three or more cups of flour well mixed dry, with three teaspoonfuls of yeast powder, flavor to suit taste.

Black Cake.

One teacupful of butter, and one and a half cups brown sugar, three quarters cup of molasses, one cup milk, three eggs well beaten, flavor to suit taste, four cups flour with two teaspoonfuls of baking powder, one pound chopped raisins, one pound currants, and one quarter pound citron finely sliced. Bake at once.

Filled Rolls.

Three-quarters pound butter, three quarters pound flour, one gill water. Filling.—Seven whites of eggs, one-half pound sugar. Rub one ounce of the butter into the flour, then add the water and make a dough, place this with the remaining butter on ice, if warm weather. After allowing it to stand ten minutes, roll out the dough into a sheet ten inches square place the butter in the centre of it, and fold the dough from both sides over it. Lightly flatten it down, and roll it a little, then work out the ends of the dough and roll them so as to cover the butter from both sides, then fold the other end of that, taking care that the paste is kept in a square, and that the butter will be filled evenly with every turn. Then roll out the dough as large as before, about ten inches square, and fold in three folds as before, from each side, roll a little more, and repeat the same, then set it aside to rest ten or fifteen minutes, covered with a damp cloth, when this same folding process must be repeated twice more. Allow it to stand again for fifteen minutes and roll out again into a sheet measuring twenty by thirty inches, with a knife cut into strips five inches square, which will make two dozen squares. Tubes of tin, one inch in diameter and five inches long, are necessary for these. With a little eggs and water wet the edge farthest from you, of each piece of dough, and proceed to wrap them around the tubes. When all are completed, wet them over the top with the egg, place them one inch apart on ungreased, lightly floured pans, and bake in hot oven. When done the tubes are withdrawn, and they are filled with the following filling from a bag or bag machine. Beat the seven white of eggs very stiff and then lightly add the sugar. Fill each roll and place on a papered pan. When all are done, return to the oven until the ends begin to work out from the rolls, take them out and sift sugar over them.

RICE CAKE.

One pound flour, one one-half pound sugar, one-half pound butter, one eighth pound rice flour, two eggs, two teaspoonfuls baking powder, one teaspoonful rose water. Rub sugar, butter, eggs, baking powder and rose water light, then mix in the flour and rice flour, and make a dough, this is to be rolled out, cut with plain cutter, and the cakes placed on greased pans. Press a piece of citron in the center of each and bake in moderately hot oven.

FILLMON FRUIT CAKE.

Stir to a cream one pound each of brown sugar and butter,

and the whites and yolks of ten eggs beaten to a froth separately, two wine glasses of brandy; mix or sift thoroughly, one pound of flour with two teaspoonfuls of baking powder, and when ready for baking add one pound chopped raisins, two of currants, one of citron, one-fourth of a pound of almonds blanched, flavor to suit taste,

Scotch Pound Cake.

One pound of sugar and three quarters of a pound of butter well beaten, beat separately to a stiff froth the whites and the yolks of eight eggs; one pound of flour with a heaping teaspoonful of yeast powder well mixed dry, and flavor with extract of lemon.

Citron Cup Cake.

· Stir three cups of sugar and one cup of butter to a cream three and one-half cups of flour well mixed dry, with two teaspoonfuls of yeast powder; one cup of milk, four eggs, yolks and whites beaten separately; one-half pound citron finely cut, sliced and floured; mix all together and bake.

Lanstry Fingers.

Bat six white of eggs to a froth only, then enough finely sifted pulverized sugar to make a dough that will admit of rolling out with rolling pin, add one pound of blanched and half dried almonds and mix them well through. Then divide this into three parts, and dye one red with cochineal, take this for a centre piece and place on each side of this the white pieces. Work this out long enough to be about one inch in thickness, and three inches wide, then with a sharp knife cut slices off it one-fourth of an inch thick. Place them on well greased and thickly floured pans one-half inch apart. Bake in moderate oven.

Love Cake.

Sift through one pound of flour two heaping teaspoonfuls of baking powder, whip to cream half-pound of butter, then stir into the butter one pound of sugar, the yolks of six eggs, and about half of the flour, then add one cup of sweet milk and the remainder of the flour, lastly, the white of five eggs beaten to a stiff froth, and flavor with extract of vanilla. Bake in moderate oven.

Tam O'Shanter.

Whites of four eggs well beaten, one and one quarter pounds pulverized sugar, two bars melted chocolate, lay them out in a bag with tube in it on floured pans the shape of a Tam O'Shanter; let them stand for one hour and then bake in quick heat, when cool take off your pans.

Kentucky Cake.

Two cups of sugar, two-thirds cup of butter, two and one-half cups of flour, half cup of water, whites of ten eggs, three teaspoonfuls baking powder, and flavor to suit taste.

Almond Pudding.

Pour boiling water on to three-fourths of a pound of sweet almonds; let it remain until the skin comes off easily; rub with a dry cloth until white; when dry, pound fine with one large spoonful rose water; beat six eggs to a stiff froth with three spoonfuls of fine white sugar; mix with one quart of milk, three spoonfuls of pounded crackers, four ounces of melted butter, and the same of citron cut into bits; add almonds, stir all together, and bake in a small pudding pan with a lining and rim of pastry. This pudding is best when cold. It will bake in half an hour in a hot oven.

Chocolate Cream Cake.

Take some cream cake mixture, put some more flour in it; this will make them bake more evenly; fill them with cream the same as the cream cakes, then chocolate them on top.

Cream Cake.

Four cups sifted flour, two teaspoonfuls of baking powder, three cups of white sugar, one cup of butter, one of sweet milk, and six eggs, flavor with lemon.

Irish Cake.

One pound and a quarter of sugar, three guarters pound butter, two pounds and three quarters of flour, three eggs; this makes a good cake and easy to handle.

Sour Apple Pie.

Peel sour apples and stew until soft, then rub them through colander, beat three or four eggs for each pie to be baked, and put in at the rate of one-half cup of butter and one of sugar for three pies, season with cinnamon. If a frosting is to be put on them return for a few moments to the oven.

Fritters.

Four or five eggs well beaten, one quart of flour, two teaspoonfuls of baking powder, little salt, milk to make a batter; fry in hot lard; sprinkle with sugar; or eat with syrup.

Fig Pudding No 1.

One-half pound of good figs, one pint of milk, yolks of two eggs, white of one, if large, one-half ounce of gelatine soaked in cold water, one-half cup of sweet fruit jelly, slightly warmed, two tablespoonfuls of white sifted sugar two teaspoonfuls of good extract of vanilla. Soak the figs in warm water until quite soft, split them, dip each piece in jelly and line a buttered mould with them. Heat the milk and stir into the well beaten yolks and sugar, return it to the saucepan and stir until it thickens. Melt the soaked gelatine by adding a teaspoonful of boiling water, when it is quite melted add it to the milk, and when well mixed, set by to cool. As soon as it begins to congeal, whisk it thoroughly with an egg beater, and add to it gradually the white of an egg, previously whipped to a stiff froth. Beat it rapidly and thoroughly until quite spongy, and fill up the fig lined mould. Set in a cool place till quite firm, five or six hours at least. Dip the mould in hot water to loosen the pudding, when you are ready for it, and serve on a glass dish. The above quantity will fill a quart mould.

Pumpkin Pie No. 1.

Pare and cut the pumpkin in pieces convenient for steaming instead of cutting in small slices and stewing in water. Put it in a steamer and steam it till soft, mash fine and prepare in the usual manner. Separate egg used, putting in the yolks with the pumpkin. When done have ready the

CREAM TOAST.

the whites whipped to a froth with a little white sugar, and spread this over the pies, leaving them in the oven with the door open for a few minutes.

CREAM TOAST.

Toast a slice of bread a nice brown, spread a little butter on it, dip sweet cream over it, set it in the oven until well heated.

MOCK CREAM TOAST.

Melt in one quart of morning's milk about two ounces of butter, a large teaspoonful of flour: freed from lumps, and the yolks of three eggs, beaten light. Beat these ingredients together for several minutes, strain the cream through a fine hair seive, and when wanted beat it constantly with a brisk movement.

COCOANUT PIE.

Three-fourths of a pound of cocoanut grated, one-half pound pulverized sugar, one quart of milk, six eggs beaten to a froth, one teaspoonful of nutmeg or cinnamon, two teaspoonfuls of vanilla or rose water. Boil the milk, take it from the fire, and whip in gradually the beaten eggs; when nearly cold, season, add the cocoanut, and pour into paste shells. Do not boil the eggs and milk together. Bake in moderate oven twenty minutes.

RICE DOUGHNUTS.

Boil three-fourths of a cup of rice in a quart of sweet milk or water, with a little salt, until cooked; add half a cup of butter, two beaten eggs and a little corn meal, make them such shapes as you like, and drop them into hot lard.

Jelly Pie No 1.

One tumbler each of jelly and water, three tablespoonfuls of cornstarch, yolk of one egg, a small tablespoonful of butter. Boil jelly, butter and water together, then thicken with the egg and cornstarch wet in water. Pour into a pie pan lined with mice paste, bake till the crust is done, then beat the white of the egg to a stiff froth, adding a tablespoonful of powdered sugar, spread over the pie and set in the oven until a delicate brown.

Raspberry Pudding.

Cook a coffeecupful of pearl tapioca until it is clarified. Stir into it a quart can of raspberries. Mould and serve with cream and sugar. Strawberry pudding made in the same way is delicious.

Apple Pudding.

Three eggs, one coffee cup of sour milk, one large tablespoon of butter, three large tablespoonfuls of sugar, one-half teaspoonful of soda, and flour enough to make a batter as stiff as cake. Add quartered apples as desired.

Lemon Pie No. 1.

Grate the rind of two large lemons and squeeze the juice into one heaping cup of brown sugar, and add two tablespoonfuls of flour, the yolks of four eggs, butter the size of an egg, stir all together and add three cups of boiling milk, and set away to cool, make crust as for custard pie, beat the white of the eggs to a froth, and add to the mixture, when cool, pour this into your pies, bake the same as custard, sprinkle with cinnamon. This makes three pies.

Apple Dumplings.

To one quart of flour, use one-half cup of lard or butter, scant measure, two teaspoonfuls of baking powder and a little salt. Mix the same as for biscuits. Roll out and put an apple in each piece, lay in a floured steamer and set on a pot of boiling water. Cover the steamer with a cloth and lid, and steam from three quarters of an hour to an hour. Forty-five minutes is long enough if the apples are good cooking apples.

One Egg Pie.

One large cup of milk, yolk of one egg, two tablespoonfuls each of sugar and flour, and a little salt. Cook by setting the dish in a sauce-pan of boiling water, stir until scalded, remove and let it cool, flavor with lemon, have your crust ready baked, pour in the mixture, and frost with the white of the egg, and one tablespoonful of white sugar. Set in a hot oven and brown slightly.

Poor Cake.

One pound of flour, one-half pound of sugar, one quarter pound of butter, two eggs, two teaspoonfuls of yeast powder, little lemon extract. Rub butter into flour well; then add the sugar, eggs, and baking powder, with the lemon, and make up into a dough. Place on lightly greased pans and

COOKING AND BAKER'S DEPARTMENT. 189

bake in moderate oven. When done, brush over with a thick syrup of white sugar.

QUICK WAFFLES.

Beat four eggs, mix well one quart of flour with three teaspoonfuls of baking powder dry, rub half cup of butter into the flour, and then add the eggs, use milk enough to make a batter, which will pour into the hot waffle irons, filling them two-thirds full.

CAROLINA CAKE.

One cup of sugar, one egg, four cups of butter, one-third cup sweet milk, one cup flour, mixed dry with one teaspoonful baking powder, and flavor to suit taste.

PIE CAKE.

One cup of butter, two of sugar, beaten to a cream; four eggs well beaten, one teaspoonful baking powder mixed dry with three cups of flour, half a cup of milk, one-half cup split peas, one teaspoonful of extract of almond.

GOOD COOKIES.

Two quarts of flour, three cups of sugar, one of butter, one cup of sweet cream, three eggs, one heaping teaspoonful of baking powder, flavor with extract of orange or lemon to taste. Turn into granulated sugar before putting into the pans.

CHOCOLATE STRIPS.

One pound of sugar, one quarter pound butter, six eggs, half cup sweet milk, flavor, extracts, mace, teaspoonful of ammonia. Mix well and add two and a half pounds of flour. Lay out into strips two inches long and dip in hot chocolate sugar. Bake in moderate heat, and when done dip them in chocolate.

POVERTY COOKIES.

One cup brown sugar, one-half cup butter, one egg, two tablespoonfuls of sweet milk, and two tablespoonfuls of currants, and two teaspoonfuls of yeast powder. Add sufficient flour to roll thin. Bake in quick oven.

TEA BISCUIT.

Beat very light one egg, pour it over a pint of flour, add a glass of milk, and chop in one tablespoonful of lard and butter mixed. Work thoroughly together, break up pieces the size of marbles, which must be rolled as thin as your nail. Sprinkle with dry flour as you roll them out to make them crisp, stick with a fork and bake.

JOHNNY CAKE.

One teacup of sweet milk, one teacup of buttermilk, one teaspoonful of salt, one tablespoonful of melted butter, one teaspoonful yeast powder. Enough meal to roll into a sheet about half an inch thick.

BREAD PUDDING.

One quart of milk, three eggs, the whites of three more for frosting, two cups very fine white dry bread crumbs, one tablespoonful melted butter, one teacupful sugar, juice and half the grated peel of one lemon. Beat eggs, sugar and butter together. Soak the crumbs in the milk and mix all well, beating very hard and rapidly. Season and bake in greased baking dishes. When almost done, cover with a frosting made of the three whites of eggs and a little powdered sugar. Eat cold.

Hot Drops.

Two tablespoonfuls each of lard, sugar and milk, two eggs well beaten, one teaspoonful of yeast powder and flour enough to roll out; fry in hot lard.

Tea Cake, Spongy.

One and one-half cupfuls of white sugar, one-half cup of butter, one-half cup sweet milk, two and a half cupfuls of flour, white of four eggs, two teaspoonfuls of baking powder, flavor with lemon.

Nice Sponge Cake.

Three cupfuls of sugar, three cupfuls flour, six eggs, one cupful cold water, a little salt, and a heaping teaspoonful baking powder, sifted in the flour. Beat the eggs (not separating the whites from the yolks) add the sugar, mixing it well with the eggs, add half the water, then the sifted flour, the rest of the water, and flavor to suit taste.

English Plumd Pudding.

One-half pound of beef suet chopped fine, one pound of raisins seeded, one pound of currants, one-quarter pound of citron, one nutmeg grated, a little cinnamon, one pound of flour, one teaspoonful of baking powder, little salt, one pound brown sugar. Sift one pound of flour, and one teaspoonful of baking powder together, then put all other ingredients in dry and mix well, then add cold water or milk to a stiff batter.

SALLY LUNN.

Two tablespoonfuls of butter warmed in two teacups of sweet milk, three eggs beaten separately, two tablespoonfuls of sugar beaten with the yolks. Sift two tablespoonfuls of baking powder and a little salt in a quart of flour; stir all together, putting the white of the eggs in last and bake at once in a moderate oven.

COCOANUT JUMBLES.

One cup each of butter and sugar, one egg, one-half teaspoonful of soda, one teaspoonful of cream tartar and one-half of a cocoanut grated. Add flour enough to make it stiff, roll very thin, cut into cakes and bake in a quick oven.

PUMPKIN PIE No. 2.

Steam the pumpkin over boiling water until soft, strain through a colander one pint of squash, one pint of milk, three eggs, one cup of sugar, one teaspoonful of ground ginger and one of extract of nutmeg, a little salt, bake without top crust.

ORANGE PUDDING No. 1.

Two oranges juice of both and grated peel of one, juice of one lemon, one-half pound stale cookies or cake, two cups of milk, four eggs, one-half cupful sugar, one tablespoonful corn-starch, wet with water; one tablespoonful butter melted. Soak the crumbs in the milk (raw), whip up light and add the eggs and sugar, already beaten to a cream with the batter. Next the corn-starch and when the mould is buttered and water boiling hard, stir in the juice and peel of the fruit. Do this quickly, and plunge the mold directly into the hot water. Boil for nearly an hour; turn out and eat witq fruit sause.

Almond Flitters.

Pound one-half pound of sweet almonds, and a few bitter ones, all blanched, orange peel, chopped lemon peel, sugar to sweeten, a teacupful of flour, and two or three whites of eggs; pound all together, adding a few drops of water or more whites of eggs to make it of a proper stiffness to roll out into balls; sprinkle a little fine sugar over them when read to serve.

Squash Pie No. 1.

Pare and grate raw squash, to one pint of the grated squash add one quart of milk, two cups of sugar one teaspoonful of ginger and one of nutmeg, little salt, three well beaten eggs, bake in custard dish without top crust.

Home Pudding.

One quart of sweet milk, one pint of bread crumbs soaked in milk, three eggs well beaten, one teacupful of sugar, a little mace, five or six good tart apples, pared, cores taken out, let them stand in the pudding and steam until the apples are done. An hour is sufficient.

Fig Pudding No. 2.

Three-quarters of a pound of bread crumbs, pound of best figs, six ounces of suet; one teacupful of moist sugar, a teaspoonful of milk, and a little nutmeg grated. The figs and suet must be chopped very fine. Mix the bread and suet first, then the figs, sugar, and nutmeg, one egg beaten well, and lastly the milk. Boil in a dish four hours. To be eaten with lemon sauce.

Squash Pie No. 2.

Pare ripe squash, slice into small pieces, boil or stew them with water enough to prevent burning, when quite tender rub through a colander; to one pint of squash, add one pint of cream or milk, two or three eggs, one cup of sugar and one teaspoonful of spice; bake without top crust.

Apple Pudding.

Put in a buttered dish, first a layer of apple sauce sweetened with light brown sugar and sprinkle with bits of butter, then a layer of cracker crumbs with a little grated nutmeg, another layer of sauce and so on, ending with a layer of crumbs. Bake and eat hot.

Corn Meal Cake.

Scald a pint of corn meal, add two eggs, a little salt and one-half teaspoonful soda. Thin enough to make stiff batter, and fry by dropping in spoonfuls on hot lard.

Boiled Pudding.

One cup of cream, one cup sugar, one-half cup of butter melted, two and one-half cups flour, two even teaspoonfuls of soda dissolved in hot water, a little salt. Mix sugar and butter together, and beat until very light. Stir in the cream and salt, make a hole in the flour and pour in the mixure. Stir down the flour gradually until it is a smooth batter.

Beat in the soda water thoroughly and boil at once in a buttered mould, leaving room to swell. Let it cook for an hour and a half.

Tart Apple Pie.

Pare and quarter enough tart apples to lay loosly in the prepared paste, the quarters should not touch each other. Fill the paste two-thirds full of thin sweet cream, then sprinkle over one spoonful of flour, butter as large as a walnut, cut in bits, sugar. Grate nutmeg over the whole. Bake slow; if a brown crust forms over the top before the apples cook, stir it under with a spoon.

Jelly Pie No. 2.

Two cups of sugar, one glass of jelly, three eggs, half a cup of butter; work sugar and butter to a cream; beat the yolks of eggs until very light, mix with sugar and butter, then the whites, last the jelly, and flavor with one tablespoonful of extract of vanilla.

Rice Pudding.

One quart of milk, one teacupful of rice, one teacupful of raisins, one teacupful sugar, butter size of an egg, grated nutmeg, and one teaspoonful of cornstarch.

Jelly Pudding.

Two tablespoonfuls cornstarch, one cup of rich cream, five eggs, beaten very light; one-half teaspoonful soda, stirred in boiling water; one glass currant jelly. Scald the milk and beat until half cold. Stir in the beaten yolks, then whites, finally the soda. Fill large pudding dish half full with batter, set in quick oven and bake half an hour. When done, tnrn out quickly; with a sharp knive make an incision in the side of the pudding, pull partly open, and put a liberal glass of the conserve within. Close the slip by pinching the edges with the fingers. Eat warm with sweetened cream.

MINCE PIE.

Boil good beef tender; when cold, chop it fine. To two pounds of chopped meat, and half a pound chopped suet add one tablespoonful each of mace, cinnamon, cloves, allspice, ginger and nutmeg, little salt, one cup of syrup or molasses, two of sugar; mix all well together and put it in a jar and cover it with molasses. When making pies, to each pound of the above add one pound of finely chopped tart apples and sweeten more if desired.

CREAM CUSTARD.

Take yolks of six eggs, one-half pound of sugar, and beat up same as sponge cake, then add ten ounces of flour; stir it well and lay it out in jelly cake pans and bake them in hot oven, and when done turn them out.

ORANGE PUDDING No. 2.

Set one pint of milk on the stove to heat. Mix one tablespoonful of cornstarch with a little cold milk and the yolks of three eggs, adding one-half teacup of sugar and a little salt. When the milk is hot, not boiling, stir in the mixture and let it boil, stirring constantly. Peel and slice four oranges, remove the seeds, and lay them in a dish, cover each layer with sugar. While the custard is still hot pour it over the oranges. Beat the whites of the eggs to a stiff froth, adding two tablespoonfuls of powdered sugar, and spread over the top of the custard. Serve when cold.

Chocolate Pudding.

Let one pint of milk come to the boiling point adding four tablespoonfuls of sugar, one bar of grated chocolate, one tablespoonful of corn starch, boil until thickened, pour into a dish and place in a cool room. Serve with rich cream, flavored with rose.

Snow Mountain Pudding.

Pour one pint of boiling water on one-half box of gelatine add the juice of one lemon and two cups of sugar. When nearly cold, strain; add the whites of four eggs beaten to a froth; beat the whole together, put in a dish and set on ice. With the yolks of the eggs, two teacupfuls of milk, one large spoonful of sugar, one teaspoonful of cornstarch make a boiled custard, flavor with lemon or vinilla. Serve cold by pouring the custard around portions of the snow placed in saucers.

Turkish Cream.

One quart sweet cream, yolks of three eggs, one-half ounce gelatine, one cup of sugar, two teaspoonfuls of bitter almond extract. Soak the gelatine in enough cold water to cover it, for an hour. Drain, and stir into a pint of cream made boiling hot. Beat the yolks with the sugar and add the boiling mixture, beating in a little at a time. Heat until it begins to thicken, but do not boil it, remove it from the fire, flavor with vanilla, and while it is still hot stir in the other pint of cream, beat to a stiff froth. Beat in this a spoonful at a time the custard until it is the consistency of sponge cake batter. Dip a dish in cold water, pour in the mixure, and set on ice to form.

Custard.

Beat four eggs with one-half cup of white sugar, and add one quart of rich new milk, flavor with lemon, stir all together. Pour into pudding mould and bake in moderate heat.

Sweet Corn Macaroons.

Make any kind of cake mixture, using three parts of ground corn and one of flour, drop on paper as for cocoanut macaroons. Bake in quick heat.

Sauce For Pudding No. 1.

Take equal quantities of sugar and molasses, boil them together, and stir in a little flour.

Zephyr Crackers.

Spread a thin layer of butter on the crackers, over which sprinkle a little grated cheese. Place in a warm oven.

Puff Pudding.

One pint sweet milk, whites of four eggs whipped to a froth, one teacupful of sifted flour, two-thirds cup powdered sugar, grated peel of half a lemon, little salt. Beat the eggs and sugar to a froth, and add this alternately with the flour to the milk. Beat until the mixture is very light, and bake in buttered mould. Turn out, sift powdered sugar over it, and eat with lemon sauce. This is delicious in taste,

Sweet Pudding.

Ingredients: Four eggs, three apples, quarter of a pound of bread crumbs, one lemon, three ounces of sugar, one-half teacupful of currants, little nutmeg, butter for same. Pare, core and chop the apples and mix with the bread crumbs, nutmeg grated, sugar, currants, the juice of a lemon and half the rind grated. Beat the eggs, moisten the mixture with these and beat all together, adding the eggs last; put the pudding into a buttered dish, tie it down with a cloth, boil one hour and a half, and serve with sauce.

Steamed Salmon.

Take the contents of a tin of salmon, pound well in a morter with seasoning and some dripping, a spoonful of ketchup or other sauce may be added. Mix with a good cupful of oatmeal. Moisten with one egg and a little milk, and steam in a dish for two hours. Serve with sauce.

Cheese and Egg Sandwiches.

Grate the cheese, and to each cupful add the yolks of three hard boiled eggs minced fine; rub to a paste with a teaspoonful of butter, season to taste with salt and pepper and spread between buttered bread or crackers. These are nice make of graham bread.

Minced Veal.

Cut the meat from the bones, and having minced it very fine with a small piece of lemon peel, grate over it a little nutmeg, and sprinkle on some pepper and salt, put the bones into a sauce pan with a large onion chopped fine and water enough to moisten well; thicken with a little flour and butter and serve on buttered toast.

Escalloped Sweet Potatoes.

Slice cold boiled sweet potatoes and place them in a buttered pie-plate, season with a little salt and pepper. Melt one-third of a cupful of butter into one-half of a teacupful of rich cream, and sprinkle some of it over the potatoes. Have your oven hot, and look at the potatoes every ten minutes until the butter and milk are all used.

Potato Omelet.

To a large coffee cupful of mashed potatoes allow three eggs, yolks and whites beaten separately, a little salt, half a teacupful of milk, a very little sifted flour, a little black pepper, and if flavor is preferred, use either parsley or celery chopped fine; heat and grease a large sauce-pan and pour mixture into it. Brown it lightly and serve hot.

Cabbage Salad.

One head of fine red cabbage, minced fine, three hard boiled eggs; two tablespoonfuls ham gravy, two tablespoonfuls white sugar, little salt, little pepper, one teaspoonful mixed mustard, one teaspoonful vinnegar. Mix and pour over the chopped cabbage.

Scalloped Eggs.

Put a layer of bread crumbs soaked to a soft paste in milk, then pepper and salt and pour into a pie pan, set in the oven until hot through. Beat five eggs to a stiff froth, add a tablespoonful of melted butter and the same of cream, and pour over the bread crumbs. Bake in a hot oven.

A Good Way To Cook Chicken.

Cut the chicken up, put into a pot and cover with water. Let it stew in the usual manner. When done, make a thickening of cream and corn starch, add butter, pepper and salt. Have ready a nice short cake, baked and cut in squares, rolled thin as for crust. Lay the cake on the dish and pour the chicken and gravy over them while hot.

Potted Halibut.

Pick to pieces cold halibut removing all the bones. Rub perfectly smooth. Put into a double boiler, having the water in the outer vessel at a hard boil, and when the fish is heated through stir into it to each cupful of fish a good teaspoonful of butter, a teaspoonful of mixed mustard, a teaspoonful of vinnegar and a little cayenne pepper. When the fish is nearly cold, pack it into small jars, and cover the top with butter. This must be prepared by melting the butter in a cup, set in a sauce-pan of hot water, removing the white cheesy scum that rises to the top as it melts, and finally straining the melted butter through a cloth. Pour in on top of the potted fish while warm, but not hot. Codfish may be prepared in the same manner; either will keep a week or ten days in a cool place.

How To Cook Veal Steaks.

Beat them very little, then broil over clear hot coals until a nice brown on both sides, season with salt, pepper and butter. Send to table while hot. A gravy made by stewing in a little hot water, some bits of veal, with a few oysters, seasoned and poured over the steak is very nice.

Fish Gems.

Take any remnant of boiled fish, chop it fine and add the same amount of bread crumbs soaked soft in milk, also two eggs beaten and a spoonfull of butter; season with salt, pepper and chopped parsley. Bake in a buttered pan twenty minutes.

How To Cook Steak.

Have a hot pan on the stove and place the steak within, do not put in any grease or water. Turn and keep turning till done enough; it is best rare. Season with butter, salt and pepper rubbed together, and a very little hot water poured over it.

Potato Sauce.

Put into a sauce-pan three tablespoonfuls of butter, a small handful of parsley chopped fine; salt and pepper to taste. Stir up well until hot, add a small teacupful of cream or new milk, thicken with one tablespoonful of corn-starch, and stir until it boils. Chop some cold boiled potatoes, put into the mixture, and boil up once before serving.

Clam Chowder.

Take the kettle in which your chowder is to be made and place within one-half pound of pork which you have cut in inch pieces. Let this fry until the fat is all drawn out, being careful not to let it burn. Remove the pork and place in the fat two onions which you have chopped fine; when they are well cooked remove the kettle from the fire and put in a layer of clams cut in small pieces, then a layer of sliced potatoes, alternately. Sprinkle on each layer salt, black pepper, sweet marjoram, a pinch of cayenne pepper and a little flour. Having saved all the water which was found in the clams, strain it and add with cold water enough to make a gallon. Return to the fire and let it boil slowly for an hour, then add five or six crackers broken in pieces, and let it cook half an hour longer.

Roast Pig's Head.

The head must first be boiled until sufficiently tender to allow the bones to be taken out. After removing these, shape the head neatly and skewer it together firmly, then mix some powdered sage leaves with pepper and salt, and sprinkle the mixture over it. Then hang it on a splint and roast it before a fire, basting it well while roasting. Serve at once on a hot dish, pouring over it a good gravy.

Chicken Pie.

Take two young chickens, cut in small pieces, season with pepper and salt, and small pieces of salt pork; put in a sauce pan with water to cover it; boil for half and hour, add flour and butter to thicken the gravy; have ready a large dish, served with paste, put all in a dish covered with a good rich paste. Bake half an hour.

Pounded Beef.

Boil a shin of twenty pounds of meat until it falls readily from the bone; pick it to pieces, mash gristle and all very fine, pick out all the hard bits. Set the liquor away; when cool skim off all the fat, boil the liquor down to a pint. Then return the meat to it while hot, add pepper and salt and any spice you choose. Let it boil for a few minutes stirring all the while. Put into a crock to cool. Use cold and cut in thin slices for tea or warm it for breakfast.

BOILED HAMS.

Soak over night. Put into a pot and boil gently for five or six hours, take it off the fire and let it remain in the water until cold. Peel off the skin and sprinkle with bread or cracker crumbs and brown in the oven; slice thin for the table.

COLORING DEPARTMENT.

COTTON GOODS.

Green.

The goods should first be dipped into home made blue; after remaining until the right darkness is obtained, take out, dry and rinse a little. Make a dye with fustic, three pounds logwood, three ounces to each pound goods, by boiling dye one hour; when cooled so as to bear the hand, put in the goods, stir quickly for a few minutes, and let it stand for one hour; take out and drain them; dissolve and add to the dye for each pound of cotton, blue vitrol one-half ounce, and dip another hour. Wring out and let dry in the shade. By diminishing or adding the fustic and logwood any shade may be obtained.

Sky Blue.

For five pounds of goods, seven ounces of blue vitriol; boil few minutes, then dip goods three hours, then pass through strong lime water.

Black.

For five pounds of goods, sumac, wood and bark together, five pounds; boil three-fourths of an hour and let the goods steep nine hours; then dip in lime water three-fourths of an hour, then let the goods drain one and one-half hours; add to the sumac, twelve ounces of copperas, and dip another hour; then run through the lime water for twenty minutes; then make a new dye with three pounds of logwood, byg boiling one hour, and dip again for two and one-half hours; now add three ounces of bi-chromate of potash to the logwook dye, and dip one and one-half hours. Rinse in clear water and dry in the shade.

Red.

For five pounds of goods—three gills of muriate of tin, add water to cover goods, bring to boiling heat, put in the goods, stir for one hour; make a new dye with two pounds of nicwood and sufficient water to cover the goods well; steep for three-fourths of an hour, then put in goods and increase for one hour, not bringing to a boiling heat at all. Take the goods out and drain for one hour; wash in clear water, dry in the shade.

Orange.

For three pounds goods—three ounces sugar of lead; boil ten minutes, let cool, and then put in the goods; let stand two hours, wring out; make a new dye with bi-chromate of potash six ounces, one ounce madder, dip until suits; if the color is too dark, dip into lime water until the desired shade is reached.

Royal Blue.

For three pounds of goods—three ounces copperas; boil and dip twenty minutes, then rinse through soap suds and back to the dye three times. Make a new dye of three-fourths onuces of prussiate potash, two tablespoonfuls of vitriol oil, boil twenty-five minutes and rinse, dry in the shade.

Yellow.

For three pounds of goods-five ounces sugar of lead; dip the goods for one and one-half hours; make a new dye with three ounces of bi-chromate of potash, wring out and dry in a shady place. If not yellow enough repeat the operation.

WOOLEN GOODS.

Pink.

For five pounds of goods—alum five ounces; boil one hour and dip the goods; then add two oz. pulverized cochineal, eight oz. cream tartar; boil and dip the goods while boiling until the desired shade is reached.

Black.

For five pounds of goods—ground argal one and one-half ounces, bi-chromate of potash two ounces; boil together and put in the goods letting it remain in the dye four hours. Take the goods out rinse in clear water, make a new dye, with one and one-half pounds of log wood. Boil one hour and add one gallon of vinegar, and let the goods lie in it all night. Rinse in clear water and dry.

Blue

For five pounds of goods—Tartaric acid six ounces, alum ten ounces; boil the goods in this for one hour. Make a new dye of warm water and the extract of indigo, using more or less indigo according to the depth of color desired; boil again until the desired shade is obtained.

Wine Color.

For one pound of goods—camwood eight ounces; boil fifteen minutes and dip the goods one hour; add the vitriol one-fifth ounce; if not dark enough, add copperas one-fourth ounce.

Scarlet.

For five pounds of goods—cochineal two and one-half ounces, muriate of tin one pound, tartaric acid two and one-half ounces; boil up the dye, put the goods in, working the goods briskly for fifteen minutes, after which boil two hours, stiring the while; rinse in clear water, drip and dry in the shade.

Green.

For five pounds of goods—fustic five pounds, alum one and one-half pounds, steep for two hours, put the goods in and let them remain until a good yellow is obtained, then filter, and add extract of chemic, one tablespoouful at a time, until the color suits. Or:

Make a strong dye of hickory bark and yellow vak, in equal quantities, add the extract of indigo, until the desired shade is reached.

Purple.

For one pound of goods—alum one ounce, pulverized cochineal one-half ounce, tartaric acid one ounce, muriate of tin one gill, boil all the ingredients except the cochineal for fifteen minutes, then add the cochineal and boil ten minutes, dip the goods for one and one-half hour, make a new dye with Brazil wood two ounces, log wood, muriate of tin two gills, one teaspoonful of chemic, alum one ounce, work again until color suits, drain, rinse slightly in salt water and dry in the shade.

Madder Red.

For five pounds of goods—five ounces of red, or cream tartar, two pounds alum; put in the goods and boil for one hour; let the goods cool in the dye; boil again for one-half hour. Make a new dye with a peck of bran and sufficient water, make it luke warm, skim the bran off and add four pounds of madder; enter the goods and raise to a boiling heat; drain one-half hour, wash in strong suds, and dry in the sun.

Tobacco Brown.

For three pounds of goods, one-half pound camwood; boil twenty minutes, dip the goods for one hour; take out the goods and add to the dye, one pound fustic; boil twenty minutes, dip the goods for one hour, add one-half ounce of blue vitriol, two ounces copperas, dip again for twenty minutes; if the color is to light add more copperas; drain, rinse in clear water and hang in the shade.

Orange.

For one pound of goods—one ounce argal, one ounce muriate of tin, boil and dip one hour; then add to the dye one-half pound of fustic, boil fifteen minutes and dip three-fourths of an hour, and add to the dye two ounces of cochineal; dip one-half hour, drain and dry in the shade.

LAC RED.

For three pounds of goods—six ounces argal, boil five minutes; then mix one-half pound muriate of tin, with one-half pound of pulverized lac; let them stand for three hours, add half of this new mixure to the dye, and dip one-half hour; add the remainder and dip three-fourths of an hour; keep the dye at a boiling heat for one-half hour, cool off and drain the goods; do not rinse but dry in the shade.

DRAB.

For three pounds of goods—two ounces of logwood, two ounces alum, boil together for one-half hour, dip the goods for three-fourths of an hour. If not dark enough add alum and logwood in equal quantities until the right shade is reached.

SLATE COLOR.

Boil beach bark in an iron vessel, filter after it has boiled sufficiently, add copperas more or less according to the depth of color desired, rinse in clear water and dry in the shade.

DOVE COLOR.

Boil a teacup of black tea in an iron vessel, with a teaspoon of copperas, and sufficient water. Dilute the goods in this.

CRIMSON.

For one pound of goods—make a paste of cochineal and water, put the goods in this for one hour; add one pound of tartar, one pound of proto-chloride, six ounces of cochineal, boil for fifteen minutes, take out, wash in clear water and dry.

Yellow.

For five pounds of goods—three ounces of bichromate of potassa and two ounces of alum, sufficient water to cover the goods; boil for one-half hour; lift the goods until well cooled and drained, then work one-half hour in another mixture with five pounds fustic. Wash in clear water and dry in the shade.

Salmon.

For five pounds of goods—one pound of soap, one pound of annotto, sufficient water to cover the goods; boil for one-half hour; if not dark enough, add more or less annotto, according to the depth of color desired.

SILK GOODS.

Yellow.

For five pounds of silk goods—one pound of sugar of lead, one and one-half pounds of alum; leave the goods in this mixture over night with sufficient water to cover, in the morning take out, drain, and make a new dye with five pounds fustic; dip until the required color is obtained.

Lavender.

For one pound silk—four ounces alum; dip one hour, wash out; make a new dye of one ounce of Brazil wood, one-fourth ounce logwood; boil together; dip in this, one-half hour, then add more logwood or Brazil wood in equal quantities, until the color is dark enough.

Light Blue.

For one pound of silk—dissolve one-half tablespoon of alum in a teacup of hot water, and put it in a gallon of cold water; then add one teaspoon chemic at a time, to obtain the desired color. The more chemic that is used, the darker will be the color. This blue works equally well on woolen silk,

Orange.

For five pounds of silk—five ounces of annotto, five ounces of saleratus, boil the goods in this fifteen minutes, drain and dry.

Crimson.

For three pounds of silk—nine ounces of alum; steep and dip for one hour; take out and drain; make a new dye of six ounces of bruised nutgalls, one ounce tartaric acid, nine ounces cochineal, sufficient water to cover the goods; boil for fifteen minutes; when the dye begins to cool, dip, raise to a boil, continue to dip one hour; wash in clear water, rinse and dry in the shade.

Green.

For three pounds of silk—two pounds yellow oak bark; boil three-fourths of an hour; filter and add one and one-half pounds of alum; let stand until cold; while this dye is being made, color the goods in wash blueing; dry and wash; then dip in the alum and bark dye; if it does not take well, warm the dye a little. Or:

One-half peck peach leaves; boil well; filter and add one-half teacup of proto-chloride of tin, stirring well; put in the goods and stir round for ten minutes; take the goods out, and add to the dye one tablespoon of indigo at a time until the desired shade is reached; put in the goods again and dip one-half hour; take out the goods, rinse and dry immediately.

Purple.

For three pounds of silk—first dip the goods in a solution of bluing water; dry the goods, then dip in one pound alum, to sufficient water to cover; steep for ten minutes; if the color is not full enough. add a little chemic; drain and dry.

Snuff Brown.

For three pounds of silk—make a solution of two gallons of water and six ounces of blue vitriol; dip in this for fifteen minutes; then run it through lime water; then run through a solution of three ounces of Prussiate of potash, to one gallon of water.

Black.

Make a week dye the same as the black in woolen goods; work the goods in bichromate of patassa, at a little below boiling heat; then dip in logwood in the same manner; if colored in blue vitriol, use about the same heat.

MISCELLANEOUS COOKING AND BAKING RECIPES.

COCOANUT CREAM CAKE.

One cup butter, two cups sugar, three and a half cups flour, whites of six eggs, one teaspoonful baking powder, one-half cup of milk, bake in layers. Filling: One-half cup sugar, one-half cup flour, whites of two eggs; beat the eggs and stir in sugar and flour; add one-half pint boiling milk and one cup cocoanut, make frosting for the top; sprinkle with cocoanut before dry.

GRAHAM BREAD.

One quart of warm water, one pint of bread sponge, one cup of molasses, one teaspoonful of saleratus, and one of salt; graham flour to make a stiff batter; add the sponge last, put it in buttered tins, and let it rise before baking. Bake in small loaves for three-quarters of an hour.

CANNED SALMON SOUP.

Drop into a quart of milk two slices of onion, a little salt, half a spoonful of pepper, and place over the fire to boil for a few minutes. While it is boiling select about a pound of finely chopped, canned salmon, from which all pieces of bone, fat and skin have been removed. Thicken the milk with two tablespoonfuls of flour wet with a little cold milk or water, or with three finely crumbled and rolled crackers. When it has thickened, add the salmon, and as soon as it boils once more, take it from the fire and add a heaping tablespoonful of butter, that has heated just enough to melt it. Serve hot.

Cream Tapioca Pudding.

Soak three tablespoonful of tapioca in a little water for three hours. Put the same in a quart of hot milk and then boil fifteen minutes. Beat the yolks of four eggs in one cup of sugar and stir them into the pudding five minutes before it is done, flavoring with lemon or vanilla. Beat the whites of the eggs to a froth, with three tablespoonfuls of sugar. Put this over the pudding and bake five minutes.

Lobster Soup.

Chop half a pound of fresh lobster into small bits and let it simmer in a quart of milk twenty-five minutes. Add a teaspoonful of salt, a little pepper and a tablespoonful of flour wet with cold milk. Remove from the fire; stir into the soup a heaping tablespoonful of softened butter, and serve at once in a hot soap tureen.

Cocoanut Chocolate Cake.

Two and a half cups of sugar, one-half cup butter, one cup sweet milk, one and one-half teaspoonfuls baking powder, four cups of flour, four eggs, bake in layers.

Corn Bread.

One quart white Indian meal, pour boiling water enough to

scald the meal without leaving any lumps or wetting to much, then one cup molasses and one teaspoonful saleratus, dissolved in a little water. Let it cool enough to mix with the hands. Use a bowl of sponge prepared the night before, and knead up with wheat flour until quite stiff then set it near the stove to rise. Bake nearly an hour.

Another Graham Bread.

One cup light sponge, two tablespoonfuls molasses, two cups graham flour, one cup wheat flour, one cup warm water, one-half cup milk, one-half teaspoonful saleratus and one of salt.

Brown Bread.

Three cups of yellow Indian meal, one and one-half cups rye meal, three cups of sour milk, one-half cup molasses, one teaspoonful saleratus. Steam three hours, then bake three hours slowly.

Cake Iceing.

Beat white of three eggs to stiff froth and add one and one-half cups pulverized sugar.

Oyster Sauce.

Drain the liquor from a quart of oysters into a kettle and place it over the fire to boil. Skim twice, and then turn in the oysters. As soon as the oysters are roughed and plump skim them out again. If there is not a pint of the liquor remaining add enough milk to make that quantity. Rub two heaping tablespoonfuls of flour into some more milk, and stir it into the hot liquid to make a smooth cream. Salt to taste, add a saltspoonful of pepper and a little ground nutmeg. Drop the oysters into this sauce after it has boiled to a thick cream, and as soon as it reaches boiling point stir into it the yolks of two eggs and two tablespoonfuls of melted butter. Serve in a shallow, broad dish, and garnish with thin angular bits of hot toast.

For Chocolate.

Scald two-thirds of a cup of milk and a tablespoonful of sugar, add two ounces of grated chocolate and boil until quite thick; cool before using.

Wheat Bread.

Put seven pounds of flour into a large bowl or tray, heap it around the sides, leaving a hollow in the centre; put into it a quart of warm water, add to it a large tablespoonful of salt, half a teaspoonful of saleratus, dissolved in a little water, and half a gill of bakers yeast; have three pints more of warm water, and with as much of it as may be necessary, make the whole in a rather soft dough; work it well with both hands; when it is smooth and shining strew a little flour over, lay a thickly folded cloth over it, and set it in a warm place for four or five hours, then knead it again, for fifteen minutes, cover it, and let it set, to rise again; when it is like a sponge, work it down again, divide it in loaves, either two or four and bake in a quick oven.

Curry Rice And Chicken.

Cut a pound of canned or cooked chicken into small pieces and season with pepper and salt. Drop them into a pan in

218   MISCELLANEOUS COOKING AND BAKING RECIPES.

which there is a heaping tablespoonful of butter, bubbling hot. If onion flavor is liked, a tablespoonful of that vegetable, finely chopped and browned in butter may be added. Stir the chicken until it is slightly browned, then remove it, and add the butter, a teacupful of rice stock or the same quantity of milk, a teaspoonful of sugar and a teaspoonful of curry powder that has been thoroughly mixed with a teaspoonful of flour and well moistened with milk or stock. Stir until all is of about the consistency of cream; then add the chicken, and boil two or three minutes, stirring all the time. Now remove it from the fire and squeeze into it the juice of half a lemon; stir again, and pour it into a dish of rice. For East India tastes one or even two tablespoonfuls of curry will be none too much. Warm and cold veal, lamb and all kinds of poultry or game may be used instead of chicken. Some cooks add half a grated cocoanut to the curry, and many think it a pleasing addition.

Griddle Cakes.

Mix one quart of sour milk with three tablespoonfuls of molasses, and salt to taste; then add slowly, four cups of sifted flour, well mixed with two teaspoonfuls of saleratus before wetting   One or two eggs will greatly improve this.

Cocoanut Pudding.

Make a custard with one one pint of rich milk, two teaspoonfuls corn starch, one-half cup sugar, whites of four eggs, a little salt and flavoring. Boil the milk, keeping a tablespoonful or two in which to dissolve the corn starch; pour the boiling milk upon it, adding the sugar and the eggs well beaten; let it boil a few minutes, then take it off and stir in half a cup cocoanut; butter a deep dish, pour in the mixture and put in the oven to brown.

Corn Meal Cake.

One quart of sour milk, two eggs beaten, two tablespoonfuls molasses, a handful of flour and litttle salt. Then add three cups of corn meal, well mixed with one large teaspoonful of saleratus before wetting. If the batter is not thick enough add more corn meal.

Cocoanut Custard.

Same receipt as for cocoanut pie; pour the raw mixture into cups and bake by setting in a pan of boiling water, stirring well once as they begin to warm. This cup custard is much liked.

Orange Dessert.

Place layers of sliced oranges on bottom of a glass dish; cover with powdered sugar and then a thick layer of cocoanut, repeating this until the dish is full.

Chicken for Dinner.

Have ready two cupfuls of cooked chicken from which the skin and bones have been removed; salt and pepper slightly, and cut into small pieces. Place in a kettle over the fire where it will not scorch, two cupfuls of milk in which a small sliced onion has boiled five minutes. To this add a little mace, a teaspoonful of celery salt and a little white pepper. Remove the onions, add the chicken and boil three minutes; after which remove from the fire and beat into it the whipped

MISCELLANEOUS COOKING AND BAKING RECIPES.

yolks of two eggs, and serve in the hollow of a dish of rice or over hot buttered or slightly dipped toast. In either case a few browned hot bread crumbs sprinkled over it adds to its appearance and flavor.

FLANNEL CAKE.

Pour about a pint of boiling water in two cups of corn meal; strain in one quart of sour milk; add flour enough to make a proper batter, first sifting the flour well, mixed with two teaspoonfuls of saleratus before wetting; mix thoroughly, and bake quickly. One or two eggs improves this receipt.

JOHNNY CAKE.

One cup sour milk, two-thirds of a cup of sugar, one egg, butter size of a walnut, half teaspoonful of saleratus; equal parts of flour and Indian meal to make it as thick as soft gingerbread.

COCOANUT CRACKER PUDDING.

To one-half cup cocoanut add one-fourth of a pound of cracker dust; and to them, one and a half pints of boiling milk, two ounces melted butter and six ounces sugar. Stir all together; beat six eggs, yolks and whites separately, stir them into the mixture, then put it in a pan and bake it, or into a pudding mould and boil it like custard; or it may be put into a dish lined with puff paste and baked.

FLANDY SAUCE.

Rub a heaping tablespoonful of butter into a cupful of sugar until it becomes a cream; then stir into it, half a cup-

MISCELLANEOUS COOKING AND BAKING RECIPES. 221

ful of cold sweet milk, a spoonful or so at a time. When all is mingled smoothly and evenly grate over it a little nutmeg; sprinkle a sifting of cinnamon upon it, or beat into it a tablespoonful rose water or any preferred flavoring.

BISCUITS.

One pint cream, one and one-half pints buttermilk, one large teacpoonful saleratus, little salt, flour enough to make stiff as bread.

STEAMED INDIAN BREAD.

Two cups of flour, four cups of corn meal, two cups sweet milk, two cups sour milk, one teaspoonful of saleratus, one egg, little salt, one cup syrup. Steam three hours.

COCOANUT LAYER CAKE.

Two cups sugar, one-half butter, three eggs, one cup milk, three cups flour, two teaspoonfuls baking powder; bake as for jelly cake. Filling: One cup cocoanut; add whites of three eggs beaten to a froth, and one cup of powdered sugar; spread this between the layers of cake. Then to one-fourth cup of cocoanut add four tablespoonfuls of powdered sugar and spread thickly over top of cake.

COCOANUT BREAD PUDDING.

One cup bread crumbs, two eggs, one-half cup concentrated cocoanut, one pint milk; butter and sugar to taste.

PUDDING SAUCE No. 1.

This excellent pudding sauce is made by beating into a pint of boiling and slightly salted milk, half a cupful of sugar and the whipped yolks of three eggs. Stir this until it become a cream, but not a custard; remove from the fire; flavor with a teaspoonful of vanilla or other extracts, and beat into it the finely frothed white of an egg.

Cocoanut Pie.

One cup cocoanut, one-half pound powdered sugar, one quart unskimmed milk, whites of six eggs beaten to froth, one teaspoonful nutmeg; boil the milk and remove from the fire, then gradually whip in the beaten eggs; when nearly cold add nutmegs and extracts and stir in cocoanut; pour in paste shells, bake about twenty minutes.

Hominy Cake.

Two cups of boiled hominy, cold; it smooth; stir in three cups sour milk and half a cup melted butter, two teaspoonfuls salt, two tablespoonfuls sugar; add three eggs well beaten, one teasoonful saleratus dissolved in luke warm water two cups flour. Bake quickly.

Graham Gems.

One pint sour milk, one egg, one tablespoonful molasses, one and a half pints of graham flour, half a teaspoonful of saleratus; beat together a few minutes. Have the tins hot and greased; drop in the batter, and bake ten to fifteen minutes in a quick oven.

Macaroni and Tomatoes.

Wash a quarter of a pound of macaroni and place it in boiling salted water. When it is done enough to be easily pierced with a fork drain it and have ready a buttered, pudding dish. To a pint of tomatoes add one sliced onion of moderate size, a teaspoonful of chopped or dried parsley, a level teaspoonful of salt and a few cloves. Boil until it is reduced one-half. Mash the tomatoes fine, pass them through a strainer, and add a lump of butter size of walnut. When this is melted arrange the macaroni in alternate layers with the tomatoes in the dish, saving enough of the tomatoes to pour over the top. Sprinkle lightly with fine bread crumbs, and bake ten minutes.

Rice Gems.

One pound of wheat flour, one pound rice flour; mix thoroughly and add one pound sugar, one pound butter, four eggs, flavor to taste. Then dissolve one teaspoonful of saleratus in enough milk to form a dough that can be rolled out and cut the same as cookies.

Cocoanut Pie 2.

Two cups cocoanut and two stale rusk; rub together one-half pound of powdered sugar and one-half pound butter; beat six eggs, or the whites of twelve eggs, very light; stir them into the sugar and butter alternately with the cocoanut and rusks; and lastly four tablespoonfuls of milk. Bake with a rich paste.

Quick Plum Pudding.

One pound each of finely chopped suet, sugar, currants, raisins, two pounds soaked bread, five well beaten eggs, little salt, two teaspoonfuls baking powder, one grated nutmeg; mix all together thoroughly; take a cotton bag, dip it in scalding hot water; flour it well and lay over it a pan; place the pudding in the sack and tie it closely, put it in a kettle of boiling water for four or five hours; have boiling hot water ready to fill the pot as it boils away so as not to allow it to get below heat.

Cocoanut Pie 3.

Three eggs, one-half cup cocoanut soaked in a pint of milk; bake without upper crust.

Chocolate Drink.

Scrape or grate two oblong bars of fine chocolate and pour a tablespoonful of boiling water upon it stirring until thoroughly mixed, then add a cupful of milk that has reached boiling point and permit it to simmer, but not boil, stirring constantly about seven minutes. Sugar may be added if desired.

Broiled Chicken.

Split the chicken down the back, disjoint but do not part it and flatten with a potato masher; broil over a hot fire from seven to ten minutes, turning frequently; sprinkle with salt and add a little butter or olive oil; lay the chicken upon a lightly browned piece of buttered toast that has its edges neatly trimmed, and serve.

Corn Cake.

Three eggs beaten light, two cups sour milk; three tablespoonfuls melted butter, one tablespoonful white sugar, one small teaspoonful of salt, one teaspoonful soda, mixed well with corn meal enough to make a thin batter. Bake in a shallow pan or small tins for half an hour in a hot oven.

Clove Cake.

One-half pound butter, one pound sugar, one pound flour, one pound raisins, one cup milk, three eggs, one teaspoonful soda, one large teaspoonful cloves, cinnamon and nutmeg.

Corn Starch Pudding.

One quart of milk, except enough to wet two tablepoonfuls of corn starch, placed in a tin pail and set in a kettle of boiling water; add the yolks of four eggs beaten, half a cup of sugar, the corn starch and a little salt; let it boil until it thickens; when cool flavor with one teaspoonful of vanilla, pour into a pudding dish, beat the whites of the eggs with half a cup pulverized sugar, flavor with lemon and place in the oven to brown.

Dark Cup Cake.

Three cups butter, six cups sugar, ten cups flour, eight eggs, two cups milk, one teaspoonful soda and spice and fruit if desired. One-third of this receipt will be sufficient for one loaf.

Plum Pudding.

Three-quarters of a cup of raisins cover with a cupful of boiling water. Let stand for fifteen minutes, drain the water. Dredge, and stir through them a heaping teaspoonful of flour. While the raisins are soaking beat a heaping tablespoonful of butter into a teaspoonful of sugar and add the beaten yolks of two eggs; mix thoroughly, and pour slowly into it half a tea cupful of sweet milk, stirring constantly. Now stir into it one and a half teacups of flour into which two teaspoonfuls of baking powder have been carefully mixed by passing them together through a sieve. After this is beaten into a smooth dough add the well beaten whites of the eggs. Pour into a pudding pan and bake in a quick oven until by testing with a straw it is found to be thoroughly cooked. Serve hot with pudding sauce.

Lemon Cake.

One and one-half cups sugar, one-half cup butter, one-half cup milk, two and a half cups flour, three eggs, half a teaspoonful of saleratus, and the juice and grated rind of one lemon.

Spice Bread Pudding.

One quart of grated bread crumbs, one quart of milk, four eggs well beaten, butter the size of an egg, one-half cup sugar, two teaspoonfuls spice, mix all well together and bake. Serve with sauce.

Sweet Potato Pie.

Boil sweet potatoes sufficient to make a pint of pulp, add a pint of milk, a small cup of sugar, a little salt, the yolks of two eggs, a teaspoonful of flour and bake in a shallow pan lined with pie paste. When done beat the whites of the eggs with powdered sugar for the top, and brown it in the oven.

Dried Apple Cake.

Three cups dried apples, soaked over night and chopped fine and stewed in three cups of molasess, three eggs, three cups flour, half a cup butter, two teaspoonfuls saleratus, one and a half pounds of currants, allspice, cinnamon and nutmegs to taste. This will make two large loaves.

COOKIES.

One cup butter, two cups sugar, four cups flour, two eggs, half a cup sour cream and half a teaspoonful of saleratus.

SUGAR COOKIES.

One-half cup butter, two cups sugar, half a cup of milk, three eggs, half a teaspoonful saleratus dissolved in milk; flavor and add just enough flour to make it stiff enough to roll out thin.

FLOUR PUDDING.

One pint sweet milk, two eggs, one tablespoonful butter, one tablespoonful of sugar, one-half teaspoonful of salt, one quart flour and two heaping teaspoonfuls baking powder; bake in cups, and serve with sauce.

CORN STARCH CUSTARD.

Two tablespoonfuls of corn starch to one quart of milk; mix the corn starch with a small quantity of milk, and flavor with vanilla, beat up two eggs; heat the remainder of the milk to near boiling, then add the mixed corn starch, the eggs, half a cup sugar, a little butter and salt, boil five minutes stirring it briskly.

RAISIN CAKE.

Three pounds of raisins, two pounds currants, half a pound

MISCELLANEOUS COOKING AND BAKING RECIPES.

citron, one pound butter, one pound sugar, one and one-quarter pound of flour, ten eggs, half a cup molasses, one tablespoonful of mace, cloves, cinnamon, allspice and nutmeg, one teaspoonful saleratus dissolved in sour cream.

GINGER SNAPS.

One cup molasses, one cup sugar, one cup butter, seven cups flour, one egg, one large teaspoonful of saleratus, one tablespoonful of vinegar and ginger to taste.

FRUIT COOKIES.

Two cups sugar, one-half cup butter, two eggs, two cups raisins, two tablespoonfuls sour cream or sour milk, two tablespoonfuls cinnamon, one tablespoonful nutmeg, one teaspoonful saleratus. Roll a few at a time.

BOILED PUDDING.

To one quart of bread crumbs soaked in water, add one cup of molasses, one teaspoonful of butter, one cup of fruit, one teaspoonful each of all kinds of spices, one teaspoonful of saleratus, three-quarters of a cup of flour. Boil one hour and serve with sauce.

YEAST CAKE.

One cup butter, four cups of flour, half a pint of milk, one egg, a little yeast, spice to taste, one and a half cups of sugar.

PEACH PIE.

Line a pie plate with a nice crust, pare and slice tart peaches, fill the plate quite full, cover with another crust and bake; when done, cut around the edge and remove the top crust; mix with the peaches two-thirds of a cupful of sugar, butter half the size of an egg; flavor to suit the taste and replace the crust; or turn the top crust over and spread in it a part of the peach and lay it crust side down on the bottom part, forming a double peach pie with out a top crust.

Pudding Sauce No. 2.

One cup sugar, one teaspoonful butter, one pint boiling water, spice to taste, flavor with lemon and thicken a little with corn starch.

A Good Cake.

Three-quarters of a pound of butter, one pound of sugar, one pound of flour, one pint sour milk, two teaspoonfuls of saleratus, four eggs and half a nutmeg.

Holliday Pudding.

One and a quarter pounds of flour, two teaspoonfuls of good baking powder well mixed dry, one pound chopped suet, quarter pound sugar, one pound English currants, one pound chopped raisins, two ounces citron, flavor, ten well beaten eggs; mix all thoroughly wringing out the pudding bag in hot water, flour well inside, pour in the mixture, tie and boil five hours; serve with pudding sauce.

Potatoes for Supper.

Pare eight medium sized potatoes and let them remain in cold water for half an hour; wipe dry and place them in boiling salted water; as soon as they are cooked drain and set them back on the stove to permit the steam to escape, then let them dry; then mash fine and mix with them a tablespoonful of butter, a little salt and pepper and two raw eggs that have been beaten; now form them into cakes and brush them over with the yolk of an egg into which has been stirred a teaspoonful of water; now set them into the oven to brown; bake five minutes.

GINGER COOKIES.

Half a pound of butter, one pint of molassess, two teacups sugar, two tablespoonfuls ginger, two teaspoonfuls saleratus, spice to suit the taste and flour enough to make a stiff dough.

CRULLERS.

One-half cup butter, one cup sour milk, one and one-half cups of sugar, two eggs, one teaspoonful soda, and one cup of new milk; bake in a slow oven.

STEWED OYSTERS.

Put the juice into a saucepan and let it simmer, skimming it careful, then rub the yolks of three hard boiled eggs and one large spoonful of flour well together, and stir into the juice; cut into small pieces quarter of a pound of butter, half a teaspoonful of whole allspice, a little salt, a little cayenne and the juice of a fresh lemon; let all simmer for ten minutes, and just before dishing add the oysters. This is for two quarts of oysters.

COTTAGE CHEESE.

Heat some sour milk until whey rises to the top; pour it off, put curd in bag, and let drip six hours without squeezing it; put in a bowl and chop fine with a wooden spoon, salt to taste, and work to the consistency of soft putty adding gradually a little cream and butter; mould with the hands into pats or balls and keep in a cool place. Best eaten when fresh.

Lobster Rissoles.

Boil the lobster, take out the meat, mince it fine, pound the coral smooth, and grate for one lobster the yolks of three hard boiled eggs, season with salt and pepper; make a batter of milk, flour and well beaten eggs, two tablespoonfuls of milk and one of flour to each egg; beat the batter well, mix the lobster with it gradually until stiff enough to roll into balls the size of a walnut; fry in fresh butter, or best salad oil, and serve.

Composition Cake.

Two cups of sugar, five cups of flour, one cup sour milk, three eggs, one teaspoonful of saleratus, one cup butter. Fruit to taste,

Noodles for Soup.

Beat one egg light, add a pinch of salt and flour enough to make a stiff dough, roll out in a very thin sheet, dredge with flour to keep from sticking, then roll up tightly. Begin at one end and shave down fine like cabbage for slaw.

Strawberry Cordial.

Rinse ripe berries in cold water and press them thoroughly; to each gallon of juice add three pounds of sugar, put in demijohns or other suitable vessels, which must be completely filled and stand away in the cellar to ferment. The matter thrown off in fermentation must be cleaned away at intervals and the vessels kept filled by adding sweetened water once a day, if necessary. When the fermentation has entirely ceased, strain and bottle for use.

ANYTHING AND EVERYTHING.

TO WASH KID GLOVES.

Put a little new milk in one saucer and a piece of brown soap in another, a towel folded three or four times; spread the gloves out smoothly on the towel, take a piece of flannel, dip it in the milk, then rub off a good quantity of soap to wet the flannel, and commence to rub the glove downward toward the fingers, holding it firmly with the left hand. Continue this process until the glove, if white, looks of a dingy yellow, though clean, if colored until it looks darker and spoiled. Lay it to dry, and the operater will soon be gratified to see the old gloves look nearly new; they will be soft, smooth, glossy and elastic.

TO WASH RIBBON.

Lay the ribbon on the table and rub it with a sponge; if soap has to be used, put it on the sponge and rub it thoroughly; after all the dirty spots have been cleaned dip the ribbon into clear water until all the suds are washed out; care should be taken not to wring them, for this has a tendency to wrinkle and break the silk.

TO REMOVE IRON RUST FROM CLOTH.

Wet the spot with cold water and place the cloth in the sun shine, then mix equal quantities of cream tartar and table salt, and sprinkle the mixture upon it until the dampness has absorbed a great deal, then lay on enough to hide the spot. Wet the spot with cold water every half hour, and if the stain is then seen, cover it again with cream tartar and salt, keep in the sun shine and continue these applications till the stain is gone, if recently contracted two or three applications will remove it.

Cure for a Felon.

Take common rock salt, such as is used for salting pork and beef, and mix it with spirits of turpentine in equal parts; put it on a rag and wrap it up well; as it gets dry put on more, and in twenty-four hours the felon will be dead.

How to Judge Canned Goods.

Note when about to purchase the condition of the tin, if bulged outwards don't have it, even as a gift. On the contrary, if the tin has sunk it is an infallible sign of goodness; it proves a vacuum, which is natural, as the meat shrinks when any air is left in the tin.

Whooping Cough.

Whooping cough can be very much relieved by covering the patient at night with a blanket upon which a five per cent. solution of carbolic acid has been sprinkled. A five per cent. solution would be about twenty drops of acid to an ounce of water.

To Remove Mildew from Roses.

Mildew has been successfully removed from roses and pelargoniums, by dissolving one ounce of nitre to one gallon water, and watering the plants with it occasionally; another way is to wash the diseased parts with a decoction of elder leaves; but the most effectual remedy is flowers of sulpher dusted over the foliage by means of a dredging box with very fine holes.

To Cultivate Corn.

Cultivate the corn as long as it can be done. It is a crop that should have the ground plowed deep before the seed is planted, but frequent and shallow cultivation should be given while it is growing. The surface of the ground alone should be stirred, and the oftener it is mellowed and loosened, the better for the crop.

How to Preserve Eggs.

To each pailful of water add two pints of fresh slacked lime and one pint of common salt; mix well. Fill your barrel half full with this fluid and put your eggs down in it any time after June and they will keep two years if desired.

How to wash Lace.

Lace may be washed by winding it around bottles or sewing it on muslin and boiling it in soft water with white castile soap. It should be rinsed in soft water after removing from the suds.

How to Save Stair Carpets.

Stair carpets should always have a strip of paper put under them, at and over the edge of every stair, which is the part where they wear first, in order to lessen the friction of the carpet against the boards beneath. The strips should be within an inch or two as long as the carpet is wide and about four or five inches in breath. A piece of old carpet answers better than paper if you have it. This plan will keep a stair carpet in good condition for a much longer time than without it.

Checking Hemorrhage.

To stop hemorrhage of the lungs, cord the thighs and arms above the elbows with small strong cords tightly drawn and tied. It will stop the flow of blood almost instantly.

The Cellar.

To keep the air of a cellar sweet and wholesome, use whitewash made of good white lime and water only. The addition of glue or size, or anything of this class, is only a damage by furnishing organic matter to speedily putrify. The use of lime in whitewash is not simply to give a white color, but it greatly promotes the complete oxidation of effluvia in the cellar air.

To Clean Kid Gloves.

Rub the gloves with very slightly dampened crumbs of bread. Or scrape French chalk upon them while on the hands, and wash them in a basin containing diluted spirits of ammonia.

Air in the Sleeping Room.

Most people, even many intelligent reformers, have the idea that to sleep in a cold room is essential to health. But this is a great mistake; it is better to have an open fire in your bedroom. The atmosphere is not only by this means constantly changed, but you will keep the window open, which will add greatly to the needed ventilation. But more than this, with the fire you will have fewer bed clothes over you, which is a gain, as a large number of blankets not only interferes somewhat with the circulation and respiration, but prevents the escape of those gases which the skin is constantly emitting. Even furnace or stove heat, with an open window, is better than a close, cold room.

Rust Stains on Nickel Plating.

Rust stains on nickel plating may be removed by thoroughly greasing, and after several days, rubbing with a cloth moistened with the water of ammonia. Any visible spots may then be moistened with dilute hydrochloric acid, and immediately rubbed dry. Washing and the use of some polishing completes the process.

An Excellent Mouth Wash.

Salol is recommended as an excellent antiseptic wash for the mouth, and is to be preferred to the solution of salicylic acid, as it does not effect the teeth. As it is insoluble in water, it is separated from its alcoholic solution by the latter in form of minute droplets which adhere to the teeth and gums, and exert there a protracted antiseptic effect. It should be dissolved in alcohol, and enough of the solution adder to water to make the mixture contain three per cent. of salol.

To Clean Carpets.

Take a pail of cold water and add to it a gill of ox gall. Rub it into the carpet with a soft brush. It will raise a lather which must be washed off with clear cold water; rub dry with a clean cloth; in nailing down a carpet after the floor has been washed, be certain that the floor is quite dry, or the nails will rust and injure the carpet. A weak solution of alum or soda is used for reviving the colors. The crumbs of hot wheaten loaf rubbed over a carpet has been found effective.

To Prevent Pie Juice From Soaking into the Crust.

The preventive is this: beat the white of an egg and brush the crust with it. If the oven is too hot when baking place a small dish of cold water in it or place a stick of wood in the oven which will take up part of the heat.

How to Stamp a Cake.

To stamp flowers, figures, monograms or mottoes on cakes, put the first coating on the cake and let it dry, then take the pattern to be stamped, lay it on the cake burr side up, and with a little sack of pulverized charcoal go all over the pattern; remove the pattern with the greatest care, then take a No. 1 tube, fill it with some of the prepared frosting and outline the design, then fill in to suit individual taste and talent.

To Clean the Scalp.

To clean your hair and scalp, beat up the yolk of an egg, rub it all through the hair, wash and rinse in warm soft water, dry with a towel as much as possible. Avoid going out before the hair is thoroughly dry, as you will be likely to catch cold. Ammonia is also very good to cleanse the hair and hair brushes; a teaspoonful of liquid ammonia in a pint of warm water is the right proportion; add a little soap, wash the hair in this and rinse well in clear, warm water. When dry, brush ten or fifteen minutes and soften with some harmless oil.

Another handy hair wash, is to take one ounce of borax, half an ounce of camphor; powder these ingredients very fine and dissolve them in one quart of soft boiling water; when cool, the solution will be ready for use; dampen the hair frequently. This wash effectually cleanses, beautifies and strengthens the hair.

To Blind a Window.

This method renders the glass impervious to sight, though not impervious to light. Dissolve five parts of sandaric and three parts of mastic in fifty parts of either, and add to the solution such an amount of benzine that a portion of the liquid, when spread upon the glass, will leave after drying, a dull uniform coat, causing the glass to appear as if ground. It is advisable that the window be laid in a horizontal position when the solution is applied. Finely, when a sufficient coat has been produced, a spray of benzine may be passed over it to give it more uniformity.

Food to be Avoided.

Very greasy food should be avoided as it is indigestible and requires of the stomach that which is almost imposible. One should eat slowly, chew thoroughly, and chat pleasantly while at the table. Pork should be eaten only by people in rugged health and of strong constitution. Nice fresh beef and mutton are the most desirable food, if not over done; veal is villianous and should not be eaten; most hot bread is indigestible; do not discuss the question whether this or that dish will hurt you; that is doing violence. A habit of this sort of discussion promotes dyspepsia, even if the food is good.

In-growing Toe Nails.

Cut a notch the shape of a V in the end of the nail, about one-quarter the width of the nail distance from the in-growing side; cut down as near to the quick as possible, one-third the length of the nail. The pressure of the boot or shoe will tend to close the opening you have made in the nail and thus afford relief. Allow the in-grown portion of the nail to grow without cutting it until it gets beyond the flesh.

To Take Pitch off of the Hands.

Mix together pulverized extract of licorice, and the oil of anise, to the consistency of a thick cream, rub it on the hands or the parts with the pitch on, then wash off with soap and warm soft water.

Remedy for Cold in the Head.

Sulpher flour sprinkled on a heated shovel and the fumes inhaled while they are fresh, will cure a cold in the head. A teaspoonful of sulpher is sufficient, and it does not cause disagreable sensations.

Emery Bag for the Invalid.

A very convenient article for the sick-room is the emery or sand. Procure some fine emery sand, or, the common sand will answer the purpose; dry it thoroughly in a kettle on the stove; make a bag, about 10 inches square of flannel; fill it

ANYTHING AND EVERYTHING.

with the dry sand, sew the opening carefully together, and cover the bag with cotton or linen. This will prevent the sand from sifting out, and will also enable you to heat the bag quickly by placing it in the oven or even on top of the stove. After once using this you will never again attempt to warm the hands or feet of a sick person with a heated brick or a bottle of hot water. The sand holds its heat a considerable length of time, and the bag can be tucked up to the back without any inconvenience to the invalid. It is a good plan to make two or three of the bags and keep them on hand, ready for use at any time when needed.

How to Make a Telephone.

A very handy and serviceable telephone can be made with two small wooden boxes and enough wire to stretch the required distant. In your boxes make a hole an inch in diameter in the centre then place one box in each of the houses you wish to connect. Then get five pounds of wire, (the common stove pipe wire) make a loop in one end and put it through the hole in your box and fasten it with a nail, then draw it tight to the other box, supporting it when necessary with a stout cord, and you have your telephone complete.

When You Eat Onions.

A cup of strong coffee will remove the odor of onions from the breath.

Wax for Grafting and Other Purposes.

Dissolve in an earthen vessel over a slow fire, six ounces of resin, six ounces of opich, four ounces of beeswax, four ounces of lard, and you will have an excellent wax. By spreading this mixture on paper it makes grafting paper. For an application where limbs have been removed in pruning, nothing is better than this wax.

The Table.

Put aside business cares when you come to the table. This is a good time to cultivate acquaintance with your family. It is not only strictly polite, but a great compliment to the entertainer, for a guest to ask for a second help from any dish.

Bed Airing.

The most effectual way to air beds and bed clothing is to throw the clothes over a chair and lift the mattress partly over the foot board in a round, hoop like fashion, and if a feather bed is used, pull it off upon a chair, then open the windows and the doors so that a current of air can pass through the room, and let it remain so for two or three hours, or even longer. Beds thus aired are always healthful, and will induce sound sleep to their occupants.

Remedy for Headache.

Pains in the head arise from such a variety of causes that no remedy will answer in every case. But the following is said to be an excellent preparation, and from the simple nature of the ingredients we think it worth trying. Put a handful of salt into a quart of water, and one ounce of spirits of hartshorn, and one ounce of spirits of camphor; put them quickly into a bottle and cork tightly to prevent the

ANYTHING AND EVERYTHING. 243

escape of the spirits; soak a piece of cloth with the mixture and apply it to the head.

To Preserve Potatoes from Rot.

Dust over the floor of the bin with lime, and put in about six or seven inches of potatoes, and dust with lime as before, then more potatoes, using about one bushel of lime to four bushels of potatoes. The lime improves the flavor of the potato, and effectually kills the fungi which causes the rot.

To Banish Flies From The Barn.

Scatter chloride lime on a board in the stable, to remove all kinds of flies, but more especially biting flies. Sprinkling beds of vegetables, with even a weak solution, effectually preserves them from caterpillars, slugs, ect. A paste of one part powered chloride of lime and one-half part of some fatty matter placed in a narrow band round the trunk of the tree, prevents insects from creeping up it. Even rats, mice, cockroaches and crickets flee from it.

To Purify The Air of The Sick Room.

Oils of lavender, thyme and rosemary, in the proportions of two and one-half, two and one-half and ten parts respectively, are mixed with water and nitric acid in the proportion of thirty to one. The bottle should be shaken before using, and a sponge saturated in the compound and left to diffuse by evaporation. This compound is said to possess extraordinary properties in controlling odors and effluvia.

"Mrs. or Miss".

A lady should always sign her name Mrs. or Miss, as the

case may be, in writing business letters or to persons who are not acquainted with her. If all ladies would do this, much embarassment might be saved, both to themselves and their correspondents.

Stammering.

Impediments of the speech may be cured where there is no malformation of the organs of articulation, by perseverance for three or four months, in the simple remedy of reading aloud, with the teeth closed, for at least two hours each day.

To Prevent Churns Overflowing.

Take the body of the churn and cut a grove around the inside of the mouth, about three inches from the top and three-eights inch deep, and then remove half the thickness of the wood, making a shoulder all around, then take the cover and fit nicely inside, and you have now done away with cloths, pans, etc., heretofore required to save the cream from flowing over.

To Kill Docks, Dandelions, etc.

Cut the tops off in the spring or summer time, and pour some gas tar, or sprinkle salt on the wound. Either of these will kill the root by eating to the very extremity.

To Destoy Insects on Plants.

Boil five drachms of larkspur seed and four ounces of quassia chips in seven pints of water until the decoction is reduced to five pints. When the liquid is cooled it is to be strained and used with a watering pot or a syringe, as may be most convenient. This is a most excellent method of destroying insects on plants without injury to the latter.

Manufactured Cream.

Take two or three whole eggs, beat them well up in a basin or bowl, then pour boiling hot tea over them, pour gradually to prevent curdling. It is difficult for the taste to distinguish it from rich cream.

Insect Destroyer.

Hot alum water is the best insect destroyer known. Put the alum into hot water and let it boil until all the alum is dissolved, then apply it hot with a brush to all cracks, closets, bedsteads and other places where any insects are found; ants, bedbugs, cockroaches and creeping things are killed by it, while it has no danger of poisoning the family or injuring property.

How to Open a Fruit Jar.

It is not always easy to start a fruit jar cover. Instead of wrenching your hands and bringing on blisters, simply invert the jar and place the top in hot water for a minute. Then try it, and you will find it turns quite easily.

Parched Rice.

Parch rice a nice brown as you would coffee. Throw it into boiling salted water, and boil it until thoroughly done. Do not stir it any more than necessary, on account of breaking the grains. Serve with cream and sugar.

Shaving Cream.

One ounce each of white wax, spermaceti and almond oil;

melt, and while warm, beat in two squares of Winsor soap previously reduced to a paste with rose water.

Liquid Blacking.

Ivory black, one half-pound; molasses, one-half pound; sweet oil, one-quarter pound; rub together till well mixed then add oil of vitriol, one-quarter pound; coarse sugar one-eighth pound, and dilute with beer bottoms. This cannot be excelled.

When You Swim.

No one can possibly sink if the head is thrust entirely under water. In this position a novice can swim as easily as walk, and get to shore readily by lifting the head at intervals for breath.

Noisy Beds.

If a bedstead creaks at each movement of the sleepers, remove the slats and wrap the end of each in old newspaper. This will prove a complete silence.

Caramels.

Two cups of sugar, one cup of molasses, one-half cake of chocolate, one tablespoon of butter, one-half cup of cream. Flavor with vanilla and boil twenty five minutes, stirring all the time. Pour into buttered pans and cut into squares.

Always Remove

The contents of tin cans the moment they are opened. It is positively dangerous to leave contents in the can after opening. The action of the air upon the soldering form an oxide which renders the food unfit for use. Cases of poisoning from this cause happen from time to time.

To Remove Mildew.

Soak the parts in butter-milk and expose to the sun's rays. Or soak the parts previously wetted, and apply salt and lemon juice to both sides, or apply finely powdered pipe clay, or pulverized chalk. Expose it for several hours to the atmosphere.

To Prevent Chapped Hands.

Chapping of the hands, which is one of the most disagreeable inconveniences of cold weather, can be easily prevented by rubbing the hands with powdered starch.

Fastening Knife Handles.

To fasten knife handles, melt rosen, add brick dust, and mix well together. This is a very good cement for this and other purposes. Shellac and prepared chalk, intimately mixed, answers well. Heat the part to be inserted, and fill the aparture with the mixture; press it in.

Parrot Food.

The best food for a young parrot is soaked bread or crackers, squeezed dry with the hand; cornmeal is also an excellent article for young birds. Keep seed and water in the cage, and cover the bird at night.

Some Uses of Salt.

To keep stove polish from flying and make it last, put in a little molasses and salt.

Salt extracts the juices from meat in cooking, steaks ought not therefore to be salted until they have been broiled.

It has been declared that the excessive use of salt is one of the main factors in the destruction of human body.

To clean brass or copper ware, use a tablespoonful of salt and a teacupful of vinegar; apply it with a piece of flannel and rub till dry.

Salts and soaps mixed together makes a good blind for the pastry or pantry window.

If you drop soot on the carpet, cover it with salt, and it may be swept up without blacking the carpet.

To remove tea stains from the cups, and saucers, scour with salt.

Colored stockings washed in strong salt water and dried, and then washed again in another solution, finishing in clear water, will prevent the dye rubbing off on the feet.

By using soda water and salt as a wash you can clean ceilings that have been smoked by a kerosene lamp.

A crack in the stove can be mended by a mixture of ashes, salt and water.

To brighten carpets, sprinkle with salt before sweeping.

Glossy Starch.

Make a mixture of one pint of boiling water and two ounces of white gum arabic powder; cover it and let stand over night; in the morning pour it carefully from the dregs into a clean bottle, keep it for use; a teaspoonful of the gum water stirred into a pint of starch that has been made in the usual manner will give lawns, either black or printed, a look of newness when nothing else can restore them after washing. It is also good, much diluted, for the white muslin and bobinet.

Molasses Candy.

West India molasses one quart, brown sugar one-half pound; boil the molasses and sugar in a preserving kettle over a slow fire, when done enough it will cease boiling; stir frequently, and when nearly done, stir in the juice of a lemon or a teaspoonful of essence of lemon; afterwards butter a pan and pour out to cool.

Cure for Warts and Corns.

This cure will be effected in ten minutes. Take a small piece of potash and let it stand in the open air until it slacks, then thicken it to a paste with pulverized gum arabic, which prevents it from spreading where it is not wanted.

Hair Invigorator.

Alcohol, one-half pint, castor oil one-half ounce, carbonate of amonia, one-quarter ounce, bay rum, one pint, tincture of cantharides, one-half ounce. Mix them well. This compound will promote the growth of the hair, and prevent it from falling out.

Grapes to do their best

And rot the least, require high, dry ground. Grapes growing where the vine is sheltered from excessive rains and hot sun are induced to rot but little. We believe a trellis made with a wide board cover at the top would in a measure prevent rot and mildew. On high gravelly soil we have had no trouble with either.

Tomatoes.

Tomatoes are a slow growing plant, and if desired reasonably early in the summer, the seed should be sowed early in the spring in boxes in the window garden.

A Feather Brush.

To make feather brushes to use in greasing pans or brushing eggs over tarts or pastry, boil the wing feathers of a turkey or chicken for about ten minutes, then rinse them in tepid water, and tie up in bunches.

The Luster of Morocco

Is restored by varnishing it with the white of an egg applied with a sponge.

Remedy for a Cough.

Roast a lemon very carefully without burning it; when it is thoroughly hot, cut and sqeeze into a cup upon three ounces of pulverized sugar. Take a teaspoonful whenever your cough troubles you.

Delicate Glue.

A delicate glue for mounting ferns, leaves, sea weeds, etc., is made of five parts gum-arabic, three parts white sugar, two parts starch, and a very little water. Boil until thick and white.

To Prevent Wet

From penetrating boots, take half a pound of tallow or

mutton suet, four ounces of lard and two ounces of new beeswax and olive oil; dissolve over the fire, mix well and apply it to the leather.

Home Made Cologne.

One-eighth ounce each of oil of lavender and bergamot, one-quarter ounce each of oil of lemon and rosemary, fifteen drops each of oil of cloves and rose, eight drops oil of cinnamon, two quarts best deodorized alcohol; shake two or three times per day for a week or ten days.

In Whitewashing.

The interior of a poultry house do not leave a spot even as large as the head of a pin untouched anywhere; splash the whitewash liberally into every nook and corner, crack and crevice. If the hennery has a floor of cement, stone, brick or boards, whitewash that alone.

To Remove Ink Stains.

Soak in sour milk over night.

To Prevent Vermin in Cellars.

Mix copperas with whitewash and apply freely.

To Preserve Milk.

Wrap well in a wet cloth the tin or jar in which the milk is kept.

Where the Making of New Lawns

Is contemplated, all available manure should be spread over the surface as soon as possible; the winter rains and snows will carry the soluble parts into the soil and prepare them for immediate assimilation by the young grass roots.

A Very Good Cement.

This cement is to fasten on lamp tops and consists of nothing more than melted alum. Use as soon as melted and the lamp is ready for use as soon as the cement is cold.

To Take out Scorch.

Scorch caused by using a too hot iron may be taken out by laying the garment where the bright sunshine will fall directly on it; it will take scorch entirely out.

To Remove Grease from Wall Paper.

Lay several folds of blotting paper over it and place a hot iron over it until the grease is absorbed.

Relief for Rheumatism.

Cloths dipped into hot potato water are recommended for immediate and complete relief in the severest cases of rheumatism.

Cold Tea

And tea leaves laid about the roots of potted plants fertilizes and keeps the soil light.

To Purify Water.

Pulverized alum possesses the property of purifying water; a large spoonful stirred into a hogshead of water will so purify it that in a few hours the dirt will sink to the bottom, and it will be fresh and clear as spring water. Four gallons may be purified by a teaspoonful.

Butter Scotch Candy.

Take one pound of sugar and one pint of water, dissolve and boil; when done add one tablespoonful of butter and enough lemon juice and the oil of lemon to flavor.

To Remove Scratches on Furniture.

Melt together beeswax and linseed oil and rub the marred places with it, using a woolen cloth or chamois skin.

Lotion for Cherries.

To have a fine crop of cherries and no worms, simply spray them with purple water right after the blossoms are dropped, and then two or three times afterwards. Use a teaspoonful of the purple water to a large pail of well water.

Foot Lotion.

If the feet are painful after long walking or standing, great relief can be had by bathing them in a lotion of salt and water. A handful of salt to a gallon of water is the right proportion. Have the water as hot as will be comfortable and immerse the feet and throw the water over the legs as far as the knees with the hands. When the water becomes too cool, rub briskly with a fresh towel. This method, if used night and morning, will cure neuralgia of the feet.

To Tell the Age of Eggs.

Dissolve two ounces salt in a pint of water. When a fresh laid egg is placed in this solution it will descend to the bottom of the vessel, while one that has been laid the day previous will not quite reach the bottom. If the egg be three days old it will swim in the liquid, and if it is more than three days old it will float on the surface, and project above the water more and more in proportion as it is older.

To Clean Paint.

Use but little water at once, keep it warm and clean by changing it often. A flannel cloth takes the fly specks off better than a cotton one. Soap will remove the paint, so use but little of it. Cold tea is the best liquid for cleaning varnished paint, window panes and mirrors. A saucer of sifted ashes should always be standing at hand to clean unvarnished paint that has become badly smoked, it is better than soap. Never put soap upon glass unless it can be thorougly rinsed off, which can never be done to window glass. Wash off the specks with cold tea, and rub the panes dry, then make a paste of whiting and water, and put a little in the center of each pane. Take a dry cloth and rub it all over the glass then rub it off with a chamois skin or flannel, and your glass will shine like crystal.

The Preperation of Night Soil.

So prepare night soil for use as a fertilizer, mix it with about four times its bulk of dry loam or road dust; keep under cover and mix thoroughly. When used harrow under lightly.

To Cure Enlarged Neck.

Take two tablespoonfuls of salt, two of borax and two of alum, dissolve in a small quantity of water and apply three times a day for three weeks. For cough, take suet, boiled in milk. For burns, take a tart apple and simmer in lard till it forms a salve. It heals quick, and always without a scar. Another remedy: liveforever and sweet clover leaves, cammile and sweet elder, the inner bark, a handful of each; simmer them in fresh butter and mutton tallow, one-quarter of a pound of each; when crisped, strain out and add a sufficient quantity of beeswax to form a salve, spread very thin on a thin cloth.

To Prevent Stoves From Rusting.

By applying kerosene with a rag when you are about to put your stoves away for the summer, you will prevent them from rusting. Treat your farming implements in the same way before you lay them aside in the fall.

To Preserve Milk. No. 2.

Milk often turns by an acid developed in the liquid. To prevent it, add to the milk a small portion of bicarbonate of soda. This is not injurious to the health, but rather aids digestion. Many of the great dairies on the continent adopts this method.

How to Ventilate a Room.

In ventilating a room open the windows at the top and the bottom. The fresh air rushes in one way while the foul air makes it exit the other; thus you let in a friend and expel an enemy. Well ventilated bed-rooms will prevent morning headaches and lassitude.

To Remove Grease from Glass.

A teaspoonful of hartshorn in the hot suds of the dish pan

will remove grease instantly and gives a fine polish to silver and glass ware.

To Test Nutmegs.

If nutmegs are good when pricked with a pin, oil will instantly ooze out.

To Remove Mortar or Paint from Windows.

Mortar and paint may be removed from window glass with hot, sharp vinegar.

Pen-wiper.

A good pen-wiper for steel pens is a raw potato; it removes the ink crust and causes a smooth flow of ink.

To Banish Flees.

The oil of pennyroyal has been found to be the best destroyer of flees. If the oil cannot be obtained and the weed flourish, dip dogs and cats into a decoction of it once a week, scatter in the beds of pigs once a month. Strings saturated with the oil and tied around the neck and tail of horses, will drive off lice; the strings should be saturated once a day.

Head Wash.

When one has had a fever, and the hair is falling off, take a teaspoonful of sage steeped well in a quart of soft water, strain off into a bottle with an ounce of borax added.

An Attack of Indigestion.

Caused by eating nuts, will be immediately relieved and cured by the simple remedy, salt. Medical men recommend

ANYTHING AND EVERYTHING.

that salt should be used with nuts, especially when eaten at night.

How to Keep Cider.

To keep cider perfect, take a keg, in the bottom of it bore some holes; spread a woolen cloth at the bottom, then fill with sand closely packed; draw your cider from the barrel just as fast as it will run through the sand; after this put it in clean barrels which have had a piece of cotton or linen cloth two by seven inches dipped in melted sulphur and burned inside of them, thereby absorbing the sulphur fumes (this process will also sweeten sour cider), then keep in a cellar or room where there is no fire, and add one-half pound of white sugar to each barrel.

Removing Fruit Stains from Linen.

To remove them, rub the part on each side with yellow soap then tie up a piece of pearl ash in the cloth, etc., and soak well in hot water, or boil; afterward expose the parts that are stained to the sun's rays and air until no trace of the stains can be seen.

The Use of Charcoal.

Charcoal is recommended as an absorber of gases in the milk-room where foul gases are present. It should be freshly powdered and kept there continually, especially in hot weather when the unwholesome odors are most liable to infect the milk. Another use of charcoal is for burns. This was successfully used in a very bad case; bound all over the face and neck, in five minutes from the application, the patient was asleep, the pain king soothed and quieted, and not a particle of a scar left. Take the charcoal just as it comes from the fire, powder it and apply to the burned place.

To Extinguish a Burning Chimney.

If it is desired to extinguish the fire in a chimney which has been lighted by a fire in the fire-place, shut all the doors of the apartments, so as to prevent any current of air up the chimney, then throw a few handsful of common fine salt upon the fire in the grate or stove, which will immediately extinguish the fire in the chimney. The philosophy of this is that in the process of burning salt, muriatic acid gas is evolved, which is a prompt extinguisher of fire.

Rubber Glue.

Make a mixture of soft soap, glycerine and salicylic acid each four ounces, then add one pint of water. Shake thorougly and add to it a mixture of mucilage made with gum arabic and water, let it stand over night and it is ready for use. Keep it in an air tight bottle or it will evaporate.

To Remove Grease Spots from Carpet.

Remove the grease spots by placing a piece of blotting paper under the stain and one immediately above it, then pass a hot iron over the paper and in this way extract the grease without injury to the carpet.

How to Use Gas Lime.

Do not spread gas lime directly on your land. It is destructive to plant life, unless modified by atmosphere influences. It should first be worked into compost with old turf, wool mol 1, marl or muck. A mass of green vegetable matter such as weeds, may be used with it as a compost, and it should not be spread until the white heap has been reduced to a fine condition.

Relief for Neuralgia.

This receipt has been used by myself for a number of times and has always been found to give immediate relief. Boil a teaspoonful of lobelia in a pint of water, till the strength is out of the herb, then strain off and add a teaspoonful of fine salt. Wring cloths out of the liquid as hot as possible, and spread them over the part effected. Change the cloths as soon as cold, till the pain is all gone, then cover the place with soft dry covering till perspiration is over, so as to prevent taking cold. Another remedy, when the pain is in the face, take two large teaspoonfuls of cologne and two teaspoonfuls of table salt, mix them together in a small bottle; every time an acute pain is felt, simply breath the fumes into your nose from the bottle and relief will be had. When the pain is in the temples, prepare horseradish by grating and mixing with vinegar, the same as for the table, and apply to the temple, or apply to the wrist when the pain is in the arm or shoulder.

To Prevent Sore Throat.

It is said a gargle of strong black tea used cold, night and morning, is a preventative for sore throat.

Use of Borax.

A teaspoonful of borax put in the last water in which cloths are rinsed will whiten them surprisingly. Pound the borax so it will disolve quickly. This is especially good to remove the yellow that time gives to white garments that have been laid aside for a number of years.

SOFT SOAP.

Make a mixture of stone lime, two pounds; sal-soda and lard, each four pounds; soft water, three gallons. Dissolve the lime and soda in the water by boiling, stirring, settling and pouring off, then return to the brass kettle and add the lard and boil until it becomes soap, then pour it into a dish or moulds, and when cold, cut it into bars and let it dry.

CULTIVATION OF TREES, GRAPES, ONIONS, ETC.

Success cannot be expected in soil that holds much water in it. Grapes begin to change their color from two to three weeks before they are fully matured. It is now conceded to be the best plan in the cultivation of onions to dig the soil away from the bulb and never allow it to become covered with the soil. Trees in a cultivated field are troublesome, but when they are numerous they add enough to the beauty of the landscape to compensate. Sweet alyssum can be easily propogated by cutting. In the old wheat fields, where the late weeds have started up, turn in the sheep. They are not dainty in the choice of food, and weeds that are pushed forward by the late rains might as well be converted into mutton as to remain and make the field foul.

WHALE BONES, ETC.

Bent whale bones can be restored and used again by simply soaking in water a few hours, and then drying them in the shade. To restore crushed velvet, hold it over the tea kettle spout, and let it steam well, then with a soft brush comb up the nap. Kid shoes may be kept soft and free from cracks by rubbing them once a week with a little pure glycerine or castor oil. A piece of zinc placed on the coals of a hot stove will clean out the stove pipe. The vapor produced carries off the soot by chemical decomposition. Brooms dipped for five or ten minutes into a bucket of boiling soap suds, at least once a week will last much longer than they otherwise would.

To Clean Silverware.

One teaspoonful of amonia to a teacup of water applied with a rag will clean silverware or goldware perfectly. To avoid a general cleaning of silver or goldware, wash with a chamois skin saturated with silver soap, each time after use.

To Destroy Moss.

The mossy parts of meadow land should be well manured with good well rotted stable dung in the autumn, and if practicable the grass should be fed off the following spring with sheep or cattle. Nitrate of soda sown on the mossy parts of the field will also kill the moss, and is an excellent manure for the grass, but this should not be sown at the rate of more than one and one-half hundred weight to the acre.

To Remove Anything from the Eye.

Take a bristle, double it so as to form a loop. Lift the eyelid gently and insert the loop over the eyeball, which will cause no disagreeable feeling or pain. Now close the lid down upon the bristle, which may now be withdrawn. The dirt will surely be upon the bristle. Or insert a flax seed into the eye and close and shut the eye several times. Then take a glass of clear cold water and wink the eye in this and the flax seed will come out and almost certain to have the particle sticking to it.

Remedy for a Felon.

Common salt roasted on a hot stove to throw off the chloride gas, or get the salt as hot as possible. To a teaspoonful of the salt and the same quantity of pulverized castile soap, add same quantity of turpentine; mix well into a poultice and apply to the felon. Make as many poultices as you have felons and renew them twice a day; in four or five days your felon will present a hole down to the bone, where the pent up matter was secreted. Of course it will not restore the bone, but it will soon heal

When Boiling Any

Kind of meat, cabbage, onions, etc., put in a piece of red pepper about the size of a five cent piece, to destroy the unpleasant odor.

When Putting Down

A new carpet be sure to save the ravelings; they will furnish just the darning thread you will need when the carpet "begins to go."

To Can Fruits.

In canning most fruits a good rule is a pound of sugar and

a cup of water for every three pounds of fruit. Make the syrup and conk the fruit in it until tender and well heated through; use a porcelain or granite kettle, and a silver or wooden spoon.

To Sweeten Musty Casks.

Throw in burning coals and then cold water; or, wash the casks with lime and water mixed nearly to the consistency of paste; remain till dry and then wash well with water.

Fig Candy.

Take one pound of sugar and one pint of water, set over a slow fire; when done add a few drops of vinegar and a small lump of butter, and pour into pans in which split figs are laid.

The Smell of Paint.

Water neutralizes the smell of paint; vessels of water placed in a newly painted room will remove the smell, especially if impregnated with a little sulphuric acid; or straw and hay well saturated with water; or chloride of lime and water.

To Prevent Mustard Plasters from Blistering.

Mix the mustard with molasses or the white of an egg.

For Sprains and Swellings.

Strong vinegar saturated with common salt, used warm, is good for sprains and reducing swellings.

Window Supporters.

This is performed by means of a cork in the simplest

manner, and with scarcely any expense; bore three or four holes in the sides of the sash, into which insert common bottle cork, projecting about sixteenth part of an inch. These will press against the window frames along the usual groove, and by their elastictily support the sash at any height which may be required.

Fly Paper.

Coat paper with turpentine varnish and oil it to keep the varnish from drying.

To Prevent Incrustation of Kettles.

Keep in the vessel a clean marble, a cockle or an oyster shell; these will attract the particles of sand.

Cidar Without Apples.

Two pounds common sugar, two gallons water, two table-spoonfuls yeast, one ounce tartaric acid; shake well; make in the evening and in the morning it will be ready for use.

Vinegar and Fruit

Stains upon knives can be taken off by rubbing the blades with raw potato and then polishing on the knife board in the usual manner.

Night Drink.

A hot, strong lemonade, taken at bedtime, will break up a bad cold.

To Keep Rare Ripe Tomatoes.

If they are picked when just ripe and with a portion of the

stems retained, and at once covered with a brine composed of a teacupful of salt dissolved in a gallon of water, they can be kept nearly all the year without noticeable loss of their freshness.

Never Allow

Fresh meat to remain in paper, it absorbs the juice.

Fish Scales.

Fish may be scaled much easier by first dipping in hot water.

To Find the Fire Test of Coal Oil.

Pour an ounce of the oil into a small tin cup; put it on a stove or over a lamp, place the bulb of a thermometer in the oil; as the temperature rises try to ignite the oil with a lighted taper or match; if it will ignite below 110 degrees Fahrenheit, the oil is dangerous to use; the higher the point at which it will ignite, the safer the oil.

Popped Corn

Dipped in boiling molasses and stuck together, forms an excellent candy.

Lemonade.

One-half pound white sugar, fifteen drops essence of lemon, three pints water, one-eigth of an ounce of tartaric acid.

To Prevent Screws from Rusting.

A mixture of oil and graphite will actually prevent screws becoming fixed, and moreover, pretect them for years against rust. The mixture facilitates tightening up, is an excellent lubricant and reduces the friction of the screw in its socket.

CEMENT FOR MEERSCHAUM.

This cement can be made of quicklime mixed to a thick paste with the white of an egg; this is also good to unite glass or china.

CARBONATE OF AMMONIA.

An ounce of carbonate of ammonate to a pint of water is said to check mamary abscess if frequently applied.

NEVER PLACE FRESH EGGS

Near lard, fruit, cheese, fish or other articles from which any odor arises. Eggs are extremely active in absorbing power, and in a very short time they are contaminated.

HOW TO PICKLE ORANGES.

This method is to place in a barrel of brine, lemons, oranges and limes that are liable to spoil; a flavor is imparted which is very pleasant.

BLACK TRANSFER PAPER.

Five ounces hog's lard, sufficient quantity lamp black, one ounce bees-wax, one-tenth ounce Canada balsam; melt together and mix thoroughly. Apply with a sponge.

INK TO WRITE ON GLASS.

An ink that will write on glass can be made from ammonium fluoride dissolved in water and mixed with three times its weight of barium of sulphate.

To Clean Alpaca.

To brighten and clean old Alpaca, wash in coffee.

To Sweeten Sour Milk.

Put in the milk a small quantity of carbonate magnesia. This will also prevent sweet milk from souring.

Lotion for Stiff Neck and Bruises.

A strong infusion of capsicum annum, mixed with equal bulk of mucilage of acacia and with a few drops of glycerine, has been found to be an excellent application to bruises and stiff neck. Two or three successive coatings applied with a camel's hair brush, if done immediately after the receipt of an injury, will prevent discoloration.

Ginger Pop.

One quarter pound bruised ginger root, the juice of three lemons, one-half pound lemon sugar, the whites of three eggs well beaten, one gill yeast, one and one-half pounds sugar, five gallons water. Boil the root for thirty minutes in one gallon of water; staain off and put in the other ingredients while hot; make over night and in the morning skim and bottle.

Kindling Wood.

The following composition is in great demand. Six parts melted resin, four parts tar, in which the wood is dipped for a moment. Or take a quart of tar and three pounds of resin melt them, then cool, mix as much sawdust with a little charcoal added as can be worked in. Spread out on a board and when cold, break it into lumps the size of a hickory nut, and you will have enough kindling to last you a good while.

How to Corn Beef.

For one-hundred pounds of beef take seven pounds of salt, two pounds of sugar, two ounces of saltpetre, two ounces of soda; dissolve in two and a half gallons of water; boil, skim and pour on hot.

Household Measure.

One pound of sugar is a pint; ten eggs are a pound; one pound of butter is a pint; eighteen ounces of meal is a quart; one pound of flour is a quart.

Sit in a Draught,

Or by an open window when peeling onions, and thus avoid the unpleasantness to the eyes.

To Mix Mustard.

Flour and mustard equal quantities, season with salt and pepper and sufficient vinegar to mix.

To Distinguish Body Brussels Carpet.

Body brussels is easily distinguished from carpets known as tapestry brussels, by showing the wool threads on the back. So generally has this become known that a style of carpet with a slightly clouded or stamp back has recently been put upon the market. It is intended to appear like body brussels, but could not for a moment deceive the eye of an expert. Tapestry brussels is printed like calico or cambric, fast colors are laid on with a brush and set by heated cylinders over which the carpet passes. The weave of tapestry carpets is much less durable than that of body brussels, as the wool surface threads simply pass under a thread of the warp that holds them.

To Drive Away Ants.

To drive away ants, scrub the shelves or drawers that they frequent with strong carbolic soap, after which sprinkle red pepper in every crack and crevice.

How To Preserve Orange Peel.

Weigh the orange whole, and allow pound for a pound. Peal the oranges neatly and cut the rind into shreds. Boil until tender, changing the water twice, and replenishing with hot from the kettle. Squeeze the strained juice of the oranges over the sugar, let this heat to a boil, pour in the shreds and boil twenty minutes. Lemon peel can be preserved in the same way, allowing more sugar.

House Painting.

Done during the autumn or early winter is much more durable than that done in the early summer or spring. The painter too, is not then annoyed by the tiny flies which are always attracted by fresh paint if applied while they are around.

How To Cool a Cellar.

The windows should be open at night. The cool air enters the apartment during the night and circulates through it. The windows should be closed before sunrise in the morning, and kept closed and shaded through the day. If the air of the cellar is damp, it may be thoroughly dried by placing in it a peck of fresh lime in an open box. A peck of lime will absorb about seven pounds or more than three quarts of water, and in this way a cellar or milk room may be dried.

FURNITURE POLISH.

Melt over a slow fire four ounces of white wax, when cool, add six ounces of turpentine, stir until cool when it is ready for use. Apply with a cork or piece of chamois.

TO PREVENT MILK FROM SCORCHING.

Put a small piece of butter in the pan or dish in which milk is to be cooked, and it will not scorch.

TO DRY RUBBER BOOTS.

If you fill rubber boots half full of oats when they are taken off at night they will be nice and dry inside in the morning.

OX MORROW POMADE.

Melt together one ounce of white wax, four ounces of ox tallow, six ounces of fresh lard, when cold add one and one-half ounce of oil of bergamot.

THE NEW YORK SUN CHOLERA MIXTURE.

Take equal parts of tincture of opium, tincture of rhubarb, essence of pepermint, and spirits of camphor, mix well. Dose, fifteen to thirty drops in a wine glass of water, according to age and the violence of the attack. Repeat every fifteen or twenty minuter until relief is obtained. A cheap and effective remedy and should be kept handy at all time. Use also for diarrhœa or dysentery.

To Preserve Celery.

Celery may be kept indefinitely by wrapping around it a heavy towel wrung out of cold water. When the towel gets dry renew the water.

How to Cure a Ham.

If this mixture is followed, the hams are sure to keep and will be noted for their excellent flavor. For one hundred pounds of meat take four pounds of fine salt, four ounces of saltpetre and one pound of brown sugar. Rub the hams with the mixture every other day, until all is absorbed. No more salt is required.

Sovereign Pop.

One and one-half ounces of ginger, five pounds of white sugar, five gallons of water, one pint of yeast, one drachm of the essence of lemon, one pound of cream tartar; bottle and tie the corks down.

How to Keep Eggs all Winter.

Wrap eggs in paper, twisting the ends hard; put them in a box in a good cellar and they will keep all winter.

How to Make Vinegar.

Two gallons molasses, two quarts yeast, five pounds acetic, put them into a fifty gallon cask, and fill up with soft water; stir it up, and let it stand two or three weeks, letting it have all the air possible, and you will have a good vinegar. The more molosses added the stronger the vinegar will be. Make in a strong place.

How to Make Beer.

Two quarts corn, one gallon molasses, ten gallons water; put all into a keg, shake well and in a few days a nice fermentation will have been brought on; keep it bunged tight. It may be flavored with the oil of spruce or lemon, if desired, by pouring on the oils one or two quarts of the water boiling hot. The corn will last several makings.

Treatment of Plants.

With plants received by mail, some care and precaution have to be taken on arrival. If plants are in the least wilted on arrival, put them in luke warm water in a shallow pan for about an hour, leaving the paper undisturbed. This will soon restore their vitality. After potting them, keep in the shade and from the wind or draft for four or five days. Sprinkle the leaves every day, but take care not to wet the soil in the pot too much, which would make the roots rot. In any case avoid extremes in watering or drying out.

Blackberry Cordial.

Press the berries, weigh one of sugar to every pound of juice, put the sugar and juice in a porcelaine kettle; add one-quarter of an ounce of cloves and allspice, one-half ounce of powdered nutmeg, one-half ounce of cinnamon bark, to each quart of liquid. Start it on a quick fire and let it boil one hour, removing all scum that may gather on the top. Let it cool and then add one-half a pint of brandy for every quart of cordial. Strain through a fine hair seive, bottle and cork tight.

Cure for Cow Itch.

To cure cow itch between the toes, tie a blue yarn thread around each toe separately.

To Pickle Celery.

Separate the stalks from the head, clean them thoroughly, and put them into salt and water strong enough to bear an egg, let them remain in this a week or ten days, or until wanted to pickle, then take them out, wash them clean in water, drain dry, place in a jar and pour boiling vinegar over, to which any approved spices may have been added, keep well covered with vinegar. If the celery is allowed to remain any length of time in the salt and water it will be necessary to soak it a day or two in clean fresh water, changing the water occassionally.

To Clean Furniture.

For cleaning bed-steds, chairs, tables, etc., mix sweet oil and kerosene together, and apply with a sponge or flannel cloth. For cleaning pianos, mix sweet oil and turpentine together and apply with a chamois.

Tomatoes for Supper.

Take as many eggs as there are members in the family, boil two-thirds of them hard, dissolve the yolk with sufficient vinegar, and about three teaspoonsfuls of mustard, and mash as smooth as possible, then add the remaining one-third of the eggs, (raw) yolk and white, stir well then add oil to make altogether, sauce sufficient to cover the tomatoes well, and plenty of salt and pepper; beat throughly until it frosts. Skin and cut the tomatoes a fourth of an inch thick, and pour the sauce over them.

Relief for Croup.

Mix together one-half teaspoonful of white sugar and one-half teaspoonful powdered burnt alum. It is better to give it to the child dry, but if too young it may be given in water. I know from personal experience that this recipe will give immediate relief. I have used it in my own family for a number of years and without a single failure.

To Remove Warts and Corns.

Soak them until they become soft, then with a sharp knife pare the top until it bleeds, then tie them up in spirits of turpentine.

How to Make Gooseberry Marmalade.

Press a sufficient quantity of gooseberries, and add three-quarters of their weight in lump sugar. Boil the fruit and sugar into a jelly so thick that when it is dropped upon a cold plate, just dipped into cold water, it will not adhere to it. Turn it into cups or bowls, and cut in thin slices for bread and butter. It makes nice sandwiches for children.

A LIST OF NEW AND ORIGINAL NAMES FOR CHILDREN.

GIRLS.

Aur.	Frost.	Keel.	Quake.
Anece.	Fissil.	Love.	Quola.
Auz	Ferda.	Lyma.	Qunell.
Adoll.	Forrest.	Lila.	Rita.
Agkell.	Giz.	Lura.	Reena.
Armory.	Gire.	Lava.	Restella.
Adot.	Gay.	Lieve.	Ronna.
Beela.	Goudelle.	Lennox.	Ransen.
Borna.	Geza.	Mona.	Rota.
Burra.	Gavre.	Merl.	Ray.
Beryl.	Gaker.	Mra.	Savanna.
Bassir.	Hayx.	Merza.	Sola.
Bunorr.	Hyzar.	Marsailles.	Samantha.
Bernice.	Hayda.	Myrtle.	Selna.
Corazz.	Hadd.	Marguerritte.	Sena.
Conn.	Husta.	Ort.	Saunda.
Cozut.	Heza.	Oda.	Suita.
Coy.	Hest.	Odellant.	Tina.
Cultz.	Inez.	Odiria.	Tuna.
Culitt.	Inare.	Ozarell.	Tot.
Conny.	Irna.	Onid.	Tulura.
Della.	Ilynn.	Onquest.	Tooze.
Davy.	Illis.	Navy.	Tonna.
Devere.	Isa.	Nankeent.	Topaz.
Dyke.	Ibon.	Nastell.	Ursurla.
Daphue.	Java.	Nervalee.	Use.
Dorris.	Jura.	Norman.	Unnis.
Durena.	Jean.	Nona.	Ulna.
Ernis.	Jise.	Nook.	Urn.
Estol.	Jove.	Petit.	Ulmata.
Eloise	Janet.	Pearl	Umarita.
Elite.	Jackey.	Partasia.	Valarie.
Eureka.	Kalen.	Parnell.	Verona.
Etna.	Knox.	Palm.	Verna.
Elcore.	Kissane.	Pern.	Vera.
Fawn.	Kinnell.	Pinkie.	Valparii.
Fern.	Karta.	Quezt.	Vazz.
Faisy.	Kiro.	Queena.	Vennzuee.

Wave.	Wanby.	Yon.	Yoc.
Wannetta.	Wrinky.	Yolla.	Zula.
Willamette.	Xida.	Yeal.	Zarcella.
Winona.	Xylo.	Yez.	Zoe.
Wilda.	Xynphe.	Yates.	Zella.
Wilma.	Xyrua.	Yanta.	Zoy.
Zelma.			

NAMES FOR BOYS.

Albreta.	Evans.	Joy.	Orville.
Adiar.	Eulan.	Jurman.	Oar.
Alzene.	Everette.	Jave.	Orkan.
Addison.	Frazier.	Jese.	Oakley.
Alwood.	Farmer.	Jacky.	Ogden.
Anvil.	Faut.	Kosair.	Octavus.
Armory.	Foss.	Kaleen.	Orvery.
Burnis.	Farrell.	Kay.	Payson.
Boyd.	Fenton.	Knox.	Peerey.
Beryl.	France.	Knott.	Percy.
Bayard.	Gny.	Kater.	Pai.
Benard.	Grey.	Kruse.	Peruda.
Bruce.	Gistine.	Levi.	Pileha.
Byron.	Gracie.	Louis.	Pontius.
Caddie.	Ghraham.	Lennex.	Quintus.
Conrad.	Gormal.	Lonsay.	Queta.
Channcey.	Grave.	Londa.	Qunicy.
Chase.	Harmon.	Lavanda.	Quietus.
Coke.	Harvey.	Loyd.	Quota.
Clyde.	Havre.	Minnian.	Quip.
Claudus.	Hoyt.	Maurice.	Quoin.
Cloudy.	Hayward.	Marx.	Rebecc.
Dana.	Hansell.	Milifant.	Renel.
Durnard.	Hanse.	Messellee.	Rodolph.
Donald.	Iven.	Markey.	Renn.
Devore.	Irvin.	Maney.	Roxana.
Dart.	Inky.	Niox.	Ross.
Doyer.	Ivy.	Napher.	Rylvan.
Darleigh.	Ival.	Narkel.	Selba.
Envil.	Istel.	Noel.	Sylvanus.
Elward.	Inware.	Neice.	Solome.
Ennis.	Jay.	Nurbach.	Serene.
Eustace.	Jarvell.	Nayvel.	Seled.

NEW NAMES FOR CHILDREN.

Syene.	Uzza.	Weser.	Yedd.
Sotia.	Ulrica.	Weimar.	Yretot.
Trebia.	Urania.	Wallachia.	Yonda.
Taree.	Undecemviri.	Wythe.	Yac.
Tebinm.	Vivian.	Weymont.	Yemen.
Tybalt.	Vincent.	Xenophon.	Zante.
Tryphosa.	Valentine.	Xenocles.	Zynder.
Tristran.	Vierre.	Xnil.	Zaire.
Thraso.	Vane.	Xenia.	Zabdile.
Ulai.	Vendee.	Xingre.	Zoreah.
Uriel.	Volga.	Xanthicus.	Zenas.
Urban.	Wilhelm.	Xuriel.	Zaccia.
Uzan.	Wady.	Yagoo.	Zavan.

CHARACTERS FOR MASQUE BALL.

GIRLS.

Peasant girl.	Dudess.	Edith.	Toboggan.
Bopeep.	Milkmaid.	Valentine.	Astronomer.
Queen of hearts.	Sweet sixteen.	Squaw.	Bridget.
Popcorn girl.	Japanees fan.	Buoy.	Rosebud.
Carnation pink.	Apple girl.	Cook.	Witch.
Princess Louise.	Ballot girl.	Rebecca.	Sunflower.
O'Conner child.	Princess.	Page.	Domino.
Golden slippers.	Queen of diamonds	Cupid.	Dress.
Goddess of Liberty	Starry night.	Lilly.	Morning star.
Mother hubbard.	Fishing girl.	Queen.	Spanish Queen.
Grecian woman.	Chinawoman.	Waitress.	Grandma.
Tambourine girl.	School girl.	Actress.	Nun.
Butterfly.	Old maid.	Huntress.	Juliet.
Jockey.	Samantha Allen.	Fairy.	Confidence.

BOYS.

Baker.	Divine.	Sailor boy.	Fairy king.
Mikado.	Priest.	Scotchman.	Connocht Moran.
School boy.	Devil.	Baseball boy.	Irish lad.
Page.	Romeo.	Sir Walter Scott.	Spanish bucaro.
Jocky.	Kaffir.	English nabob.	D'Anjou.
Dude.	Bicyclist.	Grandpa.	Butcher.
Prince.	Shepard.	Spanish Cavalier.	Cook.
King.	Clown.	Prince Mathusala.	Carpenter.
Louis XIV	Soldier.	Josiah Allen.	Green horn.
Lawyer.	Policeman.	Nankipoo.	Irish Mick.
Doctor.	Sambo.	Lord Byron.	Barber.
Chinaman.	Marionette.	Geo. Washington	Drummer.
Actor.	Indian.	Duke.	Reporter.
Professor.	Bardit.	Father hubbard.	Spanish dancer.

INDEX.

GENERAL INDEX.

It will help those who consult this book to remember that the recipes for each department are arranged in the simple order of the alphabet, so far as has been possible, both in regard to the recipes and the subjects treated.

PAPER FLOWERS — PAGE.
- Butter Cup....................10
- Dahlia.........................10
- Fuchia.........................8
- Poppy..........................8
- Petunia........................9
- Pink...........................9
- Plaque.........................9
- Rose...........................7
- Tulip..........................7
- Water Lilly....................6

WOOL FLOWERS.
- Rose..........................12
- Rose Woven...................12
- Tiger Lilly..................11

HAIR FLOWERS.
- Materials....................13

FEATHER FLOWERS.
- Materials....................14

TINSEL FLOWERS.
- Materials....................15

CHRISTMAS TREE ORNAMENTS.
- Description..................15

FEATHER WORK. — PAGE.
- Description..................17

BEAD WORK.
- Fischu.......................21
- Lamp screen..................20
- Purse........................21
- Watch case beaded............22

KNITTING DEPARTMENT.
- Astrakan knitted.............38
- Babie's knitted shirt........32
- Breakfast cape...............59
- Child's knitted shirt........48
- Edging.......................35
- Edging knit..................45
- Edging.......................34
- Edging nice knitted..........39
- Edging knit..................44
- Edging knitted...............54
- Edging saw tooth.............56
- Infant's knitted shirt.......25
- Insertion knitted............53
- Insertion knitted............55
- Insertion pretty.............24
- Insertion bead...............27
- Jacket.......................49
- Leggins, child's.............41

GENERAL INDEX.

KNITTING DEPARTMENT.

	Page
Lace, infant's	29
Lace, baby	30
Lace, Basket	24
Lace, bead	27
Lace, fern	30
Lace, six inches wide	25
Lace, Louis	31
Lace, Oregon	29
Lace, new pattern	37
Lace, knitted	47
Lace, knitted	51
Lace, rose leaf	54
Lace, knitted	53
Lace, knitted	55
Lace, knitted	57
Lace, knitted	58
Lace, clyde	32
Lace, Tidy	24
Lace, German	58
Lace, rose leaf	38
Lace, zig zag	56
Mats	40
Mittens	46
Play thing for baby	32
Robe for carriage	60
Rug	61
Shawl pattern	60
Shawl, shoulder	41
Scarf	40
Straps for curtain	57
Slippers, knit	28
Tidy, knitted	36
Tidy, knitted	45
Twilight	59
Twining leaf pattern	36
Wristlets	43

CROCHET DEPARTMENT.

	Page
Abbreviations	62
Baby carriage robe	73
Carriage Robe	81
Child's crochet hood	85
Crochet ball	86

CROCHET DEPARTMENT.

	Page
Edging	65
Edging, simple	85
Gent's leisure cap	69
Lace edging	84
Lamp mat	67
Lace	70
Lace	84
Opera cape	74
Rose	70
Rolipicot edging	83
Sacque for baby	63
Silk watch chain	65
Skull cap	77
Sofa pillow	66
Sofa afgan	82
Scarf	67
Shoe	71
Trimming	68
Trimming	74
Trimming	78
Trimming narrow	83
Twine bag	72
Tidy in tricot	73
Wool tidy	71

STAMPING DEPARTMENT.

	Page
Indelible or liquid process	87
Perforated patterns	86
Powder process	87
Stamping powder	88

PAINTING DEPARTMENT.

	Page
Black satin	90
Embroidery	90
Glass painting	89
Light satin	90
Painting on oilcloth	88
White velvet	89

MISCELLANEOUS DEPARTMENT.

	Page
Blocks for children	95
Beautiful dress	98
Chemisette	98

GENERAL INDEX.

	PAGE.
Crazy patchwork	95
Dainty Ottoman	97
Fancy pin-cushion	97
Fancy wall bag	92
Housekeeper's friend	99
Hair pin holder	100
Mammoth boquet	93
Moss cross	96
Odds and ends	99
Ornamental fan	96
Precious jewel case	95
Picture frame of pit work	97
Pen wiper	100
Rag bag	101
Traveler's bolster	94
Table cover	101
Table scarf	96
Toboggan hood	100
Watch case	101

HOME DEPARTMENT.

Bed, foot of	105
Boy's marquerit ecaps	128
Bathing slippers	127
Broom case	114
Book mark	129
Baby basket	129
Bath room picture frames	130
Bed spread and shams	131
Baby comforter	134
Bureau scarf	124
Bed valance	125
Boy's Jersey caps	122
Bed room rug	118
Bed room commode	119
Collar box	114
Cord rack	116
Comb pocket	119
Chair cushion	124
Convenient letter carrier	126
Children's bibs	126
Chain stitch embroidery	127
Child's carriage cushion	127
Child's ball	132

HOME DEPARTMENT.	PAGE.
Chair cushion	133
Child's leggins	134
Cap basket	131
Crape veils	109
Cleaning carpets	109
Chest for soiled linen	111
Dolls furniture	104
Decorated fans	121
Dining room pictures	106
Door brick	120
Dressing old frames	108
Dinning room crumb cloth	130
Doyleys	133
Dress for flower pot	133
Delevine	135
Double stitch embroidery	136
Decorated fans	142
Embroidery rings	128
Eylet hole embroidery	134
Embossed top for lamp orn't	137
Fancy knot embroidery	125
Folding screens	125
Fancy pen-wiper	126
Fancy apron	144
Glove sachet	109
Home savings	102
Handkerchief sachet	120
Hair receiver	128
Herring bone sticth embroid'y	119
Hem stitch embroidery	134
Lamp shade	121
Ladies' purse bag	106
Lace lamp shade	138
Lambrequins	112
Lattice stitch	113
Lambrequins for cup boards	117
Letter sachet	123
Match receiver	121
Monograms	134
Nurserys baskets	104
Needle book	113
Night dress case	116
Oil cloth splasher	114

GENERAL INDEX.

HOME DEPARTMENT.   PAGE.
- Ornamental bracket 117
- Outside stitch embroidery 135
- Ornamental scarf 143
- Plaques, clay pipes 109
- Parlor wood bracket 123
- Parlor door mat 112
- Pretty room 102
- Paper receiver 107
- Porcupine pin-cushion 108
- Piano cover 136
- Perfume sachet 111
- Photograph case 139
- Pocket pin-cushion 132
- Paper pocket 144
- Railway stitch embroidery 132
- Racks for keys and hooks 117
- Sofa ball 115
- Sofa pillow 110
- Satin stitch embroidery 128
- Shaving case 121
- Stove mat 116
- Spittoon mat 118
- Sitting room basket 122
- Sachet 142
- Scrap book, embroid'y and pt. 120
- Table, gipsy 115
- Toboggan cap 139
- Table cover 138
- Tam O'Shanter cap 139
- Table scarf 131
- Transom, tidy 119
- Toilet sets 123
- Tray cover 135
- Tissue paper dresses 136
- Toilet cushion 143
- Umbrella case 115
- Umbrella and cane holder 137
- Use of perfumeries 111
- Warm baby blanket 105
- Waste paper basket 107
- White oilcloth slipper case .. 112
- Women who read 110
- Waste basket 122

HOME DEPARTMENT.   PAGE.
- Waste paper basket 129
- Work basket 141
- Wood box, fancy 118
- Work stand, fancy 138

COOKING AND BAKER'S DEPARTMENT.
- Albany rolls 149
- Beef pounded 203
- Buns 153
- Breakfast rolls No. 1 147
- Breakfast rolls 149
- Breakfast rolls 148
- Buns 148
- Bread, brown 147
- Biscuits 151
- Breakfast cake 154
- Bread, Graham 161
- Bread, compressed yeast 146
- Bread, corn 151
- Custard, cream 196
- Custard 198
- Chowder, clam 202
- Cracker, zephyr 198
- Chicken 201
- Cookies, poverty 190
- Cookies 158
- Cookies 159
- Cake, orange 157
- Cake, California 157
- Cake, coffee 157
- Cake, cream 158
- Cake, everlasting 158
- Cake, butter 159
- Cake, tapeworm 159
- Cake, hill 160
- Cake, layer 160
- Cake, lemon 161
- Cake, common 161
- Cake, layer 161
- Cake, layer 162
- Cake, layer 162
- Cake, excellent 162
- Cake, jelly 163

GENERAL INDEX.

COOKING AND BAKER'S DEPARTMENT

	PAGE
Cake, orange	163
Cake, wedding	163
Cake, chocolate	164
Cake, huckleberry	164
Cake, chocolate layer	165
Cake, modest	165
Cake, chocolate	165
Cake, almond	166
Cake, bread	166
Cake, orange jelly	166
Cake, small sugar	167
Cake, nut	167
Cake, peel and citron	167
Cake, white	167
Cake, soda	168
Cake, fruit	168
Cake, Illinois	177
Cake, dainty	177
Cake, kolderve	178
Cake, Columbia	178
Cake, ren	178
Cake, cinnamon	179
Cake, orville	179
Cake, walnut	179
Cake, Hill's high	179
Cake, black	180
Cake, rice	181
Cake, fillmon fruit	181
Cake, Scotch pound	182
Cake, citron cup	182
Cake, love	183
Cake, Tam O'Shanter	183
Cake, Kentucky	183
Cake, chocolate cream	184
Cake, cream	184
Cake, Irish	184
Cake, poor,	188
Cake, Caroline	189
Cake, pie	189
Cake, Johnny	190
Cake, spongy	191
Cake, nice spongy	191
Cake, corn meal	194

COOKING AND BAKER'S DEPARTMENT

	PAGE
Doughnuts, rice	186
Doughnuts	153
Drops, small sugar	168
Drops, hot	191
Doughnuts	154
Dumpling, apple	188
Eggs, scalloped	200
Flannel cakes	155
Flour drops	160
Flitters	184
Flitters, almond	193
Halibut, potted	291
Graham cake	156
Graham bread	147
Graham bread	148
Graham Bread	148
Graham biscuits	147
Griddle cake	150
Griddle cakes	151
Griddle cakes	156
Gems	152
Gems, fish	202
Ginger bread	153
Ginger bread	155
Hot cakes	150
Ham boiled	204
Jumbler cocoanut	192
Langtry finger	182
Muffins	153
Morning cake	155
Macaroons, common almond	165
Macaroons, cocanut	168
Macaroons, sweet corn	198
Minced veal	199
Pudding, almond	183
Pudding, fig	185
Pudding, raspberry	187
Pudding, apple	187
Pudding, bread	190
Pudding, English plum	191
Pudding, orange	192
Pudding, home	193
Pudding, fig	193

GENERAL INDEX

COOKING AND BAKER'S DEPARTMENT

	Page
Pudding, apple	194
Pudding, boiled	194
Pudding, rice	195
Pudding, jelly	196
Pudding, orange	19?
Pudding, chocolate	197
Pudding, snow	197
Pudding, puff	198
Pudding, sweet	199
Potatoe, bread	146
Potatoe, omelet	200
Potatoes, escalloped	200
Pie, sour apple	184
Pie, pumkin	185
Pie, cocoanut	186
Pie, jelly	18?
Pie, lemon	187
Pie, one egg	188
Pie, pumkin	192
Pie, squash	193
Pie, squash	194
Pie, tart apple	195
Pie, jelly	195
Pie, mince	193
Pie, chicken	202
Pig's head roasted	203
Rolls, filled	180
Rolls, jelly	164
Rolls	156
Rolls	147
Rolls	148
Rolls	149
Rolls	150
Rolls	150
Rolls	151
Rolls	152
Rusks	151
Rusks	152
Rosettes	155
Short cake, strawberry	157
Short cake, strawberry	159
Short cake, strawberry	161
Sauce for pudding	198

COOKING AND BAKER'S DEPARTMENT

	Page
Sauce, potatoe	202
Salmon, steam	199
Sandwiches, cheese & eggs	199
Salad, cabbage	200
Steak, veal	201
Steak	202
Tea cakes	154
Tea cones	156
Toast, cream	186
Toast, mock cream	186
Turkish cream	197
Waffles	152
Waffles, quick	189
Wafers, cinnamon	168
Yeast cake	145

COLORING DEPARTMENT.

Cotton Goods.

Black	205
Green	205
Orange	206
Red	206
Royal blue	206
Sky blue	205
Yellow	207

Woolen Goods.

Black	207
Blue	207
Crimson	210
Darb	210
Dove	210
Green	208
Lac red	210
Madder red	209
Orange	209
Pink	207
Purple	208
Slate	210
Scarlet	208
Salmon	211
Wine	208
Yellow	211

Silk Goods.

GENERAL INDEX.

COLORING DEPARTMENT.

	PAGE.
Black	213
Crimson	212
Green	212
Lavender	211
Light blue	212
Orange	212
Purple	213
Snuff brown	213
Yellow	211

MISS COOKING AND BAKING RECIPES.

Biscuits	221
Bread, graham	214
Bread, corn	215
Bread, wheat	217
Bread, graham	216
Bread, steamed Indian	221
Bread, brown	216
Custard, corn starch	227
Chocolate	217
Curry rice and chicken	217
Chicken for dinner	219
Chicken, broiled	224
Chocolate drink	224
Cheese, cottage	230
Cordial, strawberry	231
Crullers	230
Custard, cocoanut	219
Cookies	227
Cookies, sugar	227
Cookies, fruit	228
Cookies, ginger	230
Cake, cocoanut cream	214
Cake, cocoanut chocolate	216
Cake, icing for	216
Cake, corn meal	219
Cake, flannel	220
Cake, Johnny	220
Cake, cocoanut layer	221
Cake, hominy	222
Cake, corn	224
Cake, clove	225
Cake, dark cup	225

MISS. COOKING AND BAKING RECIPES

	PAGE.
Cake, lemon	226
Cake, raisin	227
Cake, yeast	228
Cake, good	229
Cake, composition	231
Griddle cakes	218
Gems, graham	222
Gems, rice	223
Macaronia and tomatoes	222
Noodles for soup	231
Orange, desert	219
Oysters, stewed	230
Potatoes	229
Pudding, cream tapico	215
Pudding, cocoanut	218
Pudding, cocoanut cracker	220
Pudding, cocoanut bread	221
Pudding, quick plum	223
Pudding, corn starch	225
Pudding, plum	225
Pudding, spice bread	226
Pudding, flour	227
Pudding, boiled	228
Pudding, holiday	229
Pie, cocoanut	222
Pie, cocoanut	223
Pie, cocoanut	224
Pie, sweet potatoes	226
Pie, peach	228
Rissoles, lobster	231
Sauce, pudding	221
Sauce, oyster	216
Sauce, flandy	220
Soup, canned salmon	214
Soup, lobster	215
Snaps, ginger	228

ANYTHING AND EVERYTHING.

Alpaca, to clean	267
Amonia, carbonate	266
Ants, to drive away	269
Borax, use of	259
Burning chimney to extin'h	258

GENERAL INDEX.

ANYTHING AND EVERYTHING.

	Page.
Blackberry cordial	272
Beer, to make	272
Beef, to corn	268
Brush, feather	250
Bed, airing	242
Blacking, liquid	246
Beds, noisy	246
Caramels	246
Canned goods, to judge	234
Corn, to cultivate	235
Cellar, the	236
Carpets, to clean	237
Cake, how to stamp	238
Cold, in head	240
Churns, prevent overflowing	244
Cream, to make	245
Cream for shaving	245
Candy, molasses	249
Cough, remedy for	250
Cologne, home made	251
Cement, to make	252
Candy	253
Cherries, lotion for	253
Corn, popped	265
Coal oil, fire test of	265
Cider, without apples	264
Candy, figs	263
Casks, to sweeten	263
Croup, relief for	274
Celery, to pickle	273
Cow itch to cure	272
Celery, to preserve	271
Cholera	270
Cellar, to cool	269
Carpets, to distinguish	268
Carpets, putting down	262
Charcoal, use of	237
Cider, to keep	257
Docks, etc, to kill	244
Draught, sit in a	268
Eggs, to preserve	235
Eggs, to tell age of	253
Emery bag	240

ANYTHING AND EVERYTHING.

	Page.
Eggs, to keep	271
Eggs, never place	266
Eye, to remove cinder	261
Flees, to banish	256
Felon, cure for	234
Food, what to eat	239
Flies, to banish	243
Fruit jar to open	245
Food for parrot	247
Foot, lotion for	253
Furniture, polish	270
Fly paper	264
Fruits, to can	262
Felon, remedy for	262
Glass to clean	255
Grapes	249
Glue	250
Grease, to remove	252
Gooseberry marmalode	274
Gas lime, to use	258
Hemorrhage, to stop	236
Headache, remedy for	242
Hands, chapped	247
Hair invigorator	249
Ham, to cure	271
Indigestion, cure for	256
Inkstains	251
Insects on plants, to kill	244
Iron rust, to remove	233
Insect destroyer	245
Ink, to write on glass	266
Kid gloves, to wash	233
Kid gloves, to clean	236
Knife handles, to fasten	247
Kindling wood	267
Kettles, to keep clean	264
Lace, to wash	251
Lawns, to prepare	235
Lemonade	265
Morocco	250
Mildew, to remove	247
Mildew from roses	234
Mouth wash	237

INDEX.

	PAGE		PAGE
ANIMALS AND EVERYTHING		**ANYTHING AND EVERYTHING**	
Mrs. or Miss	233	Sore throat to prevent	259
Milk, to preserve	251	Stains, to remove	257
Milk, to preserve	255	Stair carpet, to preserve	235
Masquerade characters	278	Sleeping rooms	236
Milk, to prevent scorching	240	Scalp, to clean	238
Mustard, to mix	268	Sick room, to purify	243
Measure, household	68	Stammering	244
Milk sour, to sweeten	257	Swimming	245
Meerchaum, coloring	266	Salt, uses for	247
Mustard plaster	273	Starch, glossy	248
Meat, boiling	262	Shoes, protection of	250
Moss, to destroy	264	Scorch, to remove	252
Nutmegs, to test	266	Scratches to remove	253
Night drinks	264	Stoves, to prevent rusting	255
Never allow	265	Transfer paper, black	266
Night soil, to prepare	254	Toe nail, ingrowing	240
Neck enlarged, to cure	254	Trees, cultivation of	260
Neuralgia, relief for	259	Telephone, how to make	241
Names for children	275	Tomatoes	250
Oranges, to pickle	266	Table, the	242
Orange peel, to preserve	269	Tea, cold	252
Onions, when you eat	241	Tomatoes, to keep	264
Penwipe	256	Tomatoes, for supper	273
Paint, to clean	254	Vinegar, to make	264
Pie, to bake	238	Vermin, to prevent	251
Pitch, to remove	240	Wash, for head	256
Potatoes, to preserve	243	Wart, cure for	249
Plants, treatment	272	Whooping cough	234
Pop ginger	267	Windows, how to blind	239
Pomade, ox morrow	270	Wax, how to make	241
Painting, house	269	White wash	251
Paint, smell of	263	Water to purify	252
Ribbon, to wash	233	Windows to clean	256
Rice, parched	245	Window support	263
Rheumatism, relief for	252	Whalebone, etc.	260
Room to ventilate	255		
Rubber boot, to dry	270		
Rubber glue	258		
Stiff neck, to cure	267		
Screws, to prevent rust	265		
Sprains, etc.	263		
Silverware, to clean	261		
Soap, soft	260		

www.ingramcontent.com/pod-product-compliance
Lightning Source LLC
Chambersburg PA
CBHW032054230426
43672CB00009B/1592